The Ancient Greeks
For Dummies®

S0-ALJ-073

Map of Ancient Greece

Pella
Pella
Amphipolis
Eion
Samothrace
Phrygia
Chalcidice
Aegospotamos
Olynthus
Potidaea
Mount Athos
Imbros
Abydos
Mount Olympus
2317 m
2033 m
2637m
Mende
Torone
Troas
Mr Ossa
Scione
Lemnos
1878 m
Larissa
Northern
Sporades
Crannon
Pelion
Mysia
Thessalia
Pheres
AEGEAN
Corcyra
Pharsalus
SEA
Lesbos
Phthiatis
Arginusae
Ambracia
Malis Cape Artemisium
Trachis
Skyros
Aeolis
Lydia
Leucas
Mount Parnassus
Sardis
Aetolia
Delphi
Chaeronea Delium Eretria
Ithaca
Coronea Thebes Tanagra
Ionia
Chios
Gulf of Calyaon
Plataea Leuctra
Gulf of Corinth
Megara
Marathon
Ephesus
Cephalonia
Achaia
Sicyon Athens
Andros
Samos
Elis Corinth Salamis
Attica
Cape Mycale
Zacynthus
Olympia Mycenae Aegina
Ceos
Tenos
Icaria
Miletus
Arcadia Epidaurus Saronic
Mantinea Troezen Gulf
Mykonos
Elis
Argos Gulf
Syros
Delos
Southern
Carta
Peloponnese
of
Seriphos
Paros
Sporades
Mount Ithome
Argolis
Calydna
Messene Sparta
Naxos
Amorgos
Cos
Sphacteria Pylos
Siphnos
Laconia
Cyclades
Ios
Gulf
Gulf
Melos
Astypalaea
Doris
of
of
Telos
Messenia
Laconia
Thera
Anaphe
Rhodes
Cythera
Carpathos

0
150 km
100 mi
Mount Ida
Cnossus
2456 m
Crete

The Ancient Greeks For Dummies®

Cheat Sheet

Timeline

2600 BC	Beginning of the Minoan Period	479 BC	Battle of Plataea (Greece wins . . . eventually!)
1450 BC	Development of Linear B writing	477 BC	Athens establishes the Delian League
1400 BC	Foundation of Mycenaean Palaces	461–445 BC	First Peloponnesian War: Athens versus Sparta (draw)

BRONZE AGE

1370 BC	Palace complex at Knossos destroyed. Minoan civilisation comes to an end	431–404 BC	Second Peloponnesian War: Athens versus Sparta (Sparta wins)
c.1250 BC	The Trojan War	430 BC	Plague in Athens
1200 BC	Destruction of Mycenaean Palaces. Doric invasions	429 BC	Death of Pericles
		415 BC	Athenian expedition to Sicily defeated
1000 BC	End of Mycenaean civilisation	399 BC	Socrates tried and executed
		359 BC	Philip II becomes King of Macedonia

IRON AGE

776 BC	First Olympic Games	356 BC	Alexander the Great born
c.750 BC	The *Iliad* and the *Odyssey* composed. Greek alphabet established. Greek colonies established in Sicily and Southern Italy	331 BC	Alexander the Great defeats the Persians at Gaugamela and becomes the new King of Persia!
630 BC	Colony of Cyrene established	323 BC	Death of Alexander the Great
594 BC	Solon renews the laws of Athens	322 BC	Death of Aristotle
508 BC	Kleisthenes reforms the Athenian constitution and Athens becomes a democracy!	300 BC	Ptolemy the Great founds the library at Alexandria
490 BC	Battle of Marathon: Greece versus Persia I (Greece wins!)	214 BC	Philip V of Macedonia defeated by the Romans
483 BC	Athenians discover silver in the mines at Laureion	172 BC	Macedonia becomes a Roman province
480 BC	Battle of Thermopylae: Greece versus Persia II. Battle of Salamis	146 BC	Romans invade Greece and take control. Ancient Greece comes to an end

For Dummies: Bestselling Book Series for Beginners

The Ancient Greeks

FOR

DUMMIES®

The Ancient Greeks
FOR
DUMMIES®

by Stephen Batchelor

John Wiley & Sons, Ltd

The Ancient Greeks For Dummies®

Published by
John Wiley & Sons, Ltd
The Atrium
Southern Gate
Chichester
West Sussex
PO19 8SQ
England

E-mail (for orders and customer service enquires): cs-books@wiley.co.uk

Visit our Home Page on www.wiley.com

For general information on our other products and services, please contact our Customer Care Department within the U.S. at 800-762-2974, outside the U.S. at 317-572-3993, or fax 317-572-4002.

For technical support, please visit www.wiley.com/techsupport.

Wiley also publishes its books in a variety of electronic formats. Some content that appears in print may not be available in electronic books.

British Library Cataloguing in Publication Data: A catalogue record for this book is available from the British Library

ISBN: 978-0-470-98787-2 (P/B)

Printed and bound in Great Britain by TJ International, Padstow, Cornwall

10 9 8 7 6 5 4 3 2

WILEY

About the Author

Stephen Batchelor has taught Ancient History and Classical Studies for a number of years to a wide variety of student groups and is currently Head of School for Creative and Visual Arts at Mid-Kent College. He has travelled extensively in the Mediterranean and worked there as an archaeological tour guide. He has written book reviews for *Current Archaeology* and *History Today*. *The Ancient Greeks For Dummies* is his first book.

Author's Acknowledgements

This is my first book and there are several people that I would like to thank: Rachael and the team at Wiley for all their supportive comments and feedback, Dr Neil Faulkner for all his help over the years and his recommendation for this project, both my parents for their continued support, and my partner Samantha for putting up with so many lost weekends while I just did 'a bit more on the book'.

I'd like to dedicate this book to my father, Alan Batchelor, and thank him for absolutely everything. I know you've always preferred the Romans, but this one is for you, Dad.

Publisher's Acknowledgements

We're proud of this book; please send us your comments through our Dummies online registration form located at www.dummies.com/register/.

Some of the people who helped bring this book to market include the following:

Acquisitions, Editorial, and Media Development

Project Editor: Rachael Chilvers

Content Editor: Nicole Burnett

Development Editor: Brian Kramer

Copy Editor: Charlie Wilson

Proofreader: Rachael Wilkie

Technical Editor: Dr Ian Rutherford

Executive Editor: Samantha Spickernell

Publisher: Jason Dunne

Executive Project Editor: Daniel Mersey

Cover Photos: © Roger Cracknell 05/London/Alamy

Cartoons: Rich Tennant (www.the5thwave.com)

Composition Services

Project Coordinator: Erin Smith

Layout and Graphics: Reuben W. Davis, Stephanie D. Jumper, Tobin Wilkerson

Indexer: Christine Spina Karpeles

Special Help

Brand Reviewer: Carrie Burchfield

Publishing and Editorial for Technology Dummies

Richard Swadley, Vice President and Executive Group Publisher

Andy Cummings, Vice President and Publisher

Mary Bednarek, Executive Acquisitions Director

Mary C. Corder, Editorial Director

Publishing for Consumer Dummies

Diane Graves Steele, Vice President and Publisher

Joyce Pepple, Acquisitions Director

Composition Services

Gerry Fahey, Vice President of Production Services

Debbie Stailey, Director of Composition Services

Contents at a Glance

Table of Contents

Introduction

When I think about it, I've always been interested in Ancient Greece but I spent a lot of my time not realising that I was. When I was very young I went to Cyprus on holiday and was fascinated by the ruined statues and mosaics. As I grew a little older I loved films like *Jason and the Argonauts* and *Clash of the Titans* that were endlessly repeated on television at Christmas. What I didn't understand was the 'Greekness' of these things. I knew that I liked the great stories and scary monsters but it was only when I got older that I realised that they were just a tiny part of the fascinating world of the ancient Greeks.

What interested me most was the fact that, despite the gap of over 2,000 years, the world of the ancient Greeks seemed very real and contemporary. They had the same concerns and problems as people do today and went about dealing with them in tremendously imaginative ways. The Greeks were hugely creative and although they lived in a world with a very dominant religion, they never stopped looking for new solutions to age old problems.

About This Book

Studying the ancient Greeks can be a bit frustrating because an awful lot of their story doesn't take place in Greece but elsewhere in the Mediterranean. The other big frustration is that Greek history isn't really a continuum. By that I mean that it doesn't start at Point X and finish at Y. The Greeks were a fractious bunch, always fighting amongst themselves and with other people, so tracing their story can get quite complicated!

It's worth the effort though. The most wonderful thing about the Greeks is the legacy that they left behind, which you can see, touch, and immerse yourself in. The huge amount of archaeological evidence that still survives is breathtaking. From massive buildings like the Parthenon in Athens to the tiniest coin, each piece of physical evidence reveals something interesting about the way the Greeks lived and what they did.

Another fantastic resource is the huge amount of written evidence that's survived; plays, poems, works of history, philosophy, science, medicine, and epic poetry that read like the plot of a Hollywood action film have all survived for over 2,000 years. Throughout this book I try to quote as much as possible from these original sources because it's always best to hear it from the horse's mouth!

This book introduces you to the world of the ancient Greeks – a world part bizarre, part visionary, and part bloodthirsty. It's not an attempt to tell you *everything* about the Greeks; more a way of getting started so that you can carry on exploring their world – and there's enough to keep you going for the rest of your life!

Conventions Used in This Book

The two main issues when looking at any period of ancient history are language and dates!

The biggest of the two is language. The ancient Greeks used an entirely different alphabet to ours, and consequently the words seem strange and different, although a great many English words come from ancient Greek ones. To try to make things easier throughout the book I put any Greek word in *italics*. So, for example, when I'm talking about an elected official in ancient Athens I call him an *arkhon* because that's the word that the Greeks used.

You might find that in other books some Greek words are spelt differently (often using a c instead of a k) or that the author uses the proper Greek punctuation marks on words. Don't worry – it's still the same word but I choose to use the simpler version.

The other issue is using dates. Virtually every date that I use in the book has BC after it, meaning 'Before Christ'. That's because the bulk of ancient Greek history took place during the two thousand years or so before the accepted date of Jesus's birth. (I go into more detail about BC and AD in Chapter 1). Of course, this is our dating system, not the one that the Greeks would have used.

Oh yes, one other thing – places. I mention place names all the time. In most cases you can find the places on the map on the Cheat Sheet at the front of the book. In the case of battles, the Greeks often fought in a big open space like a field or a beach, and they'd avoid fighting near towns if possible. Pinpointing these out-of-the-way places can be really difficult so I try to refer to the town nearest the battle.

Differences of opinion

One of the exciting things about history is that it is always up for debate. Answers are never 100 per cent right or wrong and interpretation (understanding the 'why' rather than the 'when') is the most important thing. You can probably expect to read some things in this book that seem to disagree with things you've read elsewhere. When you're dealing with events that took place over 2,000 years ago there'll always be differences of opinion, just as there'll always be new archaeological discoveries that completely blow older theories away. In a few years' time whole new schools of thought on many of the issues that this book discusses might emerge. I hope so, because that's what keeps history fun!

How This Book Is Organised

This book is split into five specific parts, all covering a different aspect of ancient Greece.

Part 1: Travelling Back in Time

Part I is all about establishing who the Greeks were and where they came from, which isn't quite as straightforward as you might think – even the Greeks weren't sure! Modern historians have established that the really ancient Minoan and Mycenaean cultures were the forerunners of the ancient Greeks and I look at them in Chapter 2. After that comes the story of how the Greeks came into being and spread all over the Mediterranean. I also look at how they developed into such amazing warriors. It was just as well they did because the last chapter in Part I focuses on the wars with the Persian Empire when it seemed as if ancient Greece might actually be wiped out.

Part 11: Athens to Alexander: The Rise and Fall of Empires

Part II is a fantastic rollercoaster of a story! It looks at the period of greatest Greek success following the Persian Wars and how the city of Athens became so wealthy and dominant. However, after a difficult period a new power emerged in the north: Macedonia. Under Alexander the Great the Macedonians went on tremendous military campaigns and built up an empire that stretched as far as India. This didn't last either, as after Alexander's death the empire broke up and new kingdoms emerged. The last chapter in this part deals with how the kingdoms fought amongst themselves until they all finally succumbed to the threat of the Romans. Ancient Greece was effectively at an end.

Part III: Living a Greek Life

So what was being an ancient Greek actually like? Part III looks at life in the towns and cities of ancient Greece from the food they ate to what sort of exercises people did at the gym, to what happened when people got divorced. I include specific chapters on theatre, art, architecture, and what life was like in the countryside.

Part IV: Mythology, Religion, and Belief

One of the things that people find most interesting about the ancient Greeks is the world of mythology. The stories about gods, heroes, and monsters were dominant themes throughout Greek life, influencing their plays, literature, and art. Religion was a major part of public life, full of strange and bizarre rituals. Part IV is all about these themes with a focus on how the Greeks lived their lives surrounded by these ideas and based a lot of what they did on examples from mythology.

This part ends with a look at the Greek philosophers, the men who challenged these beliefs in gods and monsters, and set out to make sense of the world using their own powers of logic and reason. They were an odd bunch but their ideas are fascinating!

Part V: The Part of Tens

This final part has four brief chapters intended to give you an idea of where to go next to further your experience of the ancient Greeks. I include chapters on places to go and books to read. Chapter 23 is all about Greek inventions – you'll be surprised at some of the things that the Greeks came up with but they're all true, promise! Chapter 25 is about interesting but slightly dodgy characters; the people in history who are worth a second look and a revaluation.

Icons Used in This Book

Throughout the book I use a series of icons to capture your attention. I hope they're as useful to the reader as they were to the writer!

As much as possible I try to use bits of what the Greeks actually said. Reading something first-hand is fascinating and the huge amount of writing that survives from Ancient Greece makes this easy to do.

Just like urban myths today, a lot of 'facts' about ancient Greece aren't actually true. Occasionally I point them out with this icon.

This icon pinpoints important information to bear in mind when getting to grips with the ancient Greeks.

Some of the stories from ancient Greece are like the plots of Hollywood films and increasingly they are being made into them. This icon means that I'm referencing a film you may want to check out.

Sometimes I include information that's interesting but not vital. This icon highlights more complicated stuff that you can skip over if you want to.

Where to Go from Here

You can start at the beginning so that you have the historical context before you start looking at how the Greeks lived their lives. Alternatively, you can start with Part IV, all about religion and mythology and where the Greeks considered that they came from. This is just as important to understand as the historical background.

Each chapter in the book is written around a specific topic so you can really dive in anywhere. If you want to know about Alexander the Great, go to Chapter 11. If Greek drama is your thing then Chapter 16 is the one for you. I include cross-references in the chapters so if something comes up that's mentioned in more detail elsewhere, you're directed to it.

Whichever way you choose to enjoy the book, I hope you find it fun and interesting.

Part I
Travelling Back in Time

The 5th Wave   By Rich Tennant

"Well, that was just terrific! We pull up to shore, announce that we're Minoans bearing the framework for civilisation, and you start eating houmous with your fingers."

In this part . . .

So who were the Greeks? Well, it isn't as obvious as you might think. In this part I look at where the Greeks came from and what made them Greek. I go on to look at how these people spread out all across the Mediterranean until the Greeks were living as far away as modern Spain and Turkey.

Oh yes, and I also consider the Minotaur, human sacrifice, and huge battles with the Persians . . .

Chapter 1

When, Where, What, Who? Meeting the Ancient Greeks

*M*odern Greece is very different to the Greece of the ancient world.

Today, Greece is a medium sized member of the European Union that uses the euro as its currency. To the north-east it's bordered by Macedonia and to the north-west Albania. Most people think of it as a popular tourist destination, and during the summer months people from around the world flock to the seaside resorts on the mainland and on islands like Crete and Rhodes.

For these visitors, the material remains of the ancient world are still visible. Tourists can look at ruined temples and statues while they sit drinking Mythos beer in bars and restaurants named after Greek gods and heroes. Often, they stay in towns whose names are redolent of the ancient world, like Athens, Delphi, Olympia, and Corinth.

Much like the rest of the Mediterranean, visitors to Greece find great food, friendly people with a strong sense of honour and family values, and a seductively relaxed way of life that seems to go at a slower pace than the rest of the world.

This idyllic and fascinating holiday destination, however, is in sharp contrast to the focus of this book – the Greece of the ancient world. Ancient Greece is about huge events, incredible battles, and tremendous advances in science and understanding that took place over 2,000 years ago.

In this chapter I put the ancient Greeks in historical and geographical context – answering the questions 'When?' and 'Where?'. I also address the fundamental questions about them – precisely who they were, where they came from, and why what they did is still incredibly important.

Understanding Why the Ancient Greeks Matter

Hopefully, you have already decided that the ancient Greeks are worth bothering with – otherwise you wouldn't be reading this book.

Falling for all things ancient Greek

Simply put, the ancient Greeks were amazing. Their society and culture is endlessly fascinating. If you don't believe me, try the following for size:

- Zeus, the ancient Greeks' most powerful god, changed himself into a bull, a swan, and a shower of gold so that he could make love to beautiful women without his wife finding out. Oh yes, and his wife was also his sister. (See Chapter 19 for more on Zeus and the rest of the ancient Greek gods.)
- Ancient Greeks thought that the world was an island entirely surrounded by water that looked rather like a fried egg. (See Chapter 19.)
- They invented the Olympic Games, and their greatest Olympian trained by carrying a cow around for four years. (See Chapter 16.)
- The Greeks had elaborate religious cults that participated in strange rituals, including swimming with pigs. (See Chapter 21.)
- One of their philosophers jumped into a volcano to prove he was a god. When he didn't come back, people realised that he wasn't one. (See Chapter 22.)

Noting the Greeks' contributions

Everybody goes on about the Romans and the massive advances in civilised life that they were responsible for such as central heating, straight roads, and Latin. Well, the Romans certainly did a lot, but they were preceded by the Greeks, who were pretty inventive too.

The ancient Greeks are responsible for a fascinating number of creations and inventions: money, democracy, written history, bras, satire, and musical notation are all things that the Greeks are at least partly responsible for creating. You can read more about these and other inventions in Chapter 23.

While inventions are all well and good, the most impressive thing that the Greeks came up with was civilisation itself. *Civilisation*, the whole idea of living together in large towns and cities, was a fairly new concept that the Greeks initiated in Europe.

So who were these fascinating, inventive, and civilised people?

Meeting the People of Ancient Greece

Modern Greece is very different from the Greece of the ancient world. The biggest difference is that what you may think of Greece and being Greek is nothing like the ancients' experience.

'Being Greek' in the ancient world meant that you shared a way of life with people, rather than the citizenship of a single country. Greeks lived all across the Mediterranean: Spain, North Africa, Sicily, southern Italy, Asia Minor (modern-day Turkey), the Aegean islands, and of course the land mass that folk call modern Greece. This way of life included:

- The language that you spoke (see the later section 'Talking the Talk: Ancient Greek Language').
- The gods that you believed in (see Chapter 19).
- The food you ate (see Chapter 15).
- All the other things that make up an individual's identity.

Furthermore, the Greeks of the ancient world didn't necessarily consider themselves to be Greek; rather, they classified themselves as being citizens of the towns or cities from which they came. Greeks only really considered themselves to be Greek in comparison to foreigners. So an Athenian talking to an Egyptian described himself as a Greek, whereas if the same Athenian was talking to somebody from Corinth (another Greek town), he called himself an Athenian.

Locating Ancient Greece

Ancient Greece was very spread out, which means that the people, ideas, and events that I talk about in this book came from and took place all around the Mediterranean and sometimes beyond, as Figure 1-1 shows. Eventually, there were people who considered themselves to be Greek in Spain, France, Italy, North Africa, Libya, and Asia Minor – and in Greece itself of course.

The most densely populated area was the land mass known as Greece today. It's an area that is really dominated by two things – the sea and very large mountain ranges. For the ancient Greeks, the mountain ranges meant that sections of this big slab of land were sometimes very disconnected from each other. This is one of the reasons why people tended to think of themselves in local terms rather than national ones.

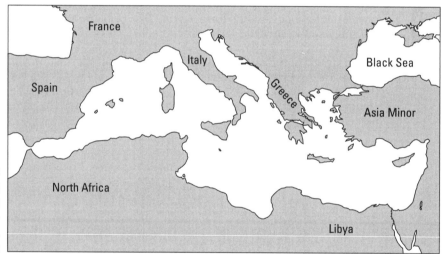

Figure 1-1:
The Ancient Mediter-
ranean.

Greece isn't a very large land mass, and wherever you stand in it you're unlikely to be more than about 50 kilometres from the sea. The land is fertile but also very hilly, which means that it doesn't have vast plains of workable farmland. These two factors are important when considering why so many Greeks decided to leave the land mass and create new towns on the nearby islands and elsewhere in the Mediterranean (see Chapter 7).

Separating the region

You can divide Greece in two at the Gulf of Corinth, the large body of water that runs through the middle of the region:

- **To the north:** North of the Gulf was the larger part of mainland Greece, although the south was much more heavily populated. The biggest city in this part of Greece was Thebes and also located in the region was the sacred site of Delphi, which was home to the famous oracle. (See Chapter 21 for more.)

- **To the south:** Southern Greece was divided in two by the Peloponnese mountain range. Most of the famous cities of ancient Greece were here: Sparta, Olympia, Corinth, Argos, and, to the north-east, Athens.

Touring the islands and beyond

Although the Greek mainland is fairly small, bits of what historians consider to be ancient Greece were spread all over the eastern Mediterranean. All the places that people now go to on holiday – approximately 1,400 islands – were part of ancient Greece, as well other more distant lands.

Here's a brief guide to some of the most notable parts of ancient Greece:

- **Euboia:** The big peninsula that's just off the eastern coast of Greece. Its people considered themselves to be very different and separate from those on the mainland.

- **The Cyclades:** The big group of islands in the south, including places like Naxos, Paros, and Delos. The ancient Greeks called this group 'The Circle'.

- **Asia Minor:** The western coast of modern-day Turkey. During the Dark Ages, loads of Greeks from the mainland moved there and created the new Greek areas of Aeolia and Ionia (for more, see Chapter 3).

- **Thrace:** At the top of Figure 1-1, the area is now southern Bulgaria. For the ancient Greeks, this area was wild, hilly country full of warlike tribes – definitely a place to avoid!

- **Crete, Rhodes, and Cyprus:** Big important islands to the south-east that developed their own civilisations independent of the Greek mainland. In fact, civilisation started on Crete; read all about it in Chapter 2.

- **The western islands:** Important islands to the west of mainland Greece. Corcyra (modern-day Corfu), Cephallenia, Ithaca, and Zakynthos were all in this part of the Mediterranean.

- **Other islands:** Of the 1,400 islands, only about 250 were inhabited and many of those by not more than about 100 people. Each of the islands has its own fascinating stories and episodes. Islands like Lemnos, Miletus, Samos, and Lesbos are important to the story of the ancient Greeks.

You can visit these islands and many contain fascinating archaeological evidence, some of which is remarkably well preserved, from enormous chunks of ancient temples to the small personal possessions that people used in everyday life. Chapter 26 suggests several places that you might like to visit when you've finished reading this book!

Clarifying When It All Happened

The period of history that historians consider to be the time of the ancient Greeks is very big. Broadly speaking, it dates from the very early beginnings of the Minoan civilisation in Crete around 2800 BC up until the defeat of the Macedonian king Perseus by the Romans in 168 BC. That's more than 2,500 years – 500 years longer than the time that's passed between the birth of Jesus and the present day.

Clearly, a book of this size can't cover everything that happened during this vast expanse of history – and I don't intend to try! Most scholars and historians agree that the history of Greek civilisation went through several distinct phases (see the later section 'Establishing chronology'). Of these I devote most pages to discussing the period between 900 and 300 BC. That's the period that I think of as ancient Greece: Homer, the Persian Wars, Socrates, Greek tragedy, the Parthenon, and Alexander the Great all came about during this time.

Playing the dating game: BC or AD?

All the dates that I use in the book are followed by the suffix *BC*, meaning 'Before Jesus Christ'. This means that something taking place in 545 BC occurred 545 years before the year in which Jesus Christ is thought to have been born. You count dates BC backwards, so that the year 344 BC was the one that immediately followed 345 BC.

Events that took place *after* the birth of Jesus are preceded by *AD*, which stands for the Latin phrase *Anno Domini*, meaning the year of Jesus's birth (AD 1 – there's no year zero). So I'm writing this book in the year AD 2007, 2007 years after the birth of Jesus. You count dates AD forwards. So this book was published in 2008, the year immediately following 2007.

Sometimes when you read a book or visit a website about the ancient world, you see dates followed by *BCE* and *CE*, meaning 'Before the Common Era' and 'Common Era' (confusingly, also known as 'Before the Christian Era' and 'Christian Era'). This convention has come about so that people who don't recognise Jesus as the son of God can use a dating system to represent the years in question without the assumption of Christ's divinity. In this book I decided to stick with BC and AD because I've always used them and it's never done me any harm.

Figuring out dates for the ancient Greeks

Obviously, the Greeks didn't think about things in terms of BC and AD, but they also didn't think in terms of the year having a number.

- Generally speaking, people in the ancient world used major events as a method of dating rather than specifically numbered years. So, for example, an ancient Greek may describe himself as having been born five years after the battle of Marathon (see Chapter 6).

- Another common method was to date an event by its proximity to the Olympic Games. For example, 'The Spartans attacked our town two years after the 25th Olympiad'.

Of course, things were often not this simple. For a mind-reeling discussion of the intricacies of the ancient Greek calendar, check out Chapter 15.

Establishing chronology

The following is a brief chronology of the whole of ancient Greek history. Of course, the ancient Greeks themselves wouldn't have thought about their history in these terms and their ideas of how the world was progressing were very different (see Chapter 19), but modern historians generally agree on the following sequence of periods.

The Bronze Age: 2700–1100 BC

This period is the earliest of Greek history. During these years the first European civilisation appeared on the island of Crete and became known as *Minoan*. This period was strange and wonderful and seems very alien to modern sensibilities.

Civilisation soon sprang up on mainland Greece, and historians refer to this culture as *Mycenaean*. Around 1300 BC something cataclysmic happened in Crete; the Minoan period came to an end, and the people scattered. Read all about these earliest ancient Greeks in Chapter 2.

The Dark Ages: 1100–900 BC

The Dark Ages are so named because historians know very little about what was going on. Most scholars describe it as time of travelling, and that pretty much sums it up. All the people who left mainland Greece after the end of the Bronze Age travelled far and wide, setting up new towns all around the Mediterranean. As a result trade and diplomacy began in earnest too.

Archaeology: Answering the impossible

Written source material from ancient Greece reveals a phenomenal amount about the Greeks and their lives. But this source material is never truly complete. The science of archaeology has been hugely useful in understanding who the Greeks were and where they came from. A little over 100 years ago we didn't know anything about the Minoans or Mycenaeans. Now, thanks to archaeological discoveries in the early years of the 20th century we know how influential these civilisations were on the development of the ancient Greeks (see Chapter 2 for more on this). New archaeological discoveries are continually being made, producing more and more 'material culture' to sit alongside the written sources that we've always had. In this book there's a bias towards written evidence (because it really helps to emphasise points that I make!) but don't ignore the impact of archaeology!

Early Greece: 900–490 BC

This period was when Greece started to grow up. The hundreds of communities and colonies that had been established during the Dark Ages grew into new societies and what became known as *city-states*.

These city-states had different forms of government, but remarkably the market town of Athens decided upon the system of *democracy*. You can read about how it happened in Chapter 4.

All the city-states soon faced a major challenge, however, when the immense Persian Empire launched a series of attacks against them. Look at Chapter 6 to find out how they got on.

The Classical period: 490–350 BC

After dealing with the Persians, the Athenians began throwing their weight around and soon possessed an empire. The money that the empire generated was responsible for some of the fabulous culture that ancient Greece is famous for. You can read more about Athens in Chapter 7 as well as nearly every aspect of Greek life during the Classical period in Part III.

Athens's domination, of course, came to an end when the Peloponnesian War began with Sparta (see Chapter 8). After its defeat, Athens declined in influence and a whole series of squabbles between the city-states broke out with no clear winner. Until . . .

The Hellenistic period: 350–150 BC

. . . the Macedonians arrived on the scene. Under King Philip II, the Macedonians dominated the whole of Greece through both war and diplomacy. Philip's son Alexander then took things further by invading Persia, seizing control of the Persian Empire, and journeying as far as India in a quest of discovery and conquest. You can read more about this brilliant story in Chapter 11.

After Alexander died without a strong heir, his empire broke up into warring territories ruled by his former generals. Eventually, the Romans arrived in the middle of the second century BC, and what we call the Greek period came to an end.

Talking the Talk: Ancient Greek Language

The language that historians and scholars call *ancient Greek* came into being around 1100 BC and first appeared in written form around 750 BC. As I note in the earlier section 'Establishing chronology', this is a time period when all the travelling and colonisation was going on, after the collapse of the Minoan civilisation in Crete.

Developing differences

Language-wise, ancients Greek came in roughly three different types:

- **Dorian Greek** was spoken by people who lived on most parts of the Greek mainland and on the islands of Cyprus and Crete.
- **Ionic Greek** was spoken by people who lived on most of the smaller islands, as well as on the eastern coast of mainland Greece (such as the people of Athens) and the south-western coast of Asia Minor.
- **Aeolian Greek** was spoken by everybody else! This included people who lived in the northern part of the Mediterranean Sea (called the Aegean Sea) and on the north-western coast of Asia Minor.

Just like today, people also spoke in their own localised dialect. These individuals would all have been able to understand each other, but regional differences existed, even within the three types of Greek mentioned in the preceding bulleted list. (For example, people who lived in Athens spoke a slightly different form of Ionian Greek called *Attic*.) It's the same today: Think of the differences in accent between people in Glasgow and Texas. They speak the same language but with huge regional differences.

(Not) lost in translation

You can read a huge number of ancient Greek dramatic, literary, historical, poetic, and philosophical texts in translation. Many translations are available and they often vary quite considerably. Some people argue that you can never really appreciate the true nature of these works unless you read them in the original Greek but, quite frankly, that's a load of old rubbish!

Translation of these ancient texts has been going on for centuries. It's only because of the work of medieval monks (who zealously made copies) that we still have these amazing works

of literature. Modern translators are incredibly skilful at producing work that captures the spirit of ancient Greek literature while still making it accessible to readers.

Try the translations of *The Iliad* and *The Odyssey* by Homer and *The Oresteia* by Aeschylus that have recently been completed by Robert Fagles (available in Penguin Classics). They are vibrant and powerful, retaining all the chutzpah of Homer and Aeschylus while still feeling contemporary today.

In the film *Alexander* (2005), Colin Farrell, who plays Alexander the Great, speaks in his own natural Irish accent, as do all the other Macedonian officers. The more refined Greek characters (the Athenians, for example) speak standard British. This use of modern dialects was a great way of showing that, despite all speaking Greek, the Macedonians would have spoken in a slightly rougher rural dialect as opposed to the more refined Greek of the folks in Athens.

Creating the Greek alphabet

If you spoke ancient Greek, people pretty much all over the Mediterranean could understand you. Part of the reason for this is that some time around 750 BC the Greeks began to use writing to record business transactions and contracts. In doing so, they came up with a method of reproducing the sounds of their language in symbols. The result was the ancient Greek alphabet.

The Greek alphabet was made up of 24 symbols that represented letters or groups of letters, like alpha α and beta β. Figure 1-2 shows the letters of the Greek alphabet.

The ancient Greek alphabet was heavily influenced by the eastern world and ancient Mesopotamia. Indeed, initially the Greeks wrote their script from right to left, like modern Arabic. However, by the Classical period, when many of the great works of literature were produced, the Greeks had adopted the left-to-right writing style familiar to writers of English.

If you look at a modern version of ancient Greek text, it includes accents and marks to suggest where you should leave gaps for breathing when reading it out. These are all modern additions. The Greeks didn't use punctuation initially (it developed during the Hellenistic period) – just plain text. Mind you, as they invented writing as we know it, we can probably let them off for skipping the commas and full stops! The Greeks used spaces between lines of dialogue to indicate a change in the speaker. This system was known as *paragraphos* and the English word 'paragraph' comes from it.

A	B	Γ	Δ	E	Z
Alpha (al-fah)	**Beta** (bay-tah)	**Gamma** (gam-ah)	**Delta** (del-ta)	**Epsilon** (ep-si-lon)	**Zeta** (zay-tah)

H	Θ	I	K	Λ	M
Eta (ay-tah)	**Theta** (thay-tah)	**Iota** (eye-o-tah)	**Kappa** (cap-pah)	**Lambda** (lamb-dah)	**Mu** (mew)

N	Ξ	O	Π	P	Σ
Nu (new)	**Xi** (zie)	**Omicron** (om-e-cron)	**Pi** (pie)	**Rho** (roe)	**Sigma** (sig-mah)

T	Y	Φ	X	Ψ	Ω
Tau (taw)	**Upsilon** (up-si-lon)	**Phi** (phe)	**Chi** (che)	**Psi** (sigh)	**Omega** (oh-may-gah)

Figure 1-2: The letters of the Greek alphabet.

Ancient Greek was a *phonetic* language (the letters of the alphabet represented a single sound) but certain stresses were employed, especially on vowels.

Chapter 2

Encountering Prehistoric Civilisations: The Minoans and Mycenaeans

*T*hese days you can very easily find out about what happened in the past. TV, the Internet, and books like this one mean that you can very quickly and painlessly have dates and facts at your fingertips.

The ancient Greeks didn't have that ability. People living in the first millennium BC didn't know very much about what existed before them, so they filled in the big gaps in knowledge about their own past with myths and legends that explained how their town or city came to be. (See Part IV for more on the ancient Greeks' rich mythological past.)

Indeed, up until about 100 years ago, researchers were still in the dark about what existed *before* the ancient Greeks. Historians relied on myths, poems, stories, and a few ancient historical writings that mention a very successful, pre-Greek civilisation based on the island of Crete, the largest of more than 1,400 islands that lie off the coast of the Grecian mainland.

This chapter is about this early civilisation – the Minoan – as well as the Mycenaean civilisation that followed. These two unusual and hugely successful groups started the chain of events that resulted in what eventually became ancient Greece.

Starting at the Beginning: The Minoan Civilisation

At the beginning of the 20th century, archaeological digs on the island of Crete led by Englishman Sir Arthur Evans revealed the existence of a wealthy, complex civilisation that had built huge palaces. Evans named these people the *Minoans*, after the legendary King Minos (see the later section 'Mythologising the Minoans' for more info). Evan's rediscovery of Minoan culture finally provided a solution to the origins of ancient Greece.

What historians and researchers call the Minoan civilisation flourished from around 2200 to about 1450 BC on the island of Crete. The Minoans weren't Greek, but the culture that grew out of their civilisation had a huge influence on the people living on mainland Greece who eventually become the ancient Greeks.

The archaeological discoveries on Crete show that people had inhabited the island since 7000 BC. Sometime around 2600 BC a great deal of disruption and moving around seems to have happened. At this point Crete became an important centre of civilisation. Historians refer to this period (roughly 3000 to 1200 BC) as the *Bronze Age* because bronze (an alloy of copper and tin) was the most commonly used metal at the time.

Unfortunately, knowledge of the Minoans is limited because they didn't use writing in the way that the later Greeks did. Early Cretan writing seems to have been writing in pictures – like Egyptian hieroglyphics – and later developed into a more recognisable form, a series of letter-like symbols that we would think of as writing; what you might call a *script* like a letter or document. Around 3,000 Minoan tablets have been discovered, and these tablets were written in *Linear B script*, a method of writing that was used in the formation of the early Greek language (see Chapter 1). Unfortunately, because the Minoan tablets are mostly lists of goods or inventories of resources, they're very difficult to translate and don't tell much about Minoan society.

Because no Minoan texts or documents exist, historians have to use the results of archaeology to interpret and make judgements about the civilisation. Hence, the Minoan culture is considered *prehistory*, rather than history.

Organising the civilisation

Researchers do know that at the height of Minoan power (around 1850 BC) the island of Crete was divided into six different political regions, as Figure 2-1 shows. Other palace complexes were on the island, but these six seem to have been the most influential due to their evident wealth and prosperity.

Figure 2-1:
Map of
Minoan
Crete.

The remains of great palace complexes, which have been uncovered during the past hundred years or so, tell researchers that Crete was politically organised. The presence of a palace implies that a monarchy ruled a society, and the towns and cities on the Greek mainland were highly influenced by this arrangement. Later, Greek cities tended to organise themselves around a palace complex.

Of all the Minoan palace complexes, by far the biggest was constructed at Knossos on the north of the island (a 5-acre site with a main building that covered more than three acres by itself). Knossos is one of the most impressive sites that people can still view today (see Chapter 27).

Knossos wasn't just a palace; it was also a seat of government, a stronghold against invasion, and a place for storing goods and wares. The main building contained around 19 rooms, the vast majority of which were used for storage.

Wealth – and in particular the visible display of it – was a prime qualification for rulers in early societies (hence, the impressive scale of Knossos). People during the Minoan period didn't have bank accounts, so they displayed their wealth through the size and contents of their houses. The Minoans didn't have the fast cars or impressive stereo systems of today to spend their money on, so they spent it on wine, olive oil, wool, and grain. Although these items were fairly ordinary, they were vital for existence, and having a lot of them was impressive. Another reason for stockpiling so much stuff was that the Minoans made their money from trade.

Engaging in retail therapy

The Minoans were serious traders. Their economy was based on buying and selling. Have a look at the position of Crete on the Cheat Sheet map. Being down in the south-east of the Mediterranean meant that the civilisation was ideally placed to carry out lots of trade.

Human sacrifice?

One unpleasant religious practice that's often been associated with the Minoans is human sacrifice. Even today academics can't agree on whether this practice actually took place.

Several sites on Crete contain shrines with possible evidence. The best example is a shrine at Anemospilia, where a body of a young man was found in a very unnatural position on top of a platform. He was in a constricted position as if he'd been trussed up in preparation for sacrifice, and a dagger was found on top of the body. This may well have been an isolated incident. But given the fact that Minoans routinely sacrificed hundreds of animals, they could possibly have switched to sacrificing humans on occasions, perhaps when a town or city was facing major problems.

The Minoans were hugely involved in the trade of tin. They didn't mine it themselves but imported it, manufactured, and sold it on. By combining tin with copper from nearby Cyprus, they were able to make bronze. Bronze was used for everything during the Minoan period, especially weapons and tools. Bronze was also in great demand throughout the Mediterranean. A good comparison would be with how important oil is in modern society.

But tin was far from the only thing that the Minoans had for sale. Other popular Minoan products included the following:

- **Ceramics:** The Minoans produced huge amounts of pottery and decorative items that they sold all around the Mediterranean region, including Greece, Asia Minor, and as far west as Spain. These must-have items were quite simple in design – usually a dark background with decorative images such as trees, fish, and animals.

- **Gold and silver:** The most valuable of metals, gold and silver were highly prized and used only for jewellery. Wearing it was a sign of real social status. It wasn't until around 600 BC that the Greeks started using coins. Accordingly, amounts of gold and silver were used as a substitute for exchanges of high value.

- **Timber:** The mountains on Crete were thickly wooded during the Bronze Age; even more so than they are today when forest fires are still a real risk. All the available lumber enabled the Minoans to build many ships. Minoan wood was also highly prized abroad, in places such as Egypt where timber was scarce.

- **Saffron:** This rare spice was the most exclusive Minoan product. Saffron was highly prized and incredibly expensive – only the very rich could afford it. The spice had a number of uses from flavouring and preserving foods to treating various medical ailments.

> ✔ **Wool:** Wool has always been a central part of the Greek economy, even at this early stage. Sheep's wool was most commonly used and was taken as raw fibres straight from the sheep before being dyed and spun using a spindle.

As Crete became the leading supplier for many essentials and luxury goods, the island also developed a powerful hold on some of its customers on the nearby Aegean islands. Historians don't know exactly how the relationship between Crete and the surrounding area worked, but the ties must have been a mixture of dependency and colonisation. When the Athenians built a powerful empire more than 1,000 years later (see Chapter 7), contemporary historians made comparisons with the Minoans. Most likely, a lot of neighbouring islands became trading outposts that enabled the Minoans to take Cretan goods farther across the Mediterranean.

Trying to meet the mysterious Minoans

All their wealth and influence presumably brought the Minoan aristocracy a high standard of living, but knowing for sure is difficult. Aside from the spectacular remains of the palace complexes, historians know very little about the lives of these puzzling people.

Getting dressed, Minoan-style

Some illustrations that have survived on fragments of pottery show men wearing clothes rather like kilts or loincloths. Given the hot climate and active lifestyle it was a fairly common form of dress and can be found elsewhere at the time, such as in Ancient Egypt.

Women's outfits were slightly more unusual. The Minoans seem to have invented the bra. The women shown in paintings wear a type of girdle that goes round the back and supports the breasts while leaving them exposed. This unusual garment was certainly not passed on to the Greeks, who were incredibly scrupulous and controlling of female dress and appearance (see Chapter 15).

Worshipping

The one area in which historians do have a little more information is religion. The Minoans often represented their gods through animal symbols, in styles much like the decoration on their pottery.

The Minoans worshipped female deities that represented different aspects of life – a mother goddess who was associated with fertility and others that represented protection of cities, animals, the harvest, and households.

The bull was also an important symbol in Minoan religion and represented a male god that was associated with the sun. In fact, some Minoan art shows young men (and occasionally women) engaging in the bizarre practice of bull leaping. This trial of strength and dexterity required individuals to leap across the back of an untethered, fully grown bull – not dissimilar to the rodeo events in modern America.

Mythologising the Minoans

Of course, this talk of bulls and human sacrifice leads to the most famous story associated with the Minoans: Theseus and the Minotaur. This story is probably a very early example of how the Greeks used myths to explain the gaps in knowledge of their own history.

Theseus and the Minotaur

According to the story, Theseus was a great hero of the city of Athens. (Indeed, a huge number of stories are associated with his legend.) His mother Aethera brought Theseus up in the city of Troezen. When he became a young man, he left home to claim his birthright as the son of Aegeus, the king of Athens, and after many adventures he succeeded in becoming heir to the Athenian throne.

At the time, Minos, the king of Crete, was exacting a grisly annual tribute on the city of Athens: Seven girls and seven boys were taken to Crete and fed to the Minotaur that lurked in the labyrinth beneath Minos's palace. The *Minotaur* was the illegitimate half-man, half-bull son of Minos's wife Pasaphae. The creature fed on human flesh.

In the third year of the tribute, Theseus volunteered to go as one of the seven boys in order to kill the Minotaur and bring the practice to an end. Theseus did kill the Minotaur and was helped by Minos's daughter, Ariadne, who gave Theseus a ball of wool that allowed him to find his way out of the labyrinth and escape with her.

Separating history and 'mythtory'

The story of Theseus has many layers – indeed, I write more about it in Chapter 4. But for now, consider how much the story tells about what the later Greeks knew of the Minoans. The story includes many of the elements I talk about in this section: foreign colonisation, bull worship, large palace complexes, human sacrifice, and bulls.

You can easily see how later Greeks put together some of the elements of Minoan civilisation and came up with a great story that explained the

Minoans' previous dominance over their own part of the world. You can almost call this practice 'mythtory' – a creative filling-in-the-blanks between what you do know.

The story of Theseus shows how myths work – a topic I cover in Chapter 19. But the myth is particularly relevant at this point because the end of the Minoan civilisation certainly involved an intervention from mainland Greece.

Going out with a bang

At some point around 1450 BC, most of the large palaces on Crete were turned to rubble. With Minoan civilisation enjoying such success, why did it come to a sudden end?

The most common explanation is an earthquake, possibly tied in with a volcanic eruption on the island of Thera (modern-day Santorini), around 150 years earlier. Many people have tried to tie this event in with the legend of the lost city of Atlantis. If the volcano theory is true, it explains why so many of the palaces were destroyed around the same time but the dates don't quite match up.

However, some people argue that human intervention may have been involved. One reason for this is that Knossos, the biggest palace of all, appears to have survived for another 50 years or so, perhaps indicating that a war won by those from Knossos led to the large-scale destruction of the other palaces half a century earlier.

Whatever the reason, by 1400 BC Knossos itself had been destroyed and Minoan dominance and civilisation was at an end. The archaeological evidence suggests that human beings destroyed Knossos. If that was the case, only one likely candidate exists: the Mycenaeans, the newly dominant force in the eastern Mediterranean.

Meeting the New Kids on the Block: The Mycenaeans

The Mycenaean civilisation flourished between 1600 BC and the collapse of what's referred to as the Bronze Age civilisation, around about 1100 BC. Later Greeks considered the Mycenaeans to be a warlike people who were bent on conquest and the expansion of their territory, and they put Greece as we know it on the map.

Mycenaean civilisation was based in mainland Greece. As Figure 2-2 shows, its main centres were the cities of Mycenae, Tiryns, Pylos, Athens, and Thebes.

Historians have struggled to identify the origins of the Mycenaean civilisation. Most researchers now agree that the Mycenaens were probably originally from Crete. When the Minoan civilisation began to spread out around 1700 BC, some travellers settled in central Greece. Within a century or so, these individuals had established a new society that was very different from their Minoan ancestors.

Figure 2-2:
The major centres of Mycenaean civilisation.

Separating Minoan and Mycenaean: Trade versus conquest

The Minoan civilisation was primarily based on trade and commerce (see the earlier section 'Engaging in retail therapy'). Although the Minoans must've fought several wars, the empire that they gained was built on trade and exchange.

This wasn't the case with the Mycenaeans. Their civilisation was dominated by a warrior elite who gained status and influence through conquest. To become an important figure a man had to be a great warrior who had conquered towns and taken booty. One great example is the conquest of Crete around 1400 BC. Whether or not the Mycenaeans were responsible for the destruction of the palace of Knossos (skip back to the section 'Going out with a bang' for more), they certainly took advantage of its demise and gained control of Crete as a centrepiece of their huge empire.

One effect of the Mycenaean conquest was that the script they used, which historians call Linear B, became probably the earliest form of ancient Greek.

However, by far the greatest achievement associated with Mycenaean civilisation is the conquest of the immense and wealthy city of Troy on the northwestern coast of Asia Minor (modern-day Turkey). The legendary events around this conquest became known as the Trojan War. Read more about this fantastic piece of 'mythtory' in Chapter 21.

Of course, Mycenaean civilisation was much more than just war and conquest, as the following sections explore.

When looking at the Mycenaeans, you're dealing with *prehistory* – no written records exist. Historians must rely on archaeology for most of their knowledge of this civilisation.

Burying the dead

Mycenaeans buried their nobles and warrior dead in beehive-shaped tombs, known as *tholoi*. The contents of many of these larger tombs have enabled modern archaeologists to come to a lot of conclusions about the Mycenaeans.

Nobles were often buried with a lot of *grave goods*, valuable possessions that tell about the person buried. Typical goods include jewellery, armour, gold masks, and weapons.

Conspiring religion

Historians know little about Mycenaean religious practices. The Mycenaeans apparently worshipped a number of the same gods that the later Greeks did, such as Poseidon. However, they probably didn't worship in the same way. Certainly no evidence exists of the sort of temples that cropped up in later periods. (See Chapter 21 for more information on ancient Greek religion.)

Organising socially

The way the Mycenaeans organised their society influenced Greek cities and culture for the centuries that followed.

Mycenaean civilisation was divided into several different centres. The poet Homer (described in Chapter 20), who was composing around 500 years later, said that these centres were based around the major cities, including Mycenae, Pylos, and Sparta. The Mycenaeans didn't have an overall ruler; their world was probably periodically dominated by whichever king was most powerful.

Each Mycenaean city had:

- ✔ **A king:** The king was probably the biggest landowner and most successful warrior within the local area and may well have become king by force. If you think about the fact that the Mycenaeans were descended from colonists, the leadership was probably the descendants of families that had originally grabbed the best land and became the most powerful.

- ✔ **The king's court:** These free individuals were courtiers to the king and lived in large residences around the royal palace complex.

- ✔ **Ordinary people:** These free individuals were known as the *demos.* The word 'demos' is very important; see Chapter 4 where I look at the birth of democracy. These merchants, farmers, and artisans lived outside the palace complex.

- ✔ **Slaves:** The few available Mycenaean texts list slaves as having been the property of the king and working at the palace. It's highly likely that the Mycenaeans captured slaves from their foreign wars, because this was the most common method of obtaining them.

Working for a living

Evidence indicates Mycenaean society had a far more developed set of social and work roles than what historians know of the Minoans. Farming was still the main profession for the majority of people, but in and around the palace complex some Mycenaeans worked as scribes, administrators, or artisans such as potters and smiths, depending on the king's patronage.

More interestingly, the Mycenaeans developed what modern people think of as industry. One of the biggest industries was metallurgy, particularly the production of bronze, which was essential for a warlike people like the

Mycenaeans. Some of the tablets that have survived suggest that a significant proportion of the population were involved in metallurgy in the town of Pylos, and historians assume that other towns had similar arrangements.

The Mycenaeans were also heavily involved in the production of textiles. Evidence shows they produced up to 15 different textile varieties, mostly from wool and flax. Other industries included ivory carving, stone carving, and perfume making.

A large amount of what the Mycenaeans produced was sold abroad. For example, Mycenaean vases have been found in Egypt, Sicily, Western Europe, and as far away as Central Europe and Great Britain.

Expanding in all directions

After the collapse of Minoan civilisation with the fall of Knossos (see the earlier section 'Going out with a bang'), the Mycenaeans became the big players in the western Mediterranean and took over much of what had been Minoan settlements. For example, they took over the town of Miletus, which had been a Minoan colony, and the same thing happened on the island of Samos.

But the Mycenaeans didn't just focus on trading with and taking over their western neighbours. They took a much more aggressive interest in the eastern Mediterranean than the Minoans – not only trading with these areas but also establishing outposts and colonies. Bases were set up on several islands like Rhodes and Cos, where merchants stayed and acted as middlemen, letting the industries in Pylos, Argos, and elsewhere know what the local markets required. The island of Cyprus and the ports on the coast of modern-day Syria were particularly big trading centres, but the Mycenaeans also traded with ports on the coast of Asia Minor.

Eventually, the Mycenaeans were in charge pretty much everywhere, including:

- ✔ **The crumbling Hittite Empire:** By around 1300 BC, expansion brought the Mycenaeans into contact with the other big, warlike civilisation at the time – the Hittite Empire.

  The Hittites had nothing to do with the Greeks; they were a completely different people. By the time that they came into diplomatic contact with the Mycenaeans, the Hittites had become the dominant force in Asia Minor, Syria, and as far east as Mesopotamia. The Hittites had come from north of the region and spoke a very different language. Their biggest enemy were the Egyptians, with whom they were continually fighting for control of Syria.

There aren't any records of the Hittites and the Mycenaeans having any military contests, but within a few years of coming into contact with each other in 1300 BC the Hittite civilisation had collapsed. Historians don't really know why, but some archaeologists have suggested that the Hittites may have experienced a devastating civil war.

✔ **The city of Troy:** The most famous of all the Mycenaean expansions was the destruction of the city of Troy around 1250 BC. Archaeology shows that the end of Troy was probably the work of a western Greek army like that of the Mycenaeans. I talk more about the myth and reality of Troy in Chapter 21.

With the Minoans destroyed, the Hittite Empire at war with itself, Troy conquered, and no real threat from anyone elsewhere in Greece, the Mycenaeans should have dominated the Mediterranean for generations to come. They were the dominant military power and economically self-sustaining, with a large trade network throughout the Mediterranean and beyond . . . but then something happened. Historians aren't exactly sure what occurred because it happened during the region's Dark Ages (see Chapter 3 for more info).

Chapter 3

Shedding Light on Ancient Greece's Dark Ages

*I*n around 1200 BC the whole of society in the eastern Mediterranean was in trouble. In the east the Hittite civilisation had collapsed and huge numbers of people fled west into Syria, Palestine, and as far as Egypt. Around the same time the Mycenaean world fell apart (refer to Chapter 2). After this civilisation's last big hurrah at Troy, something devastating happened back at home. All the big Mycenaean city centres were attacked and utterly destroyed. Mycenae and Pylos were burned and never fully recovered. And around 50 years later a second sequence of attacks finished off the remaining cities.

The damage was devastating and conclusive, and the Greek world was humbled by it. A huge amount of the learning and technology that the Mycenaeans had developed during the past 500 years was lost. The big cities were abandoned and left as permanent landmarks to the memory of those Mycenaeans who'd died, with vast numbers of people deciding to move and re-establish themselves in other areas of the Mediterranean.

It took 300 years for the Greek world to recover, but recover it did. Although the Mycenaean culture was gone, never to return, a new set of Greek people developed, with new cities, kingdoms, and – by around 750 BC – a new form of written language that scholars recognise as ancient Greek.

So although historians refer to the period of around 1100 to 750 BC as ancient Greece's Dark Ages, light was shining at the end of the tunnel. The changes ancient Greece experienced during its Dark Ages are the focus of this chapter.

The term 'Dark Ages' is actually quite a misleading one. The term suggests a time when nothing much happened – as you'll see from this chapter, that's not the case! The idea of a Dark Age comes from the fact that historians are uncertain about exactly what happened and who went where. The age is dark in terms of information, not innovation!

Surviving the Dorian Invasion

So what cataclysmic force overwhelmed the mighty Mycenaeans in around 1200 BC? Well, according to the Greeks themselves, the Dorians did it.

Later ancient Greek historians describe the destruction of Mycenae and the burning of other Mycenaean cities as being the work of a powerful army from the north that swept down over the Peloponnese mountains and into southern Greece.

The Greeks filled in the gaps in their knowledge with myth and stories – a phenomenon I describe in detail in Chapter 2. The Dorians may well have been an example of this process.

According to the Greeks, the Dorians were a people who came from the north and smashed the Mycenaeans. Many Greeks believed the Dorians descended from a group of people called the Heraclids. The Heraclids were thought to have been the descendants of the great Greek hero Heracles (or Hercules as the Romans called him) who'd once lived in southern Greece under Mycenaean control but had then been sent into exile. The Heraclids regrouped and eventually returned, led by King Hyllus, to wreak revenge on their former masters.

The famous Greek historian Thucydides, who was writing 500 years after the end of the Mycenaean civilisation, had no doubts about what had happened:

> *Eighty years after Troy the Dorians and the sons of Herakles made themselves masters of the Peloponnese. It was with difficulty and over a long period that peace returned.*

Many other versions of this story existed then and now, and all accounts seem to point to an invasion into Greece by a big army from the north or north-west.

Exactly who the Dorians were remains a mystery. What is important, however, is that by 1100 BC things had changed. The Mycenaeans had disappeared, many people had fled from their homes to a new life elsewhere, and the map of the region was very different.

Travelling into a New (Dark) Age

The movement of most people from mainland Greece during the Dark Ages had a huge effect on the rest of the Mediterranean. Imagine if today all the people living in a city like London suddenly left and began to look for somewhere else to live in Britain. The effect on the lives of people throughout the UK would be huge. Obviously big differences exist between life then and now, but some considerations are constant: The Greeks needed water, food, shelter, and enough land to be able to sustain themselves and their families.

Unsurprisingly the Greeks ranged far and wide in their search for new land. Some went east toward modern-day Turkey and beyond; others went west to Italy, Sicily, and, by the seventh century BC, North Africa. These big migrations during the Dark Ages are one of the reasons why the history of ancient Greece is so fragmented.

As I note in Chapter 1, being Greek during this time was more a state of mind than a nationality. Well, the migrations of the Dark Ages contributed significantly to this experience.

Heading east

A vast number of people leaving mainland Greece headed east across the Mediterranean toward Asia Minor. Traditional Greek myth/history says that these people fled to the city of Athens and then on to an area known as the Ionic Coast (see the map on the Cheat Sheet), establishing ancient Greece's roots in a matter of a few years. The official version of events soon became that this movement of people was a single event of colonisation, with one population group moving from their original home to make a new one.

As ever, the truth is slightly different. The transfer of people from mainland Greece to the coast of Asia Minor was a *migration* rather than a colonisation. This process took place over a number of years rather than in one big trip. For one thing, an adequate fleet of ships wouldn't have been available for such an undertaking. Furthermore, the stuff about Athens is just propaganda. Many years later, when Athens was building up its empire from many of these Greek towns, saying that the original inhabitants had come from Athens made for a good argument to go back and aggressively force the towns to join their empire and pay a tribute! (For more on this empire-building, see Chapter 7.)

A much more likely comparison of the process is that of the Pilgrim Fathers leaving England for America, a brave and adventurous group of people embarking on a journey of discovery without really knowing too much about the land that they were going to. Again like the Pilgrim Fathers, these on-the-move Greeks were a mixed group from all around the mainland. Whole towns wouldn't have moved at once and each successive migration would have been made up of a mixed bag of people. It was only when they made land and founded a new place to live that they became a new 'people'.

Those that had headed east became known as the *Ionian* Greeks because the coastland and nearby islands they inhabited were known as Ionia. Confusingly this region had nothing to do with the Ionian Sea, which refers to the stretch of water between Sicily, Southern Italy, and Western Greece. Although the two words look exactly the same in English, they meant different things in ancient Greek.

Meeting the neighbours

Although much of the territory of Ionia was uninhabited when the Greeks arrived, the areas to the immediate north and south weren't. These areas were called Aeolis and Doria (so-called because some Dorian Greeks had ended up living there) and they'd both been populated for some time.

- **Aeolis:** The people to the north of Ionia were known as the Aeolians. They were probably also Greeks who had left the eastern Greek mainland a little before the travellers who became known as the Ionians. Later Greek writers maintained that the Aeolians were the sons of Orestes, the son of the famous Mycenaean king Agamemnon. But this bit of genealogy is just a myth. The area known as Aeolia was very fertile, and the Aeolians seem to have spent their time as relatively contented farmers.

- **Doria:** To the south of Ionia was Doria, which was under the control of a very different people called the Carians. The Carians spoke an old language that was different from the Greek languages. They'd been in contact with the Mycenaeans and had absorbed a lot of Greek culture but they were definitely not Greek. Like the Aeolians they were, in the main, farmers.

The Greek writer Strabo describes the Carians as *barbaroi*, which gave rise to the modern word *barbarians*. Strabo's word choice came from his belief that when the Carians tried to speak Greek, they made a noise that just sounded like 'ba, ba, ba'! The Greeks used this word to describe anybody who was a non-Greek speaker.

Establishing new Greek cities

The new Ionian territory was made up of 12 major cities. Two of them were on the islands of Chios and Samos and the others, such as Ephesus and Smyrna, were on the mainland (see the Cheat Sheet map).

The Greeks learn to write

The Greeks in the east were in very close association with the Phoenicians and picked up from them something far more important than any treasures or fancy goods. At some point around 750 BC, Greeks in the east began to use the Phoenician system of language notation, which led to the Greek alphabet. Although some letters and forms varied depending on where ancient Greeks lived throughout the region, the basic underlying principles of the Phoenician-based system became standard throughout the Mediterranean. In fact, the Greek expression for writing is *phoinikeia grammata*, which means 'Phoenician writings'.

In the main, the new settlers built their settlements on peninsulas just away from the mainland. These areas were linked to the mainland by narrow causeways, or *isthmuses*. These locations were beneficial for a few reasons:

- ✔ The new cities enjoyed relatively cool temperatures along the hot Asia Minor coastline.

- ✔ The geography offered natural harbours that the new inhabitants used for trading supplies and receiving friends and relatives from the Greek mainland.

- ✔ The new cities were more secure from attack because they had water as a natural barrier on one side and freshly built fortifications on the landward side.

Early on, these new towns weren't particularly remarkable – but they became tremendously important later on. Constantly involved in the struggles between Greece and Persia, they were eventually used as an excuse for the invasion of the Persian Empire by Alexander the Great. (For more on Alexander the Great, march to Chapter 11.)

Soon after their foundation, the cities were nothing more than increasingly popular trading spots. The trade that they engaged in, however, brought them into contact with a culture that had a major impact on ancient Greeks – the Phoenicians.

Trading with the Phoenicians

The Mycenaeans had been adventurous traders and their kings had spent their wealth on luxuries from the east, in particular Syria and Egypt. The knowledge gained from trade routes in the eastern Mediterranean became more wide-spread on the Greek mainland and helped with the migrations that followed the collapse of Mycenaean civilisation.

The main traders in luxury goods from the east were the Phoenicians. The Phoenicians were originally from the east, possibly as far east as the Persian Gulf, and they established themselves in the city of Tyre on the Syrian coast, in the area known now as Lebanon. From there they eventually founded colonies as far away as Cadiz in Spain and most famously Carthage in North Africa.

Going west

While the great migration of people to the east took place, things continued to happen on the Greek mainland. Archaeology indicates that the tenth and ninth centuries BC (900–700 BC) was a period of great poverty on the Greek mainland. After the destruction of the Mycenaean civilisation, a great deal of the established industry and infrastructure disappeared. Society became entirely dependent on agriculture, and the number of inhabited sites decreased significantly.

The old system of Mycenaean kings was dependent on wealth, so when the kings were eliminated, society changed too. The old palace culture of the Mycenaeans disappeared (see Chapter 2), and a levelling out of social classes took place. In each community, power became shared among a group of the most influential people rather than one man. I write more about these changes in Chapter 4.

The most immediate result of these societal changes was another wave of migration. Around 750 BC new groups of people were looking to leave mainland Greece. This time, the people weren't fleeing invasion (see 'Heading east' earlier in this chapter). Instead, they were:

- Discontented nobles who'd lost influence
- Struggling farmers who were looking for new territories to cultivate

With the Ionian Greek cities firmly established to the east, these new travellers had to look elsewhere for fresh land – and they looked to the west, as Figure 3-1 shows.

Settling in Italy

One of the western-bound Greek travellers' first ports of call was southern Italy. In fact, so many early ancient Greeks migrated to Italy that the Romans later called the south of Italy and Sicily *Magna Graecia*, which was Latin for 'Greater Greece'.

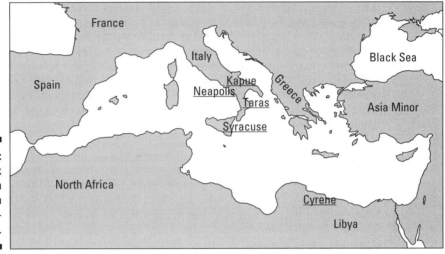

Figure 3-1:
Greek
colonies in
the western
Mediter-
ranean.

In the eighth century BC westward migrating ancient Greeks founded the
Italian towns of Neapolis (Naples), Kapue (Capua), and Taras (Taranto).
These towns became very rich and powerful thanks to their close trade links
with mainland Greece and beyond. The towns maintained their independence
for more than 500 years until the Romans finally conquered them and
absorbed them into their empire.

On the island of Sicily, the most important new town by far was Syracuse
(see Figure 3-1). Greeks from the city of Corinth founded Syracuse in around
734 BC. They were led by Archias, who named the town *Sirako* after a nearby
swamp. Due to its excellent position for trading, Syracuse grew very quickly
and became immensely wealthy. The money was spent on extending the
harbour facilities and defences and for some time Syracuse was considered
to be the most powerful Greek city in the whole of the Mediterranean.

Setting up in Egypt

Coincidence is a wonderful thing. Just around the time that ancient Greeks
were establishing more western towns and initiating trade across the
Mediterranean, the ancient civilisation of Egypt opened its doors to trade.
For thousands of years Egypt had been closed to Mediterranean society.
Egypt had no need to trade with anybody because it was so fertile and pretty
much self-sustaining. For more on the histories and mysteries of ancient
Egypt, check out *The Ancient Egyptians For Dummies* by Charlotte Booth
(Wiley).

During ancient Greece's Dark Ages, Egypt was invaded and conquered by its great rival Assyria, led by the great monarch Assarhaddon. The Assyrians ruled Egypt for several generations until Assurbanipal, one of Assarhaddon's successors, was the victim of a big revolt led by Psammetichus. Psammetichus was probably from Libya in North Africa and had raised a mercenary army from all around that included new Greeks from Ionia and Caria. After he won a tremendous victory over Assurbanipal, one of Psammetichus's first acts was to open the doors of Egypt to his new allies.

This meant that Greeks could now trade with Egypt and travel there to experience the country. As a result, many Greeks encountered the art and architecture of Egypt for the first time, and the rich Egyptian culture had a huge impact on them. For more on the Greeks' interactions with the Egyptians, see Chapter 17.

Venturing into Cyrene

Psammetichus came from present-day Libya in North Africa, and the Greeks soon established a town there too. In around 630 BC, a group left the small island of Thera and founded the town of Cyrene (shown in the map in Figure 3-1). Cyrene was in a great location, roughly halfway between Carthage and Egypt, and it very quickly became large and wealthy.

Ancient Greece's Dark Ages were actually a tremendous period of travelling and expansion, which changed the map forever. People living on opposite sides of the Mediterranean now, appropriately, claimed to be Greek and spoke a version of the Greek language. Large trade networks were building up and these new international Greeks were adopting new things such as writing.

Back on mainland Greece, however, something equally remarkable was happening: old social structures were breaking down and new rulers emerging. Read all about it in Chapter 4.

Chapter 4

Governing by Kings, Tyrants, and (Eventually) Democrats

*I*f you leave a group of people in a room together for long enough, they're bound to end up having an argument about something. TV these days is based around this concept. Usually the disagreement comes up because somebody feels unable to express a point because others aren't listening.

The same was true 2,500 years ago in ancient Greece. Back then the arguments were about who controlled the towns and cities that had developed after the big migrations that I write about in Chapter 3. Unlike most arguments, however, these ancient disagreements ended up producing something amazing.

This chapter is the story of how a bunch of farmers and aristocrats managed to invent the system of government that still exists throughout the world today – democracy.

Shaping the New Societies

When ancient Greece's Dark Ages came to an end in the eighth century BC, the communities that had survived in mainland Greece were very small and simple. The big expansions overseas involved thousands of people leaving the Greek mainland, severely weakening the old Mycenaean power centres (see Chapters 2 and 3).

Remembering Theseus

The shift from local governments to a centralised government took place before the Greeks started recording their own history. Without recorded history to rely on, the Greeks often turned to characters and events from their mythology to explain things.

Some later writers credited the mythological noble Theseus (see Chapter 2) for bringing the whole of the region of Attica under centralised control. He did this by setting up a council of nobles that met regularly and made decisions about the running of the area as a whole.

Of course, one man wasn't solely responsible for uniting the entire, and significantly large, territory of Attica. Still, the Athenians' mythological hero proved a very useful story to gloss over the years of fighting and plotting among several wealthy families in the region.

As a result most ancient Greeks at the end of the Dark Ages were likely to live in small villages ruled by local nobles and wealthier citizens with the most land. Life for most people was very tough, and the chances of improvement and advancement very small. Depending on who you were, you filled a certain place in society. You were born into your position, and change was virtually impossible.

As an ancient Greek at the end of the Dark Ages, your family and your *clan,* or extended family that you came from, were the most important considerations in your life. Your ultimate superiors were local lords to whom you and the rest of your community paid tribute.

Over about half a century, these very local communities began to come under central control by one town. This change probably wasn't the communities' choice; they were most likely forced into the new arrangement by threats and violence from another town in the area that wanted to expand its territory. Probably the most significant example of this was what happened in the region of Attica in western Greece (see the Cheat Sheet map) because it resulted in the formation of the city of Athens. Several important families in the region fought and plotted against each other for hundreds of years. But by the seventh century BC, the region was in the hands of an aristocratic elite.

Meeting the ruling class

In the seventh century BC the people of Attica were ruled by what they considered to be a king, but this leadership wasn't what modern people would understand as a king. The ancient Greeks used the word *basileus* to describe a king. This word translates as 'sovereign', so the individuals weren't actually kings in the sense of Henry VIII. A *basileus* was just one of a board of annually elected officials – like councillors or local government officials – called the *arkhons*. This board formed a ruling council that met at a spot known as the *Areopagus* on the Hill of Ares in Athens and exercised control over Athens and the region of Attica. Eventually the title *basileus* became used to describe an *arkhon* with special religious duties.

Although this combination of a *basileus* and an *arkhon* may sound like a move toward a more open form of government, the arrangement wasn't really much of a change. The opportunity to be an *arkhon* wasn't open to everybody – only those born into the leading aristocratic families in Athens had the right to stand for election. The elections were also only open for the aristocrats to vote in! So in a way the government was as much of a closed shop as it had been under the earlier king-led system. The aristocrats were still in control; there were just more of them.

The aristocrats themselves clearly recognised the exclusive nature of the system because they named the group the *Eupatridai*, which means 'the sons of good fathers'.

The power structures found in Athens and the Attica region during this period weren't all that different from the surrounding area. Throughout Greece and the Mediterranean at the time, the vast majority of people who ruled did so based largely on the qualifications of wealth and birth. The aristocrats were generally the oldest families who'd lived in the area longest – and therefore grabbed all the best land when they arrived. Consequently, they become the wealthiest and the most influential citizens.

Introducing the new middle class

People always find something to argue about, and the system of government in Athens was no different. Any agreement among the aristocrats held only for as long the entire ruling group agreed. If one man wanted to take all the power for himself, the system could break. Indeed, by the seventh century BC the relationships among the various aristocratic families in Athens had reached a breaking point, but another potentially bigger problem existed – the growing middle class.

As Athens had grown and expanded, it had become wealthier. In particular, people who made money from trade or successfully farmed less attractive land were frequently as wealthy as the leading aristocrats. Although these successful individuals made up Athens's new middle class, they were still born outside the noble families and had no chance of being elected to rule.

Around the same time big changes were happening to the way that the Athenians made war and fought against their enemies. The Athenians had adopted the *hoplite* method of fighting (see Chapter 5), which brought together and armed many male Athenians. Unsurprisingly this group soon realised they had enormous power at their disposal.

This mixture of middle-class discontent and burgeoning military strength was a time-bomb waiting to go off. All that was needed was an individual with the charisma and drive to take advantage of the situation and initiate massive change.

Surviving the Cycle of Tyranny

The Greeks used a word called *turannos* that means 'the rule of one' and is the source of the modern word *tyrant*. However, the ancient Greeks' notion of the tyrant didn't necessarily have the connotations of cruelty and harshness that it does today.

The earliest surviving instance of the word *tyrant* is in a poem by Archilochos. This piece of verse talks about the tyrant Gyges who reigned in Lydia in Asia Minor between 680 and 640 BC:

> *To me the possessions of Gyges rich in gold are of no concern, envy has not seized me, and I do not look with jealousy on the works of the gods, nor do I passionately desire great tyranny; such things are far from my eyes . . .*

Nevertheless, many of the tyrants who seized control in ancient Greece did go on to run repressive regimes, as the following sections explore.

Kylon: Discovering that tyranny is harder than it looks

The first attempt at tyranny in Athens was a failure. In 640 BC, Kylon tried to take advantage of the discontent in the city (see the preceding section).

Kylon was an interesting character. He was a former winner at the Olympic games (see Chapter 16 for more on the Olympics), which made him very popular with the common people who saw him as a hero. He also had the backing of his father-in-law Theagenes, who was the tyrant of Megara.

According to the historians Herodotus and Thucydides, Kylon acted on the advice of the Delphic Oracle by trying to sieze Athens during the Festival of Zeus when much of the city was otherwise engaged. Unfortunately for him the plan failed and he was forced to flee to the temple of Athena. Kylon was persuaded out by a promise that he wouldn't be harmed but then stoned to death! Although Kylon's plan was a total failure, it was a warning of what was to come.

Drakon: Changing the rules

Discontent rumbled on in Athens, and the *Eupatridai* responded to Kylon's action by attempting to tighten their control on the city. Around 620 BC, Drakon published the first-ever Athenian law code, defining the rules by which Athens would be governed. (These laws were deliberately harsh, and Drakon's name is the source of the word *draconian*.)

In particular the laws tried to break down the idea that people should look to their own family for justice and take vengeance when someone had been wronged. Drakon's laws made clear that justice was the role of the state. This might not seem like such a controversial idea to us but it was establishing the state as able to interfere in private affairs. This was a big change because previously it had been the role of the individual to protect his own household. The law particularly affected the aristocrats of Athens who'd previously acted as they wished. Drakon was attempting to get this group under state control – a laudable aim but probably for his own benefit rather than anybody else's.

Enter Solon: A Man of the People

With so many tensions pulling at the organisation of society, ancient Athens seemed about to break. The Athenians recognised how critical the situation had become and in 594 BC appointed Solon, a middle-class Athenian who'd made his money from trade, as *arkhon*. Solon is very interesting to historians because he's the earliest Greek historical figure who's famous, well-documented, and real.

In fact, Solon was the first ancient Greek to write his autobiography. It wasn't actually a book but he composed numerous poems for people to recite and so remember his achievements after he was long gone.

> *To the people I have given such privilege as is enough neither taking away nor adding to their honour. While those who had power and were famed for their wealth, for them I took care that they should suffer no injury. I stood, holding out my strong shield over both, and I did not allow either to triumph unjustly.*

Making changes

Boasting aside, Solon did have a tough job to do. Athens was in a difficult situation with all the classes feeling hard done by. As a result, Solon made some sweeping changes, including:

- ✔ **Cancelling debts:** Solon introduced legislation that he called the *seisakhtheia* or 'the shaking off of burdens'. Many peasants with small amounts of land were effectively paying protection money to members of the aristocracy from whom they rented it. If their crops failed they got further and further into debt and eventually had to vacate the land.

- ✔ **Defining new political classes:** Solon divided the city population politically based on agricultural wealth. This policy broke the exclusive power of the *Eupatridai,* and the wealthiest citizens in Athens now had the opportunity to become *arkhons* regardless of whether they came from one of the city's original families.

- ✔ **Establishing the new council of 400:** By far Solon's biggest change was the introduction of a new council called the *boule.* This assembly was made up of 400 citizens, 100 from each of the four Athenian clans, and gave an opportunity for the rest of the citizen body to participate in debate.

The reforms of Solon were publicised in an interesting way. All the individual laws were numbered and inscribed on wooden tables or *axones*. Each law was then quoted by number, like items on a take-away menu. Citizen were required to swear an oath that they would obey the new laws for the next ten years, the idea being that the laws would be revised a decade later.

Stepping out of the limelight

Solon's reforms seemed like real progress. His policies attempted to prevent the *Eupatridai* from lording over the rest of the population, reduce the economic problems of the lower classes, and give the lower classes a voice in the process of running the city.

Unfortunately Solon was one of the first people to discover that you can't please all the people all the time. His debt laws proved extremely popular with the lower classes and greatly helped poor farmers but the leaders of the aristocratic clans were hugely resentful. Nevertheless, it kept more people working on the land, which was Solon's intention. But his political reforms had an entirely different outcome as the aristocrats tried to seize back control (see the following section 'Bouncing Back to Tyranny').

Anarchy!

The whole point of Solon's reforms was to stop Athens from falling victim to tyrants. Unfortunately the same old problems soon cropped up again. The period immediately after Solon is another one for which historians don't have many sources. Researchers do know that in around 589 BC, Athens fell into a struggle among the aristocrats that was so bad no *arkhons* were elected for two years. The Greeks used the term *anarkhy* – meaning 'without *arkhons*' – to describe this time. Of course, this is where the modern word *anarchy* comes from.

Solon retired from public life. The details of his later life are sketchy. Some people say that he went travelling but it seems that he eventually returned to Athens. Unfortunately by the time he died in 558 BC he saw all his good work undone by the vengeful *Eupatridai* and other opportunists.

Bouncing Back to Tyranny

After the crumbling of Solon's reforms and a brief period of political anarchy, Athens was ripe for potential tyrants. Several people made attempts to seize power. By far the most successful was the man who dominated Athens in the sixth century BC – Peisistratos.

Peisistratos: Playing the system

While Solon had been trying to solve Athens's social and political problems, the city had been in conflict with the neighbouring city of Megara. During the conflict the Athenians had successfully attacked and captured the port of Nisaea, an ally of Megara. The leader of the expedition was called Peisistratos, and his military success encouraged him to launch a political career.

Solon's reforms and the chaos that followed had led to a split amongst the Athenian people. On the one side were the aristocrats and on the other were the *democrats*, from the Greek word *demos* which meant 'the people'. The democrats believed that Solon hadn't gone far enough in giving power to the whole population.

Peisistratos targeted the democrats as allies. In 561 BC he appeared in the *agora* or public square covered in blood and claiming to have been injured by his political enemies. He used the ensuing public outrage to his advantage and seized control of the city.

Essentially Peisistratos played Solon's system to his own advantage. Peisistratos didn't change anything that Solon had put in place; by using bribery and intimidation he just made sure that every year his own supporters were elected as *archons*. Eventually people were keen to vote for his supporters as they realised that their own prospects of advancement would be limited if they didn't. Simple really.

Out, in, and back out again

Peisistratos's grip on power was actually quite simple to break. He dominated Athens for five years until a faction of aristocrats led by a man named Megacles managed to drive him into exile in 556 BC.

However, Megacles was unable to keep hold on the argumentative elements within his own party, and within a few years, he sought to reconcile with Peisistratos, sealing the deal by arranging that the former tyrant marry his daughter. In 550 BC Peisistratos returned to Athens a hero.

Of course, Peisistratos didn't stick to the arrangement with Megacles. Peisistratos already had two sons from his first marriage, and he wanted them to take power after his death. Consequently, he treated Megacles's daughter badly and refused to recognise her as his wife so as not to weaken the position of his sons.

Unsurprisingly Megacles was upset about the situation and immediately betrayed Peisistratos to enemies. After a very brief power struggle, Peisistratos was forced into exile once again.

Regrouping abroad

In exile for the second time, Peisistratos learned from his mistakes. This second exile was much longer, lasting over a decade. During this period, Peisistratos realised that to truly dominate Athens he needed support from other powerful states throughout Greece. The benefits of this strategy were two-fold:

- ✔ The Athenians would see Peisistratos as the only person able to handle the foreign affairs of Athens.
- ✔ Peisistratos would be able to immediately build up an army to help him grasp and keep hold of power.

Noble failures – Harmodios and Aristogeiton

In 514 BC, two lovers named Harmodios and Aristogeiton attempted to end Hippias's rule by assassinating Peisistratos's other son, Hipparkhos, during a public festival. The plot succeeded, but Harmodios was killed during it and Aristogeiton was captured and died under torture.

But despite the relative failure, the two assassins became celebrated figures in Athens and were considered to be important heroes in the struggle for democracy. Unfortunately, this celebrated status wasn't quite based on truth. Harmodios and Aristogeiton were both aristocrats and wanted to get rid of Hippias so they could replace him with another set of aristocrats. But the romance of their story ensured their fame.

Harmodios and Aristogeiton became such celebrities that several statues were erected to their memory in Athens. The rose-tinted view of their exploits was also remembered in later ancient Greek drinking songs like this one:

In a branch of myrtle I shall bear my sword like Harmodios and Aristogeiton when the two of them slayed the tyrant and made Athens a city of equal rights.

Peisistratos spent ten years building up support in Macedonia, Thessaly, and other places to the north of Athens (refer to the Cheat Sheet map). Finally, in 540 BC, he landed with an army at Marathon and swept virtually unopposed into Athens. He declared that he was the true and legal ruler of the city. He was back in power and this time he wasn't shifting for anybody.

Enjoying the benefits of tyranny

Peisistratos stayed in power for the next 13 years, and during this time Athens undeniably went through a boom period. Peisistratos's aggressive foreign policy built up Athenian territory around Greece and generated a lot of revenues.

In fact, during this time some of the earliest of ancient Greece's impressive building projects began. Virtually all of the building programmes attributed to Peisistratos are now lost but he's said to have initiated the building of several religious buildings in the *agora* (the main town square, like the Roman *forum*) as well as a large palace for himself. The knock-on effect was that artists were attracted to Athens – like artists in Renaissance Italy, creative people went where the money was. Peisistratos's other cultural achievement was the introduction of two new elements to religious festivals; the singing of *dithyrambs* (hymns sung in honour of the gods) and also tragic drama. To do so he introduced the first *orchestra* (performance space) in the city.

Hippias: Tyranny as a family business

Peisistratos's hold on power was so complete that when he died in 527 BC he was able to hand over control to his son Hippias. Unfortunately for Hippias, his father's personality had been a big part of his success. Many people who had previously supported Peisistratos turned against Hippias.

After the assassination of his brother (see the nearby sidebar 'Noble failures – Harmodios and Aristogeiton'), Hippias became more severe, and many influential aristocrats were forced to flee Athens. Those individuals who stayed needed fresh help. The people who they turned to were something of a surprise – the Spartans.

Getting to Know the Spartans

Although the Athenians couldn't have known it at the time, the Spartans were to become their mortal enemy and also the most feared and famous fighting force in the ancient world.

The city of Sparta was to the south-west of Athens in a region called Laconia (take a look at the Cheat Sheet map). The Greek term for the region was *Lacedaemon*, and that's why the Spartans are sometimes referred to as the Lacedaemonians. Their way of life was considered to be brutal and without luxury, hence the modern word *Spartan*, which means simple and non-luxurious.

Growing up Spartan

The Spartans first came to prominence after the Dorian invasions (see Chapter 3 for more details) when the old inhabitants of the region were kicked out and replaced by tribesmen from the north-west and Macedonia. Being both very warlike and very good at it, the Spartans soon gained control of the whole of Laconia. By the time that Hippias was tyrant in Athens, Sparta was the leading power in southern Greece.

Two things made Sparta very different from all the other Greeks states:

- ✔ Sparta was the only state to have a standing professional army. Read more about this in Chapter 5.

- ✔ The Spartans governed themselves. Other cities in Greece were experimenting with new forms of government and different systems (see the sidebar 'Know your ocracies', later in this chapter), but the Spartans had a form of government and social organisation that was fixed and unchanging.

Living the hellish life of a Helot

Nearly all the citizens of Sparta were involved in running the state and were brought up since childhood to perform their roles (see Chapter 5). An unfortunate group of people known as the *helots* carried out farming, labour, and all other manual work required by Sparta. These people were serfs (or workers) owned by the state. The *helots* had come to their position because their land had been incorporated into the Spartan state, and they were now forced to work for it. It was a grim existence: The *helots* worked hard for little reward and no chance of bettering their station in life.

Helots made up 90 per cent of the Spartan population. As a result, the Spartans were always worried about revolts and developed a particularly unpleasant way of keeping power over the *helots*. Because the *helots* didn't count as Spartan citizens, they could technically be considered foreigners or enemies. Consequently every year the *gerousia* would vote to declare war on the *helots* and then carry out massacres to keep the numbers down. The Spartans also considered that this brutality was a useful way of giving young soldiers practice at killing.

In short, Sparta had two kings who were the top dogs, taking the roles of generals in war and chief priests in peace. A group of elected officials called the *ephors* and a council called the *gerousia* carried out the actual administration of the state. The system wasn't particularly unusual except for the fact that many positions were for life and were full-time jobs. Thus, the aristocracy of Sparta devoted their entire lives to the official business of Sparta – which included fighting many wars.

Getting involved in Athens

The Spartans were a warlike people keen on furthering their territory, and they had a pretty brutal attitude toward violence and death – all of which makes them a surprising choice for the Athenian aristocrats seeking their help.

Yet after the failed attempt to remove Hippias, the Athenian aristocrats were forced to look to Sparta for help. According to the Greek historian Herodotus, Sparta had a reputation as being sympathetic to requests for help from states under tyranny. In addition, a prophecy from the Delphic oracle (see Chapter 21) suggested to the Spartans that they should involve themselves in the Athenian situation.

The end result was that in 510 BC, the Spartan king Kleomenes led his troops into Athens and forced Hippias and his entire family to flee. He couldn't have imagined what would happen next.

Considering Kleisthenes: The Beginnings of Democracy

When Kleomenes intervened in Athens and restored the usual form of government, fresh elections were held. One of the candidates was a man called Kleisthenes. When Kleisthenes made a series of important reforms to the Athenian constitution in 508 BC, he never imagined the impact he'd have on the history of mankind. Kleisthenes's change – arguably – created the idea of *demokratia* or 'rule of the people'.

Rather than being the product of some high-minded ideals, democracy was the result of another aristocratic squabble. Kleisthenes himself was a blue-blood Athenian aristocrat. The year before he had lost out to a fellow aristocrat, Isagoras, in the election for *arkhon*. Rather than seek revolution or look for military support, Kleisthenes appealed to the common people for support. In this case, the 'common people' were individuals who didn't really have a voice, even after the reforms of Solon; people such as traders and farmers without much land or social status.

Kleisthenes proposed new laws in the *ekklesia* that allowed all citizens to take part in the process of government. Unsurprisingly Isagoras tried to block the moves, but he didn't have enough support. As a result, Isagoras called in Kleomenes of Sparta to quell the unrest in the city.

Kleomenes and his troops turned up in Athens, but he took things a bit too far, expelling 700 pro-Kleisthenes aristocratic families from the city and then leaving Isagoras to sort things out himself. Isagoras attempted to abolish Kleisthenes's reforms, but Kleisthenes responded by returning to the city with a small number of troops and forcing Isagoras to surrender. Finally, Kleisthenes was able to complete his proposed reform.

Reforming and reorganising

In essence Kleisthenes only made one big change: He scrapped the wealth-based classes that Solon had created nearly 90 years before and instead divided the population in terms of where people lived.

To do this Kleisthenes created ten new *phulai*, or tribes. Your tribe depended on where in the city you were born rather than which class you were from or how much money you had. Each tribe was further divided into *demoi*, or *demes*. These were smaller districts, like the constituencies or wards making up a City or County Council , a few streets or a zip-code district. The *demoi* became the units in which local business was done and meant that *demoi* representatives could take the views of each local area to the *ekklesia* and get it on the agenda to be discussed.

Knowing your ocracies

Although Athens is heralded as the birthplace of democracy, many different forms of government existed in ancient Greece and democracy was just one of them. Here are some common governmental forms (and examples from ancient Greek history):

✔ **Democracy:** Literally the 'rule of the people'. In a democracy, the people make decisions about the policy and actions of their community. In the ancient world, this tended to be *participative* (people actually voted and debated themselves) rather than *representative* (where they elected somebody to do it for them). For more on democracy, see Chapter 7.

✔ **Monarchy:** Rule by a king or queen. In this form of government, an absolute ruler is unelected, and his or her authority is unquestioned. The monarch may (or may not) be able to appoint a successor. Monarchy of a type was very popular in early Greek culture and survived throughout Asia Minor and in Macedonia.

✔ **Oligarchy:** Rule by the few. In early Athens, the aristocrats descended from the region's early settlers who had claimed the best land functioned as an oligarchic governing body.

✔ **Plutocracy:** Rule of the wealthy; from the Greek word *ploutos*, meaning wealth. A minimum property or wealth requirement was usually in place for those who wanted to take part in government. Plutocracies were normally mercantile communities like several of the Greek islands such as Samos.

✔ **Timarchy:** Nothing to do with people called Tim; derived from the Greek word *time*, which meant honour or respectability. In practice, a timarchy could be anything from the strongest warrior to the most respected family ruling a region. Many people argue that Sparta was a timarchy and some Mycenaean states are good examples of warrior timarchy.

✔ **Tyranny:** Literally 'rule by one'. In ancient Greece, the individual often seized power but sometimes he was voted in. The Greek meaning didn't have the negative associations that it does in the modern world.

Throughout the ancient world these and many more systems flourished – or they were combined as suited a particular political moment. For example, the Roman Empire was essentially an oligarchy but with elements of plutocracy; at certain points it was fundamentally a tyranny!

After Kleisthenes's reform a massive section of the Athenian population that previously hadn't been able to gain citizenship now could. Theoretically the change meant that any citizen from any social status could become an *arkhon*.

In actuality, things didn't turn out like this – and it was very unlikely that Kleisthenes wanted any other result. During the next century nearly all the people that ruled Athens continued to be aristocrats.

Taking small steps toward democracy

What Kleisthenes achieved wasn't democracy in the way you think of it today. Athenian political involvement depended on citizenship, which meant no women, resident slaves, or resident foreigners were able to vote. Also, it was highly unlikely that anybody outside the aristocratic elite had the money or influence to win an election.

However, Kleisthenes did recognise the power of popular opinion (and how he could manipulate it). The changes that he made ensured that the reformers who followed him in the fifth century BC could create something truly extraordinary. I talk about how the system worked in Chapter 7.

When Kleisthenes was making his reforms at the end of the sixth century BC, the word the Greeks used for popular rule was *isonomia*, which literally meant 'equality under law' and referred to the status that the creation of the tribes brought to all citizens. The Greek word *demokratia* had a much more serious meaning and referred to the people holding all power. The Athenians would have considered that their state was a *demokratia* and would have described it as such. So *demokratia* was an Athenian invention!

Challenging the new order

The Spartans weren't best pleased with the political reforms of Kleisthenes and were quick to respond when he kicked Isagoras out. In 506 BC, Kleomenes returned with another Spartan army intent on forcing Kleisthenes and his supporters out for a second time, but the Spartan attack didn't work. The mass public support that Kleisthenes was able to call on saw the Spartans soundly defeated, and the same happened to invading armies from elsewhere the following year.

The reforms of Kleisthenes had banded the people together to a common cause in a manner ancient Greeks hadn't previously experienced.

Chapter 5

Fighting and Warring: Greece Gets Heavy

Timokritos was bold in war. This is his grave.
Ares the war-god spares the coward, not the brave.

–Anakreon of Teos (circa 550 BC)

*L*ike death and taxes, war is something that seems likely to always be part of being human. Even today, with much of the world at peace, wars are still going on all around. For the luckier individuals and nations, war is something experienced from afar through newspapers, TV reports, and re-creations in films. You might know people affected by war – but for many, war is not a close-to-home experience.

In ancient Greece, however, the situation couldn't have been more different. War was essentially ever-present. Depending on who you were, war was either a threat or an opportunity for glory. If you were male then, whatever your social status, your involvement was likely to be brutal, painful, and right in the thick of battle. In ancient Greece warfare was upfront and personal.

In this chapter I cover the basics of Greek warfare on sea and land, focusing on the experience of war and warfare in ancient Greece from the end of the Dark Ages (around 750 BC) through to the rise of Macedonia (around 350 BC).

I describe the activities and equipment involved in war, how various combat tactics developed, and why the Spartans (see Chapter 4) became famous for being so good at fighting.

I examine specific techniques as they relate to particular battles or time periods in other chapters. For example, Chapter 8 offers details on siege warfare, which was critical during the Peloponnesian War and when Athens was under siege by the Spartans.

Joining the Fight

When a war took place in ancient Greece it involved all men of fighting age. Most modern states have armed forces to fight wars for them, and fighting, patrolling, and eventually keeping peace after battle are these people's jobs. But in ancient Greece, responsibility wasn't divided up this way. If a town was attacked, it had to defend itself, and that meant that every male citizen who was old enough (and not too old) to hold a sword took part in the effort. Indeed, officers and (in the case of Sparta, kings) were required to fight in the front line in just the same way as common men. War was a great leveller in ancient Greece. The experience on the battlefield was the same for every man, regardless of station.

In short, the vast majority of the city states that I write about in Chapters 2, 3, and 4 defended themselves by using a citizen militia, an army made up of the male citizen population and led by officials chosen by the state or elected by the people. For example, if you wanted to stop somebody from attacking your farm and stealing your property, you had to protect it yourself. The only exception to this citizen-led system was Sparta, a city-state whose whole system was built around constructing and maintaining a fearsome standing army (a group of men who had no other responsibility than war, a professional force). See the later section 'Living for Killing: The Spartans' for more info.

One fascinating aspect of ancient Greek warfare is how little it changed over many centuries. Yes, tactics improved, as did the calibre of weapons, but if you took a soldier from 750 BC and put him in the middle of a battle with Alexander the Great in 350 BC, the basic experience was amazingly similar – even though 400 years had passed. So what I write about arms, armour, and tactics in this chapter goes for much of the historical period from 750 BC to 350 BC. (Of course, I make mention of any changes and differences whenever appropriate.)

IN THEIR WORDS
ΣΩΦ

Fighting like a Homeric hero

Ancient Greek males had to learn to fight and use weapons. Much of this was done through physical exercise in the *gymnasium* (see Chapter 16) as nearly all Greek sports were developed out of practising the skills needed to fight in war.

In particular, the Greeks considered Homer's *Iliad*, the epic poem of the Trojan War, a mine of information on all manner of subjects (for more on *The Iliad* and its influence, see Chapter 20). The only problem with using this great work of literature as a training manual is that the characters are a lot to live up to. Indeed, the Greek and Trojan warriors in *The Iliad* fight like superheroes – battling for hours and laying waste to scores of enemies, with seemingly no consideration for tactics, formations, or obeying orders.

In this typical scene from *The Iliad* the Greek hero Patroclus is tearing into the Trojan fighters.

Patroclus kept on sweeping in, hacking them down, making them pay the price for

Argives slaughtered. There Pronus, first to fall – a glint of the spear and Patroclus tore his chest left bare by the shield-rim, loosed his knees, and the man went crashing down.

In the next thirty lines of the poem Patroclus kills another ten warriors in equally unpleasant ways without even stopping to pause for breath!

Although the weapons and armour described by Homer are similar to those the ancient Greeks actually used, everything else was very different. In particular, real-life battle focused much less on one-to-one combat, and those lengthy introductory speeches before a fight began probably didn't happen.

Nonetheless, the tales in *The Iliad* and indeed those elsewhere in mythology were a great influence on later Greeks because they regarded the nobility and skill of the warriors mentioned as the ultimate example of what they should aspire to.

Dressed to kill: Hoplites

Ancient Greek soldiers were referred to as *hoplites*. Hoplites were standard infantrymen who fought in formation at a battle (see the section 'Getting tactical: Hoplite formations').

By far the most important development in Greek warfare was the discovery of iron in approximately 1200 BC. Prior to this, all metal weapons were made of bronze. Iron is tougher, more hard wearing, and incredibly strong in comparison. When wielded by a powerful warrior, an iron sword could literally split a bronze weapon in two.

By the eighth and seventh centuries BC, the hoplite's equipment (or *panoply*) had become fairly standard, as Figure 5-1 shows.

Figure 5-1:
A Greek
hoplite in
full armour.

Armour

Ancient Greek armour was heavy but not as heavy as the gear worn by an armoured knight from the Middle Ages. The Greek soldier needed to be able to run fast and be as flexible as possible, so he kept his armour to a minimum.

The most important piece of armour was called the *cuirass*. This piece protected a soldier's body but left his arms free to fight – rather like wearing a sleeveless t-shirt but much, much heavier.

The *cuirass* was made in two separate ways. One was to stitch together many layers of canvas and linen to fashion a kind of rigid shirt with strips of bronze sewn in to reinforce it. The other, much more expensive way was to cast the *cuirass* completely in bronze, muscled to fit the shape of the body.

The legs were protected by *greaves*, which were made of bronze and cast so that they fit the legs of the soldier without using any kind of straps. The greaves protected the front of the leg between the knee and ankle with a partial covering around the calves. Soldiers wore normal sandals with no extra armour or protection.

Helmet

Helmets were bronze, and many different styles existed. The most common was the *Corinthian* (see Figure 5-1), which had an opening at the front with a long strip of bronze as a nose-guard. Many soldiers wore a horse-hair crest on top of their helmet but this was purely for display rather than protection.

The arms trade

For the ancient Greeks, a complete *panoply* (all the armour and weapons I write about in this section) was really expensive. Every soldier had to buy his own panoply, and looking after this equipment was important. Only the very rich would have had somebody to tend to their equipment for them in the way that medieval knights did. For everybody else their panoply was their own concern and many men used armour and weapons that their grandfathers and fathers had bought because the cost of replacing these items was so great. Hence, the panoply that you owned in ancient Greece gave a good indication of the class you came from.

Anybody who owned a full hoplite panoply would've been from the wealthier middle or upper classes.

Although arms and armour were expensive, the poet Archilochos of Paros (circa 650 BC) made it clear what was most valuable to take from the battlefield:

> *I don't give a damn if some Thracian ape struts, proud of that shield that the bushes got. Leaving it was hell, but in a tricky spot. I kept my hide intact. Good shields can be bought.*

Shield

The shield was known as a *hoplon*, and that's where the hoplites got their name. By the seventh century BC, the typical shield was about 1 metre (3 feet) in diameter. It was round in shape, made of wood and reinforced with bronze. The inside most likely had two brackets. The soldier put his arm through one bracket and gripped the other.

Sometimes soldiers hung leather curtains from the bottom of their shields to use as a barrier against rocks, arrows, and missiles. The shield would've been really heavy, probably about 8 kilograms (17 pounds).

Weapons

Hoplites carried two main weapons into battle:

- **Spears:** These were the most important weapon and quite big and cumbersome – about 3 metres long, made of wood, and tipped with iron at both ends (refer to Figure 5-1). Given their size, they weren't thrown like javelins (covered in 'Cavalry' later in this chapter) but used for thrusting and defence.

- **Swords:** These weapons were quite small, only around 60 centimetres long and would have only weighed about 1.5 kilograms but they were very deadly at close quarters. They were made of iron with a bronze handle and carried in wooden scabbards. Another version of the sword, called a *kopis* meaning 'chopper', was longer, heavier, and used with a slashing motion – usually from horseback.

Considering other troops

Although hoplites dominated warfare in ancient Greece, other types of troops took part in battle.

Cavalry

Cavalry weren't a big feature of early Greek warfare, partly because providing and paying for horses was incredibly expensive. The endeavour was also very risky. The Greeks rode without stirrups and mostly only used cloths as saddles. Ancient Greek cavalry were excellent horsemen; they needed to be because their main weapon was the javelin – actually several javelins – that they threw while on the gallop. A cavalry soldier didn't carry a shield or wear any armour. His only covering was a broad-brimmed hat that helped keep the sun at bay.

By the time of Alexander the Great (356–323 BC), cavalry had become a vital part of the Greek war machine. For more on how the cavalry developed, see Chapter 10.

Light troops

Sometimes the Greeks used lightly armed troops for special missions, like scouting and ambushing the enemy. These troops were called *peltastai* because they carried the light shield called a *pelte*. The *pelte* was usually a goatskin stretched in a crescent shape across a wooden frame. It was incredibly light and only really useful for deflecting small missiles from the *peltastai*. *Peltastai* were most often armed with a small bundle of javelins, which they used strictly for hit-and-run operations.

Archers

Archers appear a lot in Greek mythology. The hero Odysseus was famed for his skill with the bow, and arguably the most famous of all Greek warriors, Achilles, was killed when he was hit in the heel by the Trojan archer Paris. It was this story that gave rise to the expression 'Achilles heel' because it was the only vulnerable point on his body. The most famous Greek archers were from the island of Crete.

Greek archers were very lightly armed. The bows themselves were made of cedar wood with animal sinew used for the string. The bow would usually be the only weapon carried by the archers because it was vital that they could move quickly as the battle changed, so they could attack fresh targets. Despite this, archers weren't often used in Greek battles. The Greeks felt that it was more honourable to fight face to face and archers were sometimes of little use when a heavily armed *phalanx* (see the following section) was fighting in formation. Some Greek armies did use archers that hailed from Scythia, the large region to the north of Asia Minor. Athens kept a troop of Scythian archers, which Peisistratos (refer to Chapter 4) introduced. These archers were used mostly as a police force and not in battle.

Getting tactical: Hoplite formations

Films such as *Troy* (2003) and *300* (2006) can make it seem as if a Greek battle just involved everybody charging at each other in the midst of a general punch up. This was far from the case. Greek battles were fought along rigid tactical lines that meant each man knew exactly what his job was.

The hoplite infantrymen were dominant in ancient Greek warfare at the expense of all other types of fighting because they were so effective. The strength of hoplites came down to the shield. The *hoplon* shield was lighter than the larger shields that soldiers had used previously. As a consequence, men began fighting closer together in battle, and the hoplite *phalanx* developed – a powerful battle formation in which the hoplites lined up in files (see Figure 5-2), probably eight men deep.

In the *phalanx* the troops set out in an open formation, marching or jogging alongside each other with weapons sheathed until it was time for battle.

When a battle began, these open formations closed up, so that each man occupied only about 1 metre of space. Moving close together meant that the right-hand side of each man was pretty much covered by the shield of the man to his right – and so on all along the line. Tightening their formations produced the effect of a wall of shields that the hoplites then thrust their spears over or in between. Figure 5-2 shows how close the men were to each other and how they covered the man to their left.

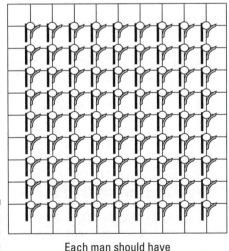

Figure 5-2:
The hoplite
phalanx
in battle
formation.

Each man should have

| = Spear /(= Shield

Let battle commence!

Hoplite tactics were very regimented, reducing the role of the individual to that of a cog in a well-oiled machine. This was a complete departure from the super-heroes in *The Iliad* (see the sidebar 'Fighting like a Homeric hero' for more points of departure).

After battle began, the role of each hoplite soldier was to push forward against the man in front. If the man in front of you fell, you moved forward and took his place in the line.

The Spartan writer Tyrtaeus, who lived in the seventh century BC, wrote about fighting as part of a hoplite *phalanx*:

> *Everyone should close up to his man with his great spear or sword and wound and kill his enemy. Standing leg to leg, resting shield against shield, crest beside crest and helmet to helmet having drawn near, let him fight with his man with his sword or great spear.*

The key element to the battle was to push forward and at some point force the line of the enemy to break. After this happened, the fight was usually all over.

Reports of ancient Greek battles usually suggest massive casualties for the losers and only very minor ones for the victors. Although the figures are probably inflated, an imbalance between winner and loser makes sense: After the losing line broke, the victorious army would chase its men down as the soldiers fled the field, resulting in most of the killing that took place. Cavalry and light troops were also brought in at this point to chase the enemy down.

Imagining the abject terror of fighting in a battle like this may be difficult given modern warfare tactics. On the ancient Greek battlefield, you had no hiding place; you were face to face with your enemy. If you didn't kill or severely injure the man across from you first, he would kill or injure you. All around you, other men were dying of the most horrific injuries. You'd have had no time to save them or offer help.

'Are you calling me a coward?'

Any soldier who ran from the ancient Greek battlefield would drop his shield to move more quickly. The Greek word for this was *rhipsaspis*, or 'one who throws his shield away'. Calling somebody a shield-dropper was a huge insult.

Although ancient Athens didn't have an equivalent to modern laws of libel or slander, you could take somebody to court if he called you a *rhipsaspis*.

Living for Killing: The Spartans

As I note in Chapter 4, the people of Sparta were different from the rest of ancient Greece – and indeed the western world – in many respects. Their attitude was that you returned from battle *with* your shield – or *on* it (as a funeral *bier* or stretcher). The Spartans didn't believe in half-measures, and their standards of military discipline were absolute.

Military training for Spartan boys began when they were just 7 years old. At this age, boys left home and joined the education system. This comprehensive curriculum including hunting skills, physical training, and also emotional training – designed to teach bravery.

One particularly brutal element of Spartan education was called 'The Gauntlet' and involved boys running around and being continually flogged by older children until they fell down or, in some cases, died.

The final Spartan training exercise, called the *krypteia*, involved sending young men (possibly as young as 14) into the countryside alone with no food or water and requiring them to live on their wits for a month. Sometimes a *krypteia* also included the task of killing *helots* (see Chapter 4 for more on these people) found wandering the countryside.

Although these young men probably stole food to survive, stealing was considered a crime. A story from Plutarch shows the lengths that one young boy went to in order to hide stolen property:

> *The boys take great care over their stealing, as is shown in the story of one who had stolen a fox cub and hidden it under his cloak, for he endured having his stomach lacerated by the beast's claws and teeth, and died rather than be detected.*

Their training and ability to endure hardship made the Spartan army more feared than any other in Greece.

After completing their training, Spartan men became part of the army in which they had to serve until the age of 30. Between 30 and 60, they became part of the military reserve, which could be called upon at any time.

Sink or Swim: At War on the Waves

As I explain in Chapter 1, ancient Greece was very spread out, with people living as far apart as modern-day Spain and Turkey considered to be Greek. Consequently the wars that took place weren't always fought on land, and the

Greeks developed quite complicated methods of naval warfare. (I only talk about war ships in this section; you can find information on other types of sailing in Chapter 13.)

Getting on board the Greek trireme

The standard Greek fighting ship was known as the *trireme*, which comes from the Greek word *trieres* meaning 'triply equipped' or 'three oared'. The triple description comes from the three banks of oars that the crew used to propel the ship forward.

These ships were 40 metres long and about 4 metres wide – long, stream-lined, and built to travel as quickly as possible. They relied on the power of oars, although sometimes they incorporated a sail. Before going into battle, the crew lowered both the sail and mast.

The construction of this sort of ship was time consuming but followed a very specific model. The keel (central long section) was assembled first and then all the additional planking fixed to it and sealed. As you can see from Figure 5-3, the finished ship couldn't sit very low in the water because the lowest oars were only a few feet above the water. The ships were fast but not very robust and wouldn't have been suited to surviving really difficult weather.

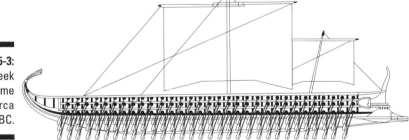

Figure 5-3:
A Greek trireme circa 500–450 BC.

Meeting the crew

Each *trireme* had a crew of about 200 – a lot of people on board a small ship. The vast majority of the crew were on board to make the vessel move. Here's the crew roster:

- **Rowers (170):** Unlike in the Roman empire, the men who rowed the ancient Greek warships weren't slaves. They were well-trained citizens from the lower classes who ended up as sailors because they could not afford the panoply to be soldiers.

Rowing was hard, back-breaking work – continually digging in to heft the 4 to 5 metre (15 foot) oars. On a *trireme*, the rowers were arranged on three different levels: 62 upper rowers (*thranites*), 54 middle rowers (*zygotes*) and 54 lower rowers (*thalamites*).

✔ **Flautist (one):** Rather like the cox or skipper on a modern row boat, this flute-player helped the rowers keep time.

✔ **Marines (14):** These individuals were usually a mixture of hoplite soldiers and a few archers (probably Scythian).

✔ **Deckhands (15):** These soldiers had the vital work of keeping the ship functioning – making repairs and working the sails and tiller (steering).

✔ **The captain:** The captain of the ship was called the *trierarch*. He was responsible for everybody on board and the tactics in battle. He'd allocate duties to the various deckhands, all of whom would take turns on watch at night. Generally the *trierarch* took responsibility for navigating and setting course because that was considered a duty of command.

With all these people on board, triremes weren't particularly useful for transporting land soldiers around. The majority of Greek wars were fairly localised, so most soldiers would march to battle but if they had to be moved across the sea, they travelled on normal merchant ships, guarded by triremes.

Being nautically tactical

Fighting at sea was completely different to land battles. The great strengths of the hoplite fighters (see the earlier section 'Getting tactical: Hoplite formations') weren't very useful on the water. The two main attack methods were ramming and boarding.

✔ **Ramming:** Because the Greek ships sat low in the water, a ramming caused damage so severe that the rammed ship would sink. Surprisingly, if it was done correctly, it would cause very little damage to the attacker.

✔ **Boarding:** When fighting at close quarters, boarding was usually the preferred attack method and often took place after a ramming. Boarding usually involved grappling hooks, ropes, and other equipment to get a hold of the enemy ship. Eventually the Greeks developed something that the Romans called the *corvus* (Latin for 'raven'), which was a kind of bridge that swung onto the enemy vessel. Hand to hand fighting did take place in naval battles but the sides would have to be close enough together to do so first! The marines could only really actively engage with each other when the ships had locked together.

With both sides relying on fairly similar equipment, the Greeks had to develop attack strategies to gain an advantage over their enemies. The three main strategies, illustrated in Figure 5-4, included:

- ✔ The *diekplous* involved targeting one ship in the enemy line and turning it, breaking open a hole in their line. Any enemy ship that turned to aid the stricken ship ended up exposing its flank to the attackers too.

- ✔ The *kyklos* was a defensive formation that was used when a fleet was outnumbered or being pursued by a faster fleet. The ships formed a circle with their rams facing outwards, projecting at their pursuers.

- ✔ The *periplous* was an attacking move that was designed to outflank the line of the enemy.

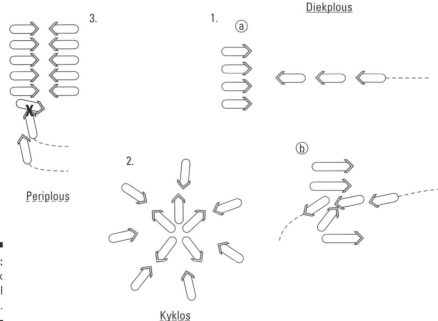

Figure 5-4:
Three Greek
naval
tactics.

Chapter 6

East versus West: The Persian Wars

*P*eople in the ancient world experienced many and varied wars. Usually the fighting was more of a local thing, with neighbours acting on long-term grievances. Occasionally one city or region attempted to bring another city under its rule. Some wars, however, were massive, international events. The Persian Wars certainly come under this category.

Struggles between the west and the east are a big feature of history. The Persian Wars were followed by Alexander the Great's invasion of Asia Minor in the fourth century BC, the struggles of Alexander's successors afterwards, and eventually ongoing trouble between the Roman Empire and the Persians' successors, the Parthians.

Today, because the differences between east and west continue to cause friction and often escalate into confrontation, the Persian Wars of the fifth century BC have never seemed so relevant. This chapter introduces the ancient Persians and examines the problems they had with the Greeks.

Powering Up the Persians

The Persian Empire came into being in the sixth century BC, around the same time that Athens was going through the changes that eventually resulted in the beginnings of democracy (refer to Chapter 4). Much of the empire's early success can be attributed to King Cyrus and his progeny.

Taking charge with Cyrus

Within a period of about 40 years, the hugely successful Persian king Cyrus the Great took control of all the territory between Asia Minor (modern-day Turkey) and the Asian Steppe (modern Russia to the east of the Black Sea). A people called the Medes previously held most of this territory, but Cyrus effectively defeated them when he occupied their capital of Ecbatana in 549 BC.

Cyrus established this new Persian empire based around the city of Susa on what became known as the Persian Gulf (modern-day Iraq). As Figure 6-1 shows, this empire was absolutely vast, covering a huge geographical area of almost three million square miles.

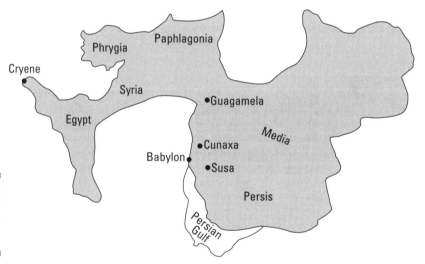

Figure 6-1:
The Persian Empire circa 500 BC.

Having gained control of such a vast area, Cyrus began to look to the west to further consolidate his territory and gain control of all the trade routes that passed through his empire to the Mediterranean Sea.

In fact, trade was what first brought the Persian Empire into contact with the Greek world. In 546 BC Cyrus fought and defeated Croesus of Lydia. During the Dark Ages, Greeks had established many new towns and settlements in Lydia (refer to Chapter 3 for more on Greek movements in the Dark Ages).

With Cyrus's victory over Croesus, the mighty new Persian power was less than a week away by sea from the Greek mainland. Furthermore, Cyrus divided Asia Minor and the newly conquered Greek mainland into provinces that were each run by a *satrap* – a local lord who controlled the area and its people and collected revenues, which he sent back to the king. The Ionian Greeks were now under foreign control.

The Greeks of the mainland were shocked to become subjects of the Persian Empire. The Ionian Greeks pondered how to respond to their new rulers, and eventually the Spartans acted. They sent an embassy to Cyrus and ordered him to leave the Ionian Greek cities alone. Cyrus's puzzled reply was, 'Who are the Spartans?' Cyrus did nothing and ignored them but confrontation with mainland Greece was inevitable.

Cyrus continued to expand the empire by attacking and conquering the fabulous ancient city of Babylon, which had remained independent of his rule to this point. After he was killed during a war in the north of the territory, Cyrus's successors continued to expand and refine the empire, and in 512 BC the Persian king Darius extended the empire's reach as far as Thrace and Macedonia.

The Greek playwright Aeschylus fought at the battle of Marathon (see the following section 'Going the Distance: The Battle of Marathon') and wrote a play called *The Persians* in 472 BC. In the play, the chorus of Persian elders give their opinion of Darius. Aeschylus was a Greek but his depiction of the Persian attitude seems authentic:

> *Alas! It was a glorious and good life of social order that we enjoyed, while our aged, all-powerful, guileless, unconquerable King god-like Darius ruled the land. Firstly, we displayed glorious armies, which everywhere administered tower-like cities.*

Rebelling with the mainland: The Ionian revolt

Greece and Persia eventually came to blows. The Persian army was much larger and more cosmopolitan than the mainland Greeks (see the nearby sidebar 'Assembling a league of nations: The Persian army'), but the main difference between the two armies was that the Greeks generally wore heavier armour and fought in a closely regulated formation (refer to Chapter 5) and the Persian troops donned light armour and were armed in a variety of ways.

Assembling a league of nations: The Persian army

The Persian Empire was huge and included many cultures; consequently its army was very diverse. Here are some of the main troops:

✔ **Persian 'immortals':** These full-time soldiers were of Persian origin and were the king's elite troops for ceremonial as well as battle purposes. They were known as the 'immortals' because of their incredible courage and fighting prowess – they fought like gods. There were always 10,000 of them and whenever their numbers dipped after a battle, more troops were brought up. The immortals' main weapons were the bow (which wasn't very effective against heavy Greek armour; see Chapter 5), short spear, and short sword. They also used large wicker shields called *gerrons* that were fairly light and quite manoeuvrable although not as strong as Greek bronze.

✔ **Mede cavalry:** Lightly armed cavalry was the Persians' other main force in battle. The cavalry's main weapons were the bow and javelins, which the horsemen fired while riding at speed. Very impressive.

✔ **Phrygian spearmen:** Recruited from Asia Minor, these were very fast spear throwers who were also highly manoeuvrable. They wore hardly any armour apart from a reinforced wicker helmet and a small round shield.

✔ **Ethiopian troops:** The vast Persian Empire even drew troops from Africa. These troops were generally referred to as Ethiopians, even though they had nothing to do with the modern country. The soldiers were very simply armed with a bow and spear and wore no armour at all.

The Persian army's mix of troops was one of its strengths, but it also inspired rebellion. During Darius's campaign in Thrace at the end of the sixth century, the contingent from Ionian Greece saved the Persian forces from defeat. The Greeks took their success in the Thrace campaign as a sign of Persian weakness and saw an opportunity to revolt.

A Greek called Aristagoras, who Darius had appointed to rule all of Ionia from Miletus, travelled to the Greek mainland to canvas support from the Ionian Greeks. The Spartans – surprisingly turning down an opportunity to be difficult and to fight – refused to join Aristagoras. The Spartan king Kleomenes apparently felt that the Persian Gulf was too far to travel for the cause of Greek liberation.

Eventually Aristagoras gained support from Athens and the city of Eretria. The revolt initially met with success, but the rebels couldn't sustain the uprising against Darius's massive forces. Darius had a whole empire to call on and could routinely devote 50,000 men to the campaign (see the nearby sidebar 'Assembling a League of Nations'). Eventually in 494 BC Darius's army attacked Miletus and razed it to the ground. The revolt ended, and Aristagoras fled to Thrace where he was eventually captured and killed while trying to drum up support for a fresh revolt. The campaign had taken over five years and Darius blamed the Greeks for it. Although the Ionian Greeks had caused the problems, Darius felt that it was the states on the Greek mainland which had been behind the uprising. His focus would now be on extending his empire west across the Mediterranean.

Going the Distance: The Battle of Marathon

In 490 BC, four years after the fall of Miletus, Darius's army crossed the Aegean Sea intent on the invasion and conquest of mainland Greece. The Persians had sent agents ahead of them to scout the land and try to arrange support from some Greek states. They'd been successful and the city of Eretria on the island of Euboia allowed the Persian army to land. From Eretria, the mainland was a simple trip by boat, landing in north-east Attica at the bay of Marathon only about 40 kilometres from Athens.

With the massive Persian army perilously close to Athens, the Athenians had to decide whether to stay in the city and face a siege in the hope that the other Greek cities would come to their aid, or go outside the city walls and march out to meet the Persians in battle.

Many believe the origin of the word *marathon* relates to an unnamed runner who brought back news of victory – the Greek word *nike* – to Athens. (This runner was also the first ever piece of product placement in history!) However, this isn't true. *Marathon* actually relates to a runner named Pheidippides who was sent from Athens to Sparta to tell the Spartans that the Persians had arrived. Pheidippides was the first Marathon runner. Only in later versions of the story was his run changed to being from Marathon to Athens.

Even though Pheidippides delivered his message, the Spartans didn't come to the Athenians' defence against the Persian invasion. The Spartans were celebrating a religious festival and refused to leave, so the Athenians were on their own. Led by the general Miltiades, they advanced to attack.

The battle: First blood to Athens

In the battle between the Athenians and Persians, the Persians were overwhelming favourites. They had a force of around 25,000 men including 5,000 cavalry. By contrast the Athenians mustered only slightly less than 10,000 hoplites (see Chapter 5 for more on the hoplites) and no cavalry at all.

The Persians made camp close to the sea in the bay of Marathon with a large marsh behind them and they marched out toward the small Athenian army with the sea to their left, as Figure 6-2 illustrates.

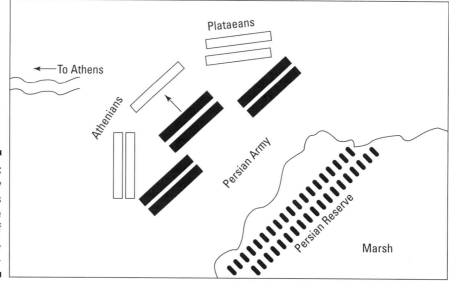

Figure 6-2:
Military
manoeuvres
at the
battle of
Marathon,
490 BC.

Additionally the Persians sent some infantry and all their cavalry by ship to Athens. The odds were almost impossible: The Athenians had to beat the Persians near Marathon and then dash back to Athens ahead of the Persian strike forces to defend their city.

The dire situation forced a bold Athenian strategy. As the Persians advanced, the Athenians ran towards the centre of its infantry line. Despite the fact that they were in arrow range, the Athenians' heavy armour protected them. The centre was the Persian army's weakest point, and it began to crumple. Many Persians were shocked and began to flee – some into the marsh and others back to their ships.

Instead of pursuing the Persians, the Athenians held their discipline and set off on an amazing forced march back to Athens, despite the fact that they'd all just fought in one of the hardest and most nerve-racking battles of their lives. They made it back about an hour before the Persian strike fleet. When the Persians arrived they saw they were outnumbered, and sailed back across the Mediterranean empty handed.

In the final reckoning the Persians lost about 6,000 men to the Athenians' 192. These few Athenian dead were buried with great ceremony in a mound that still exists. It was a magnificent victory – but the Persians would be back (see the following section 'Having Another Go: Greece versus Persia II').

Athens hits the jackpot

Marathon was a tremendous victory for Athens, but what followed was almost as important.

In 483 BC the discovery of silver in the mines at Laureion in Attica immediately brought fabulous wealth to Athens. This new wealth was a huge boom for the middle classes, but eventually the Athenians decided to spend their riches on something they desperately needed – a fleet.

The encounter with Persia showed the Athenians that mainland Greece was truly at the mercy of the Persian navy. By 480 BC the Athenians constructed a fleet of nearly 200 ships (Chapter 5 has more on Greek naval warfare). The motivator for this was the *arkhon* (elected official) Themistocles who famously told the Athenians to 'Lay hold of the sea'.

The people took him at his word as further fighting with Persian forces demonstrated.

Having Another Go: Greece versus Persia II

Darius wasn't around long enough to hold a grudge against the Athenians; he died in 486 BC. However, he was succeeded by his son Xerxes who was absolutely determined to gain revenge for his father's defeat and began to assemble a massive army and fleet.

Regrouping in Greece

The Greeks knew Xerxes would return to Athens and realised that a combined effort was required if the Greek mainland was ever to defeat the Persian forces.

In 481 and 480 BC, representatives of the major Greek cities held two big conferences at which 31 Greek states pledged to put aside their differences and join together against Persia. They erected a monument at the sacred site of Delphi as a visual symbol of their new unity. The conference also voted that the Spartans would have overall command of the joint army. For the fractious Greeks, this level of agreement was amazing.

The Greeks definitely needed to be united, because the size of the second Persian force was extraordinary. Ancient sources talk about a force of about a million, but the number was probably around 150,000 as the logistics involved in moving and feeding an army any larger than that would have made the invasion almost impossible.

Heating up at Thermopylae and Artemision

As the Greek troops made their way south, they had to choose a strategic location to make a stand against the Persians. Eventually the leaders chose a small pass in the southern Greek mainland near the mountains and the sea. The location was the famous natural sulphur springs – Thermopylae, literally meaning the 'hot gates'. It was a good choice because if they wanted to avoid going through the narrow pass, the Persians would have to take a massive diversion. Either way, they'd be held up until the Greek forces further south were fully organised.

Having chosen Thermopylae as the point at which to stand the Greeks sent their new fleet, which was mostly composed of the new Athenian ships (see the earlier section 'Athens hits the jackpot'), to Artemision, a promontory sticking out of the north-east corner of the Euboean peninsular where they hoped to stop the Persian fleet from joining up with its army.

The famous 300

Barely 7,000 Greek troops fought at Thermopylae, all under the command of the Spartan king Leonidas. The fact that only 300 of the troops were Spartan made the Greeks doubt the level of the Spartans' commitment. However, Leonidas chose the narrowest point of the pass to defend and, incredibly, he and his troops held on for two days against wave after wave of Persian attacks. Although other Greeks took part in this battle, the 300 Spartans were at the forefront, thus the famous '300' of the film!

After several attacks were rebuffed with high Persian casualties, Xerxes paid a local goatherd for information about an alternative route. This was another, even narrower track that took a longer way around the mountains. Xerxes sent a large group of his army's 10,000 immortals (see the sidebar

'Assembling a league of nations: The Persian army') on this alternate route in an effort to get behind the Greeks.

Historians don't know why, but Leonidas dismissed the vast majority of the Greek troops, leaving only his 300 Spartans and a few others. After a heroic defence that slowed up the Persian advance, Leonidas and his men were eventually overwhelmed. The Persians advanced swiftly further south but the hold up had been vital.

The heroism of Leonidas and the Spartans became legendary. The Spartan poet Simonides paid tribute:

> *Stranger, go tell the Spartans that we lie here*
>
> *Obedient to their laws.*

Simonides's lines were probably the ultimate expression of the Spartan ideals of bravery (refer to Chapter 5). Leonidas and his men had taken on a fight that they knew they could never win but had stayed and fought to the last man 'obedient to their laws'.

The action film *300* (2007) is based on a stunning graphic novel by Frank Miller and depicts the events at Thermopylae. Although the film has some fantastic elements and over-the-top scenes, the violence and brutality of the battle scenes are very accurate. It's worth seeing but is in no way a historical representation. It presents the Greeks as heroes and the Persians as evil – a very biased version. It also includes mythical beasts – none of the Greek historians mention them!

Meanwhile, at Artemision

While the battle at Thermopylae raged, the weather along the coast at Artemison was stormy, causing the Persians to lose large numbers of ships on the rocks. The Persians were further surprised by the Greek fleet, which captured several more of its ships. What remained of the Persian fleet sailed on south with the intention of meeting up with Xerxes and the land force before launching an attack on Athens.

Seeking safety in Salamis

The Greeks did exceptionally well at Thermopylae and Artemision to hold up such a massive army but it was nothing like a victory. The city of Athens was in a tricky position after these battles because it was left very exposed. The huge Persian army was moving south and looking to attack the city. The *arkhon* Themistocles realised that the city could never hold out against such vast numbers, so he persuaded the citizens to put their faith in the Athenian fleet.

The citizens of Athens abandoned their city and fled to the island of Salamis, and the Athenian fleet positioned itself near the island. The Persians took their chance and *sacked* (looted and vandalised) the empty city as the fleet travelled south. The Persian fleet then moved around the peninsular of Attica and approached the island of Salamis, but to get any farther they had to get past the Athenian fleet.

The Persians still had the advantage of numbers, but the Greeks countered with stealth and deception. The Greeks used a brilliant five-step plan:

1. They sent a false message to Xerxes the Persian king, telling him that the Greek fleet intended to flee north-east to the Isthmus of Corinth. Xerxes fell for the message and sent the Egyptian section of his fleet off to block the fake move.

2. At dawn the Greek fleet put to sea and headed north into the narrow channel between Salamis Island and the mainland. A small section of ships from Corinth went south to defend against the Egyptians who were soon to find out that they'd been conned.

3. Another small section of Greek ships hid in the small bay called Ambelaki to the south of the narrow channel.

4. The massive Persian fleet, thinking that the Greeks were fleeing, followed the Greeks into the narrow channel. The Athenians turned to face them, and the Persians were stuck. The Greeks rammed the Persian ships, and the Persian commander was one of the first casualties. Chaos ensued.

5. The small fleet hidden to the south caught the Persians as they tried to flee back down the channel, and the Corinthians (remember them from Step 2?) stopped the Egyptians from coming back to help.

The Persian fleet was *routed* (utterly devastated and incapable of recovery). They lost about 200 ships to the Greeks' 40.

Entering the endgame: The battle of Plataea

After the events near Salamis, the Persian fleet was in pieces, which meant its army was cut off from supplies. As September came – and with it the end of the sailing season – Xerxes decided to head north for the winter to rest his army and spend time organising supplies. In the event, Xerxes decided he'd had enough and headed back to Asia Minor. (He was probably worried that the Ionians may revolt again; see the earlier section 'Taking charge with Cyrus'.) Xerxes left the army under the control of his son-in-law Mardonios, who led the army south in the spring of 479 BC.

This battle really was the endgame – the Greeks faced the Persians on land in open battle. All or nothing.

The Athenians evacuated their city once more, and the Persians sacked it again. However, this second attack convinced the Spartans to finally commit to the fight (since Thermopylae their support had been in doubt). In command of the joint force was a young Spartan named Pausanias who was acting as regent for the young son of Leonidas (Leonidas was killed at Thermopylae). Pausanias led the army north into the lands around the town of Plataea.

The Persian recruitment drive

Although the Spartans had joined up again, many other Greek states refused to rally to the Athenian cause. As the Persians moved south, they were joined by contingents from Thebes, Thessaly, Phocris, and Locris, amongst others. None of the new recruits thought that the southern Greeks could possibly win. They figured they should throw in their lot with the Persians because it was odds on that the Persians would soon be their new overlords.

The battle of Plataea: A time for heroes

For a period of about two weeks, the Greeks manoeuvred around the countryside, avoiding the attacks of the strong Persian cavalry. Pausanias grew very frustrated and tried to work the Greek army into a position to attack. He attempted to make the move at night, but the plan ended in total confusion. As dawn broke the Greeks were halfway to their destination of Plataea. Mardonios, the Persian commander, sensed that this was the Persians' moment and he led an attack.

But Mardonios got it wrong. Although the Greeks had become a little split up, their hoplite training (refer to Chapter 5) kicked in as soon as they saw the Persians begin to attack. The Greeks assumed a defensive formation, which limited the effectiveness of the Persian archers' onslaught.

When the two lines of infantry came together, the Persians – despite their superior numbers – couldn't cope with the heavily armed hoplites. Slowly but surely the Greeks forced the Persians back. Mardonios was killed and soon afterwards the Persians broke, fleeing the field. As the Persians fled, the Spartans hunted and killed them by the thousands.

The Greeks scored an amazing victory against huge odds, but their success was due more to luck than wise judgement. Pausanius certainly hadn't intended to take the Greeks into battle when they ending up fighting, but at the end of the day it's the result that counts. The Persians were defeated and fled, and this time they didn't come back.

The poet Simonides recorded the epitaphs that the Athenians wrote to their dead. The following tells much about what the Greeks considered to be an honourable death:

> *If dying nobly is the greatest part of valour, to us above all others Fortune has granted this. For after striving to crown Greece with freedom, we lie here enjoying praise that will never age.*

Fighting the forgotten battle – Mykale

What happened next often gets a little bit lost in history. Marathon, Thermopylae, Salamis, and Plataea are always thought of as the biggest battles of the Persian Wars whereas it was actually at Mykale that the last act was played out.

As what remained of the Persian fleet made its way home across the Mediterranean the Greeks followed in hot pursuit and they quickly caught up. After what had happened at Salamis (see the preceding section 'Seeking safety in Salamis'), the Persians weren't keen to fight at sea, so they beached their fleet at the promontory of Mykale opposite the island of Samos, where they were joined by some Persian forces that had stayed behind in Asia Minor.

The Greeks, commanded by the other Spartan king Leotykhidas (each year Sparta had two kings), stormed the beach and burned the Persian fleet. As the Persians desperately tried to defend themselves, the Ionians who were part of Persian army swapped sides and helped the Greeks.

After Mykale, the Persian defeat was total, and the Persian Wars were at an end.

Heralding the Real Winner: Athens

The Persian Wars were huge historical events that impacted the course of western civilisation. Imagine how different things would've been if the Persians had won. Nearly everything else in the following chapters of this book would never have happened. The Olympic Games wouldn't be in London in 2012, and people wouldn't be arguing about whether the Parthenon sculptures in the British Museum (the so-called 'Elgin Marbles') should be returned to Greece. Who knows how the arts, government, and science – to name but a few critical areas – may have evolved without the Greeks' victory. History would've been very different.

Although victory in the Persian Wars benefited all of Greece, one city-state emerged particularly strong. Yes, the Spartans fought heroically to defend Greece, but the historian Herodotus gives credit for defeating the Persians to Athens:

> *And so anyone who said the Athenians were the saviours of Greece would be perfectly correct . . . they chose that Greece remain free and they roused all of Greece that hadn't medised [become a Persian ally] and played the main part, after the gods, in driving off the King.*

Athens' new fleet was without equal anywhere in the Greek world and its role at the head of the resistance made the Athenians very influential in all political and economic decisions to come. Athens' position ushered in a new era of empire building.

Part II

Athens to Alexander: The Rise and Fall of Empires

The 5th Wave   By Rich Tennant

"Okay, we've invented democracy, philosophy, and astrology. Now, Hilladius, you're working on something called pole dancing...?"

In this part . . .

The chapters in Part I look at who the Greeks were and how they forged an identity as a people by coming together to fight the wars against the Persian Empire. Well, some people did rather better out of that experience than others and in this part I look at the rise and fall of the Athenian empire and that of its ultimate successor, Alexander the Great of Macedon, who took the war to Persia. Hold on – it's a bumpy ride!

Chapter 7

Athens and Empire Building

*A*fter years of warring with the Persians, the Greeks emerged victorious (see Chapter 6) – and Athens played a massive part in the success. In the years following the end of fighting with Persia, Athens built on its successes to become the dominant Greek state in the Mediterranean with a domain comprising other cities, towns, and islands. In this chapter, I explain how the Athenians created one of history's greatest empires.

Establishing the Delian League: Athens Comes Out on Top

Although the Greeks defeated the Persians in 480–479 BC, the threat of the Persians returning to fight again was never likely to go away. All the Greek cities realised this danger, and after the celebrations of their great victories were over the big question facing the victorious Greeks was 'What do we do now?'

The Greek naval fleet continued to range around the eastern Mediterranean. In 478 BC Pausanias, the Spartan commander from Plataea, took the war to Persian-held Greek territories. First he sailed to Cyprus and managed to take control of the island. He then sailed up the Bosphorus to Byzantium (close to the site of modern-day Istanbul in Turkey) and managed to drive out the Persian garrison. Sadly, at this point Pausanius seemed to have lost the plot and was recalled to Sparta for attempting to install himself as a tyrant in Byzantium. If you want to know what happened to the power-hungry Pausanius, look at Chapter 26.

Let's stick together

Pausanius's naughty behaviour had a big effect. Despite the Spartan's military greatness (see Chapter 5), the rest of Greece began to suspect that they were not the best candidates to lead the long-term resistance against Persia. The Athenians, with their large fleet that had done so well in the recent war with Persia, seemed a much better alternative.

In the winter of 478–77 BC, ambassadors from many Greek towns and islands held a big meeting on the island of Delos. An Athenian general called Aristeides came up with the idea of a league of Greek states that worked together to protect the Greek world from the Persians – and also to financially compensate the states for damages that the Persian king had inflicted.

To prove their allegiance to this new enterprise, Aristeides proposed all the league members be required to pay an annual tribute of either money or ships to the Delian League treasury. (Aristeides himself decided how much members had to give.) Of course, the general also proposed that the Athenians supervise the entire endeavour and take on the job of treasurer, collecting and holding the cash for this new enterprise.

Essentially all the states (including Athens) were contributing for the common good because the collected resources were to be used to defend any of the member states against attack. Athens, however, was in a very strong position – having control of the entire operation made the city very powerful.

Adding another brick in the wall: Themistocles's return

Themistocles, the man who played a massive part in the battle of Salamis and persuaded the Athenians to abandon the city (refer to Chapter 6), made an even bigger contribution to Greek politics following the Persian Wars.

While the Delian League was being set up, Themistocles prompted the Athenians to begin rebuilding the walls of their city. In order to imagine the size of this undertaking, take a look at the plan in Figure 7-1. We don't know how high or thick these walls were but they were about four miles in length. Some parts are still preserved and if you go to the Naval Museum in Athens you can see a section of them.

Figure 7-1 shows Athens around 450 BC. By this point the walls of Themistocles had been joined to the 'Long Walls' that connected Athens with its port Piraeus. This meant that the city was completely encircled by defensive walls.

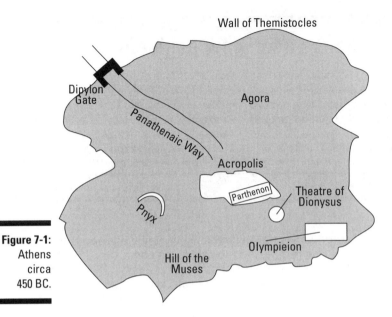

Wall of Themistocles

Dipylon Gate

Agora

Panathenaic Way

Acropolis

Parthenon

Theatre of Dionysus

Pnyx

Olympieion

Figure 7-1:
Athens
circa
450 BC.

Hill of the Muses

Athens's protective walls had been destroyed during two Persian sackings (being vandalised and looted by invaders) carried out over the preceding 25 years. The move to rebuild the walls was very controversial at the time. The Spartans (who else?) protested against Themistocles's plan, claiming that it went against the spirit of the accord that brought many Greek states together to defeat Persia. Surely, the Spartans suggested, destroying the Athenian walls was a more appropriate symbol now that all Greek states trusted each other.

More likely, the Spartans were concerned about Athens's growing power and knew that large walls would make the city more difficult to defeat in open warfare because it would be more able to withstand a siege. In any case, the Athenians ignored the Spartan's protests and carried on with the building project!

Getting together the necessary amount of stone and materials was a huge task. The historian Thucydides describes the extent that some Greeks had to go to:

> *Meanwhile the entire population of the city should build the wall, sparing neither private nor public buildings which might be of some use in the work, but demolishing everything . . .*

The project took 20 years to complete. By 450 BC, walls encircled the whole city of Athens as well as the large port of Piraeus. The Athenians then went on to build 'the Long Walls', that linked the port and the city. No other Greek state boasted defences like this.

Thanks a lot, now push off!

You may think that a hero like Themistocles was guaranteed a life of fame in Athens after initiating the city's massive wall rebuilding project. No chance. Like many others, he fell foul of the chaotic political scene in Athens. Not long after the walls were finished, Themistocles's political opponents ostracised him from the city. He ended up in the town of Argos but was driven out of there when the Spartans accused him of intrigue. Themistocles finished up living at the court of the Persian king Artaxerxes, an odd place for a Greek hero to end up! He had dreamed of Athens gaining a whole Mediterranean empire – ironically that was exactly what they did after his death in 459 BC.

Athenian construction went even further, spending money on the buildings within the city. During this period the Athenians constructed the Parthenon on the Acropolis and many other buildings (see Chapter 18 for more on ancient Greek building techniques), which attracted huge numbers of artists and poets (see Chapter 17).

Expanding its Influence: The Delian League Goes into Action

Of course the Delian League wasn't just a defensive measure. Despite the fact that the league had been created to help the Greeks defend themselves against foreign threats, fairly soon after it was founded, the Greeks started to aggressively attack the Persians. The league seemed to follow the idea that attack is the best form of defence. From around 477 BC onwards the states involved in the Delian League began to launch attacks on Persian-held territories.

Representing the Delian League – or the Athenian empire?

Kimon was the man who led the new attack on Persia. He was the son of the famous general Miltiades, who had been one of the heroes of Marathon (see Chapter 5). Kimon had two significant early successes:

- ✔ In 476 BC, he captured the port of Eion, which was the last surviving Persian port on the borders of Thrace.
- ✔ In 475 BC he took control of the island of Skyros.

Holding out for a hero: Enter Pericles

By 470 BC, Athens was experiencing its 'Golden Age'. A combination of military success, financial security, and immense creativity in the arts turned this small market town in Attica into the absolute centre of the ancient world. (You can read a lot more about the achievements of Athens as well as the everyday lives of its people in Parts III and IV of this book.)

Central to a great deal of what was happening in Athens was a dominant new player on the political scene. His name was Pericles, and he made huge changes to the way that Athens looked and acted.

In many ways Pericles was a traditional aristocrat. His family was descended from the Alkmaionids, who were among the oldest and most influential aristocrats in the city (see Chapter 4). Despite this upper class background, Pericles was always very closely associated with democratic reform in Athens. (I mention several of these reforms in the later sections 'Navigating Athenian Democracy' and 'Examining the Athenian Legal System'.) And as a patron of the arts, Pericles was dedicated to turning Athens into the greatest of all Greek cities and (at the time) he arguably succeeded in doing so. It didn't last, however.

Although Kimon's victories were all well and good, other members of the Delian League began to question whether he had won the new territories in the name of the Delian League or the city of Athens. The answer soon became clear.

The island of Skyros wasn't even a Persian territory, but the Athenians claimed to have captured it for strategic reasons. Just to back their argument up even more, the Athenians enacted an impressive piece of spin-doctoring. Soon after Skyros was captured the Athenians discovered the skeleton of a very large man, and claimed they'd discovered the tomb of the hero Theseus (refer to Chapters 2 and 3). And because Theseus was an Athenian, Skyros must therefore be Athenian territory. Hmmm. This only served to increase the cynicism of the other members of the league.

Extracting protection money

The Athenians asserted their interests within the Delian League to an even greater extent over the next few years. In 470 BC Kimon used the fleet (technically the Delian League fleet) to force the Euboian city of Karystos to join the league. The city was no threat to Greece, but after the Athenians forced Karystos into the league, it had to pay dues (see the preceding section, 'Let's stick together').

Pestering the Persians

Kimon went even further in the following decade. He took the fight to Asia Minor and beyond. In 459 BC, the Egyptians revolted against Persian rule, and Kimon took 200 ships from the Delian League to the Nile Delta. The Delian League stayed in the region for five years, supporting the Egyptians' attempt to revolt.

What had started as a means of protecting mainland Greece from Persia had turned into something quite different. The military and naval strength that had been assembled to protect Greece from external attack was now acting as a kind of international policeman in foreign wars and engaging in unprovoked attacks on Persian territory. None of this was defensive and the greatest beneficiaries were the Athenians. The arrival of a new leader in Athens took things further still.

Transforming the league into an empire

Around the time that Pericles rose to prominence in Athens, the nature of the Delian League changed forever. The key event happened on the small island of Naxos in 470 BC.

Despite the continuing threat of Persian attacks, Naxos decided that it wanted to withdraw from the league. The Athenians responded by sending the fleet to attack the island and then destroy the walls of its main city. The Athenians also forced Naxos to continue paying its taxes – only this time Naxos had to pay directly to support the upkeep of the Athenian fleet.

The league was increasingly functioning more like an empire (with Athens as enforcer) rather than a mutually supportive organisation. Compared to the Athenians, the Persians weren't really that much of a threat to the people of Naxos! (A similar bit of political and military intimidation happened to the island of Thasos in 463 BC.)

Taking all: Athens in control

The Athenians effectively put the seal on the deal in 454 BC, establishing themselves as the leaders of an empire. During that year the Athenians moved the league's treasury from the island of Delos to the Acropolis of Athens. Not only did the leadership in Athens hold on to the money, but they also insisted on taking a percentage each year as a tribute to the goddess Athene (the patron deity of Athens) under whose care the money now rested.

This shift was a clear sign that Athens now considered itself the head of an empire rather than the chair of a league. The following section looks at how Athens managed to ascend to its dominant position.

Navigating Athenian Democracy

Many ancient Athenians probably considered the city's well-developed system of government to be the main reason it had become so dominant in the Greek world and Delian League by 470 BC. In Chapter 3, I examine how Athens's aristocratic system and tyrannies finally gave way to democracy. This section covers how the system actually worked.

Democracies exist throughout the world today, but they're very different from democracy in ancient Athens. Most countries today rely on some form of *representative democracy*, in which people vote for somebody (usually from a political party) to represent them in a parliament (or other governing body) and hopefully to vote in accordance with how people feel on issues. By contrast, ancient Athenian democracy was a *participative democracy.* Although the system included elected officials, government was carried out directly by the people, who voted on all major issues such as whether to go to war, build walls around the city, or start new religious festivals.

Getting organised

Athenian democracy ran via two main bodies:

- ✔ The **ekklesia,** or general assembly, which was the main body open to all male citizens over the age of 18.
- ✔ The **boule,** or Council of 500, which had a subcommittee known as the *prutaneis* to deal with emergency situations.

In addition to these two, the highest body in ancient Athens was the Aereopagus Council. This was a throwback to the old days of aristocratic rule in Athens (refer to Chapter 4), but as I explain in the later section 'Meeting the VIPs: Very important politicians', this group was due for a shake-up!

The following sections examine these bodies in much closer detail.

The Acropolis and its temples are very famous, and many think of the site as a symbol of Greek democracy. But the Acropolis wasn't actually the home of Athenian politics – this was based in various sites around the *agora.* Figure 7-2 shows the actual political areas in the Athenian public square, or *agora.*

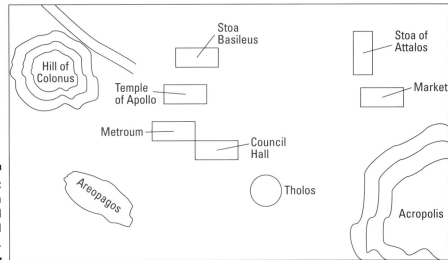

Figure 7-2:
Athenian
political
sites around
the *agora*.

Participating in the ekklesia

The *ekklesia*, or general assembly, was the main democratic body in Athens. Its job was to make major decisions and pass laws. If a male citizen registered in his *deme* (local area), he was entitled to attend the meetings of the *ekklesia*. It might seem as if this would make the meetings unmanageable but the Athenian population in 450 BC was around 250,000. Of this only around 30,000 were eligible male citizens (the rest were women, children, slaves, and resident foreigners called '*metics*'). Of these 30,000 probably an average of around 5,000 would attend *ekklesia* meetings. That's a lot but still only about two per cent of the population!

Meeting and voting

The *ekklesia* met regularly, four times a month on the big hill called the Pynx, which was located to the south-west of the city (see Figure 7-2).

Meetings were usually held early in the morning because agendas were lengthy and could take most of the day. Standing items on the agenda were defence, the election of officials, and the grain supply.

After this business was out of the way, the floor was opened by the chairman of the *ekklesia*, who was also the chairman of the *prutaneis* (see the sidebar 'Acting presidential: The *prutaneis*'). Theoretically, anybody could speak at the *ekklesia*, but matters to be voted on had to be cleared by the elected *boule* first (see the later section 'Joining the *boule*').

Votes were usually taken by a show of hands unless it was particularly close, in which case a secret ballot took place. It was a lengthy process where people dropped a stone of a different colour into a jar depending on whether they were for or against. The jars were emptied and the votes counted. The pebble and jar method was also sometimes used to decide sensitive issues such military policy and commands.

Speaking up, speaking out

Of course, some people in the *ekklesia* spoke more than others. Those people who responded most often became known as *rhetores*, which is where the words *orator* and *rhetoric* come from. Wordy modern politicians owe their name to this group of old windbags. Quite appropriate really!

The *rhetores* were regularly in attendance and became very good at speaking and quite influential. Although the *rhetores* didn't hold an official position, other attendees at the *ekklesia* looked to them to speak. Often a *rhetor* would represent a group of like-minded people, thus forming the closest thing that ancient Athens had to a political party.

Packing 'em in

So, if every male citizen over the age of 18 was eligible to attend the *ekklesia* surely every meeting was packed? Well, probably not, actually.

At the time of Pericles (circa 450 BC), estimates suggest that the citizen population in Athens was probably about 30,000. Clearly not everyone could attend the same meeting and have his say! Historians estimate that only about 6,000 people could attend a meeting of the *ekklesia* at any one time.

Citizens were unable to attend for many reasons:

- Citizens (who were mostly self-employed) lost a day's work by coming to meetings. By 400 BC, when the city was suffering after the Peloponnesian War (see Chapter 8), the Athenians instituted a system of attendance pay – citizens received 1 obol to compensate for lost earnings. For many citizens this was a mere gratuity.

- Many citizens lived all over Attica; the trip into Athens was time-consuming for these individuals.

In the middle of the fifth century, the Athenians introduced a new attendance system in which the Scythian police force (described in Chapter 15) dragged a long, red rope across the *agora* (public square) on the mornings when the *ekklesia* was meeting. People touched by the rope would already be late for the meeting on the Pnyx and that would show when they arrived with a big red stain on their clothes. They would then be fined for late attendance!

In his play *Acharnians* the Greek comic playwright Aristophanes (see Chapter 16) gives an interesting description of a day at the *ekklesia*:

> *At dawn, and the Pynx here is deserted – people are sitting in the agora and here and there avoiding the vermilion rope. Even the prutaneis haven't come, but they'll arrive late and then jostle as you might expect to try and get on the front bench.*

Despite Aristophanes's sarcasm, the Athenians loved democracy and shouted it from the rooftops. Although not every meeting of the *ekklesia* had maximum attendance, politics and the daily life of the city was on people's lips all the time in a way that may feel quite unusual to people today.

Joining the boule

The *boule*, or Council of 500, complemented the *ekklesia* as the other major element of Athenian democracy. Basically the *boule* was an administrative group that set the agenda for the *ekklesia*, where the main business was done. Subsequently, it was the responsibility of the *boule* to carry out the laws and administration that the *ekklesia* had decided on. The *boule* met in the large building to the west of the *agora* called the *bouleuterion*.

Like the *ekklesia*, the *boule* was an amateur group made up of citizens who gave their time for no financial reward. The 500 individuals who made up the *boule* had to be Athenian citizens over the age of 30. They served on the *boule* for a year at a time and couldn't serve more than twice in their lifetime.

Additionally, the 500 citizens were selected in a very specific way: Every year 50 men were elected from each of the ten tribes of Athens. This system meant that all areas of Attica were equally represented in the process.

Acting presidential: The *prutaneis*

The *boule* contained a special group known as the *prutaneis*, or presidents. This was an emergency committee that dealt with crises as and when they emerged. Serving as a president was a full-time job; citizens lived at state expense on 24-hour call in a building called the *tholos* (see Figure 7-2). The first duty for the *prutaneis* if a crisis happened was to summon a meeting of the *boule*. The *prutaneis* was a coveted position and usually only held once in a lifetime. A candidate would have to be wealthy because he needed to ensure others carried out his business or worked his farm while he served. Like other aspects of Athenian democracy, the *prutaneis* appeared to be open to all but time and money pressures meant that only the wealthy could really afford to do it.

In a sense, members of the *boule* were like a kind of civil service that administered all areas of the state. Huge numbers of people were voted in as officials on an annual basis to enforce the policies of the *ekklesia*. At points during the fifth century BC around 700 people served as registered officials although the vast majority of these posts weren't full-time and could be worked alongside the post-holder's own business.

The following are some of the more important positions:

- ✔ **The Nine:** These nine individuals (surprise) were the most senior officials. The most prominent of the Nine gave his name to the calendar year. The rest of the group dealt with public festivals, religious matters, and justice.

- ✔ **The Eleven:** Below the Nine in prominence, these eleven officials were responsible for the jury-courts and maintaining punishments and the prison (see the section 'Examining the Athenian Legal System' for more on Athenian legal matters).

Many other officials tackled other areas of civilian life. For example, some officials were elected to engage in foreign policy and foreign relations, including envoys (*presbeis*) and heralds (*kerux*), who were state-appointed.

Meeting the VIPs: Very important politicians

Despite the full democracy at work in Athens some citizens were more important than others. In many ways, the true leaders of the Athenian people were the Aereopagus Council, nine *arkhons* who were elected on an annual basis. The council was so called because it met in the space known as 'the crag of Ares' between the hill of the Acropolis and the Pynx. Although they met on their own these *arkhons* also attended all meetings of the *boule* and *ekklesia*.

Solon (described in Chapter 4) decided in 594 BC that only two people from the top two property classes were eligible to ever become *arkhons*. Dating back to the early days of Athens, any former *arkhons* had automatically become part of the Aereopagus Council. Originally, the council had administered most of the business of the city, but gradually the *ekklesia* and the *boule* took on most of these responsibilities. The Aereopagus became a court to deal with serious criminal offences.

The *arkhons* and *strategoi* (elected generals) were the most dominant people in Athens. They were very influential in the *ekklesia*, but their influence wasn't because people feared their power. Rather, the prominence of these people came from their being excellent speakers who knew how to work an audience and convince people to vote for their ideas.

One of the most notable VIPs was Pericles (see the earlier sidebar 'Holding out for a hero: Enter Pericles'). He was involved in changes that reduced the powers of the Aereopagus Council, but he also made significant changes to the other great boast of ancient Athens – the jury system.

Examining the Athenian Legal System

The legal system in ancient Athens was very complicated. I could write entire chapters – indeed books – about Athenian justice. In this section, I just give a brief guide and overview of what took place in the court of law.

The main principle of the Athenian legal system was trial by jury. The Athenians believed that, like politics, every citizen should contribute to the system of justice – and jury trials were the easiest way of doing this. Other Greek cities either decided on issues by the power of the monarch or ruling council or allowed individuals the opportunity to enact vengeance themselves. Athens was doing something really quite different.

Meeting the legal players

The *thesmothetai* – six *arkhons* who were part of the Eleven (see the section 'Identifying special roles and posts') – were responsible for administering justice, which meant staffing and running the jury-courts and ensuring that justice took place.

The jury-courts were known as the *eliaia* and were staffed by between 201 and 2,501 jurors, which the *thesmothetai* would decide upon depending on the case's significance. Immense care was taken over the selection of the jury to try and ensure that people with close relationships to those involved were not selected, but this was always difficult in such a small community.

The Athenians held a register of 6,000 citizens who were eligible for jury service. Pericles eventually introduced the system of payment for jurors, arguing that jury duty was as important as attending the *ekklesia* and so participants should be paid. The going rate was two obols a day (twice the rate of a day at the *ekklesia*). The number of cases going on meant that a juror was likely to be busy for many days of the year.

Prosecuting cases

Athens's legal system was different from modern, Western systems in that all prosecutions were brought by private citizens. The state didn't prosecute anybody. So, for example, if somebody broke into your house and stole your property, even if they were caught in the act, *you* would be responsible for taking them to court. Even crimes against the state, such as treason, were prosecuted by private individuals. When Socrates was put on trial in 399 BC for 'corrupting the youth of Athens' (Chapter 9 has the details) the charge was made by several private citizens, not the state.

Similarly, the Athenian system didn't have any lawyers, as you know them nowadays. Citizens represented themselves in court, although they sometimes got more eloquent speakers to write speeches for them – for a fee, of course!

Everything took place in front of the jury of citizens (no private discussions with a judge or meetings between lawyers). Also, trials had to be over in one day. In a sense this time limit made for a much less complicated process – although you can argue that the jury was merely swayed by clever speaking.

Determining the fitness of a witness

Given the short duration of all Athenian court cases, good witnesses were vital. In the Athenian court, witnesses merely gave their evidence; no cross-examination was allowed. The selection and use of witnesses in court was the main legal strategy employed by prosecuting citizens.

Only citizens were allowed to give evidence. This regulation meant that women and *metoikoi* (resident foreigners) weren't allowed to serve as witnesses. However, they could make a statement to a representative of the *eliaia* that a male citizen then read aloud.

Trial evidence provided by slaves was particularly controversial in the Athenian courts and was admissible only if the slave had been tortured first. This grizzly task was carried out by the Scythian archers who served as the Athenian police force and supervised by an *eliaia* official. (Indeed, the lives of these unfortunate people were in stark contrast to the experiences of citizens in highly democratic Athens; for more on slavery see Chapter 14.)

Doggone good justice

In Aristophanes's play *Wasps*, he pokes fun at the Athenian legal system and the tendency of some people to be over-litigious on trivial issues if there was any chance of gaining compensation. He stages a fake trial at which a dog called Labes is prosecuted for stealing and eating a piece of Italian cheese! The prosecuting citizen

Bdelykleon sums up the charge and suggests punishment:

Now hear the indictment. Prosecution by the Dog of Kydathenaion against Labes of Aixone that he wronged one Sicilian cheese by eating it all by himself. Punishment one figwood dog-collar!

Trying a case

At a preliminary hearing in the Athenian courts both parties stated their case. An attempt would be made to settle the issue at this point as the appointed *arkhon* would encourage both sides to negotiate. If that failed then any physical evidence was boxed up and handed to the *arkhon*, and he would set a date for the trial which could be several weeks or even months in the future.

At the trial a water-clock timed the proceedings so that neither side was allowed to dominate and both had sufficient time to make their case. Both sides presented their evidence and then the jury voted. If the jury decided on a guilty verdict then they took another vote about the form of punishment. Very often the prosecution suggested its own punishment during a case.

More often than not, the jury's punishment was a fine. The three heaviest penalties were death, exile (being expelled from the city either indefinitely or for a set period of time during which citizen rights would be lost), or *atimia*. *Atimia* involved stripping away the rights of Athenian citizenship. Although people could continue to live in Athens, they could no longer participate in any official functions. The Athenians often referred to *atimia* as a state of 'living death'. The presiding *arkhon* was responsible for ensuring that the punishments were carried out and would attend and supervise executions.

Chapter 8

Dealing with the Neighbours from Hell: The Peloponnesian War

In This Chapter

▶ Identifying the war's causes

▶ Waging the First and Second Peloponnesian Wars

▶ Surviving the plague in Athens

▶ Engaging in siege warfare

Thucydides the Athenian wrote the history of the war between Athens and Sparta . . . in the belief that it was going to be a great war and more worth writing about than any of those that had taken place in the past.

–Thucydides, The History of the Peloponnesian War

The Peloponnesian War lasted for more than 30 years. When it started in 431 BC, Athens and Sparta were pretty much unchallenged as the two dominant city-states in the whole of Greece. Athens had its international empire and dominant fleet, and Sparta had control of large sections of mainland Greece and its famous army.

By the end of the war, both sides were in a position from which they never really recovered. Essentially, their time had passed. The Peloponnesian War brought one era of ancient Greece to an end, and this chapter examines how.

Engaging in the First Cold War

A clash between Athens and Sparta was always likely. Ever since the final defeat of the Persians in 478 BC, the various Greek states had struggled for supremacy. Of all the states Athens and Sparta were the best placed to grab power. The states were rivals for several reasons:

✔ **Historically,** the Spartans were the military leaders of the Greeks, and the Athenians were the founding force behind the Delian League (see Chapter 7) and used this political entity to build an empire.

✔ **Politically,** Athens was a participative democracy (see Chapter 7), but Sparta was ruled by a dominant aristocracy and had two kings and a group of *ephors* (supervisors) that ran the state (see Chapter 4).

✔ **Culturally,** Athens had developed into the artistic capital of the Greek world, and Sparta was an austere, war-like civilisation that held fast to its strict and disciplined rules.

Athens and Sparta had a lot of differences but what they had in common was an aggressive foreign policy towards the other Greek towns and cities and they gained control over more and more of them when they could.

Like the US and USSR in the 20th century, Athens and Sparta had become too big to not be rivals. And just like the Cold War in the last century, any confrontation between the rivals had the potential to be brutal, final, and come at a massive human cost.

Sparta in the doldrums

The Athenians had done very nicely out of the Persian Wars – establishing the Delian League and creating a vast empire – but the years that followed 478 BC weren't as kind to Sparta.

The Spartans were the big players in what was known as the Peloponnesian League. This loose group of cities including Corinth and Elis banded together to face the Persian threat in the 480s BC. After Persia was defeated in 478 BC the league drifted apart, and the Spartans weren't able to call on league members for support in the way that the Athenians did with the Delian League.

In many ways 464 BC was Sparta's *annus horribilis* (awful year). During this year Sparta suffered a tremendous earthquake, resulting in massive damage to the town and the death of many people. Following the earthquake, the long-suffering helot population (see Chapter 4) took its chance to revolt. The Spartans managed to recover and pin down the revolting helots on Mount Ithome where they'd built a fortified encampment that eventually became a town. This was a huge problem for the Spartans because the helot population was massive – at least five times the number of Spartan citizens.

At this point the Spartans appealed to their fellow Greek towns – including Athens – for help to launch a final attack on the helot camp.

Kimon: A big fan of Sparta

Kimon was such a fan of Sparta and its constitution that he named his son *Lakedaimonios*, which literally means 'of Sparta' or 'Spartan'. Being sent back to Athens was a tremendous blow to him because he'd worked so hard for the campaign to be approved. He suffered the consequences on his return being *ostracised* (sent into exile) for ten years. Kimon tried (unsuccessfully) to return two years later but was eventually recalled in 451 BC when the Athenians needed his experience to help them negotiate a peace treaty with Sparta, and he resumed his leading role in the political life of the city.

Decision time in Athens

The dominant political figure in Athens in the fifth century BC was Pericles (see Chapter 7). He encouraged policies that saw the Athenians expand their empire and turn the city into a cultural centre. But Pericles wasn't a king and there were other speakers in the *ekklesia*, or general assembly, who disagreed with his reforms. (Chapter 7 has more info on *ekklesia*.) One of these was a man called Kimon.

Kimon was pro-Spartan in outlook, meaning that he felt the Greek states should work together for their own mutual interests. He believed that the Persians were still the biggest threat to all Greece and that the Athenians should seek to form an alliance with the Spartans that protected both cities from foreign, non-Greek threats like the Persians without coming into conflict with each other.

When the call for help came from Sparta in 464 BC, Kimon managed to persuade the Athenian *ekklesia* to vote him commander of an expeditionary force that would go and help Sparta. Kimon was hugely pleased with his new role, but his actions unwittingly kicked off the chain of events that started the brutal Peloponnesian War.

Things didn't turn out as Kimon expected. Although he was pro-Sparta many of his troops were Athenian democrats. When they arrived at Mount Ithome they upset the Spartans by expressing sympathy for the helots and their plight. The Spartans grew suspicious and sent the Athenians back home, saying that they were no longer needed. After all the debating, the Athenians never even lifted a sword in anger!

This incident at Mount Ithome was fatal to the relationship between Athens and Sparta and the divide between them became permanent. A few years later in 460 BC, the Athenians signed a treaty with the town of Argos, a sworn enemy of Sparta.

Thucydides: News from the frontline

Historians are very well informed about the Second Peloponnesian War, partly because of the work of the Greek historian Thucydides. Thucydides was born around 460 BC and lived through nearly the whole war and actually served as a commander for the Athenians. He was a relative of Kimon (see the sidebar 'Kimon: A big fan of Sparta') and a supporter of Pericles. Thucydides's book *The History of the Peloponnesian War* is the first real work of history ever written and it's written by somebody who was actually there, fighting in a war that took place 2,500 years ago. Amazing!

Enduring the first Peloponnesian War (460–446 BC)

By signing the treaty with Argos the Athenians officially became the enemies of Sparta. Over the next 15 years a war of sorts took place. Athens and Sparta attacked each other's allies on mainland Greece and close by. The war involved a lot of manoeuvring for position and short-term captures of territory.

Neither side managed to gain the upper hand, and victory was usually quickly followed by defeat. After early victories for Athens, the initiative gradually slipped away, with Sparta's allies the Boiotians and the island of Euboia revolting against Athens. In 446 BC, Pericles and the Athenian army were perilously cut off in Euboia when the Spartan king Pleistoanax had a chance to attack Athens itself. Pleistoanax didn't attack, and the war petered out. Pericles began negotiations, and eventually both sides signed a treaty declaring 30 years of peace. Unfortunately, the Thirty Years Truce, as it was known, was never likely to hold for that long. Fewer than half the 30 years elapsed before the beginnings of the Second Peloponnesian War.

Fighting the Main Event: The Second Peloponnesian War

Greek historian Thucydides was clear on the causes of the second, bloodier Peloponnesian War:

> *War began when the Athenians and Peloponnesians broke the Thirty Years Truce ... What made the war inevitable was the growth in Athenian power and the fear that this caused in Sparta.*

Historians largely agree with Thucydides's assessment; fear of Athenian power had been partly responsible for the First Peloponnesian War (see the preceding section 'Enduring the First Peloponnesian War'.)

However, the incident that prompted the breaking of the Thirty Years Truce was a bit more interesting and took place on the island of Kerkyra.

Initiating a crisis in Kerkyra

Kerkyra was a colony of the city of Corinth. In 435 BC, the Kerkyrans revolted against Corinth, and a war raged for two years. In 433 BC, the Kerkyrans asked Athens for help, and the Athenians, sensing an opportunity, said yes and immediately became an enemy of Corinth.

Corinth was a member of the Peloponnesian League (see the section 'Sparta in the doldrums'), and when the Athenians clashed with them again over the small city of Poteidaia in northern Greece in 432 BC, Corinth complained to the Spartans about Athenian aggression. Surely, the Corinthians argued, the Peloponnesian League would defend its members' interests?

The problem was that the Athenians hadn't actually broken the peace treaty they signed with Sparta because they hadn't done anything against the Spartans' interests, so the Spartans would be the ones breaking the agreement if they took any action against Athens. During the winter of 432–31 BC, the Spartans spent days debating whether to move against Athens. One of their kings called Arkhidamos argued long and hard that the Spartans should hold back from confrontation, but the momentum was already behind war.

Really the start of the war had nothing to do with the rights and wrongs of the Athens and Corinth situation. As Thucydides wrote, the Spartans feared Athens's growing power.

Actually, in the end, neither Athens or Sparta officially started the Peloponnesian War – rather it was the city of Thebes, another influential and aggressive Greek state who were at the time allied with Sparta. Ironic really, because the Thebans ended up doing rather well following the war (see Chapter 9).

In the spring of 431 BC, a group of Thebans managed to take hold of the town of Plataia. The Plataians were allies of Athens and had refused to go over to the Spartan-dominated Boiotian League, a small group of towns allied with Sparta in the east of Greece. The Thebans' actions were a direct attack on Athenian territory and broke the peace treaty. The Plataians managed to kick out the Theban force, but it was no good. The war had started.

This early stage of the Second Peloponnesian War (the first ten years, 431–421 BC) is often known as the Arkhidamian War. Rather unfair given that Arkhidamos was a leading Spartan general who argued *against* fighting in the first place. After the war began though, Arkhidamos had to lead the Spartan troops.

Figuring out how to fight

Athens and Sparta fighting each other presented difficulties. In addition to the contrasts I describe in the earlier section 'Engaging in the First Cold War', the Spartans were the superior force on land, whereas Athens had a supposedly undefeatable navy.

These differences made actually fighting each other very difficult because:

- ✔ Pericles proposed a strategy in which Athens avoided engaging the Spartan army directly but used its fleet to harass and attack Sparta's allies, like the small towns in the Boiotian League.
- ✔ Sparta spent a great deal of time invading Attica without ever going as far as to lay siege to Athens.

The Spartan attacks in Attica were very harmful. The Spartans would attack and kill farmers and their livestock and destroy any crops. This had two big effects: First, food became scarce, and second, all the homeless people from the countryside (with the encouragement of Pericles) came to Athens.

Dealing with the plague

As the Spartan attacks continued in Attica and the area surrounding Athens, people began to pour into Athens looking for shelter and safety. The effects of this population increase soon took its toll. In 430 BC, a terrible disease took hold in the city. Many people at the time blamed the illness on a ship from the east, but the immense overcrowding and unpleasant conditions in the city can't have helped.

Thucydides, who caught the plague but survived, gives an unpleasant first-hand account:

The bodies of the dying were heaped one on top of the other, and half-dead creatures could be seen staggering about in the streets or flocking around the fountains in their desire for water. The temples in which they took up their quarters were full of the dead bodies of people who had died inside them.

Life in Athens must have been absolutely horrific. Around 30,000 people died of the plague and its after-effects. The population in Attica didn't really recover for several generations.

The Athenian people put all the blame on Pericles because it had been his strategy to fight the war abroad and bring many people in Attica inside Athens's walls. He was suspended from his position as a *strategos* (general) and fined.

Then in 429 BC Pericles himself caught the plague and died. By this point the Athenians had already reinstated him as a *strategos* (due to a lack of alternatives). Death by plague was a sad end to the life of a great man – and Pericles's death left Athens facing a very uncertain future.

Responding to the Mytilenean revolt

The war pressed on regardless of Pericles's passing. With Athens doing badly some of her allies began to jump ship. In 428 BC, the town of Mytilene on the island of Lesbos (see the Cheat Sheet map) revolted against Athens.

The Athenian response was savage. First, an Athenian fleet was sent to blockade the island. After Mytilene surrendered, the Athenian *ekklesia* voted to execute all the male citizens and sell the women and children into slavery.

Athens had previously done everything possible to nurture its relationship with its allies. So why the drastic change in dealing with Mytilene? Well, the death of Pericles left a vacuum in the *ekklesia*, and it was filled by what Athenian aristocrats referred to as the 'new men'. These new men weren't descended from ancient aristocratic lines like Pericles, and they rose to positions of influence through their ability to rabble-rouse and speak impressively in the *ekkleisa* (see Chapter 7).

Chief among the new men were Kleon and Hyperbolos. Hyperbolos was so famed for his speaking that the word 'hyperbole' derives from his name which literally meant 'throwing beyond' (that is, exaggerating)! Both of these new men frequently gave inflammatory speeches that encouraged Athenians to take the harshest action. The response to Mytilene was a case in point.

Although Kleon had argued that Mytilene should be punished harshly, Athens was uncomfortable with this judgement. The issue was debated again the following day, and a majority voted for a lighter punishment. A ship was dispatched to take the news and arrived at Mytilene just in time to stop the massacre. Phew!

Athens's new men are mercilessly mocked by the comic playwright Aristophanes in his play *Knights*. Aristophanes had a particular hatred for Kleon, whom he called 'The Tanner', mocking his background in the trade of leather goods. In *Wasps* he went even further, naming characters 'Procleon' and 'Anticleon'. Procleon is written as a total braggart but a real wimp when it came to fighting:

> *'Here, here, what's coming over me? I've gone all limp, I can't hold the sword up any longer! All the fight's gone out of me!'*

Going international: A situation in Sicily

The Peloponnesian War from 431 to 428BC was so far, so Greek. But after 427 BC, the effects of the war began to spread around the Mediterranean. Other countries getting involved in fighting between Sparta and Athens may sound weird, but think about the way that the Second World War ended up being partly fought in North Africa, Japan, and the South Pacific as well as in Europe itself.

Additionally, a long history of Greek influence affected the region. For example, the Greeks had founded colonies in Sicily several hundred years prior to the Peloponnesian War (see Chapter 3). The island's many towns had close relationships with the Greek cities from which they'd originated through trade and population movement.

One Sicilian town was Leontinoi. In 427 BC, Leontinoi appealed to Athens for help against the attacks by Syracuse, and the Athenians agreed to assist. You would have thought that the Athenians had better things to do, what with the Peloponnesian War going on and everything, but Athens had hidden motives for wanting to help and got involved in another war that was entirely separate from their campaign against Sparta.

Unlike Attica and much of the Peloponnese, Sicily was rich and fertile, producing a huge amount of grain. In fact, a lot of the grain that the Greek cities consumed was imported from Sicily. Athenians probably saw aiding Sicily as a chance to get to grips with the grain supply – either by taking it all for themselves or stopping grain ships from reaching Sparta and its allies.

Perhaps the Sicilians worked out that Athens was likely to be a bigger threat than a help. When the small Athenian fleet arrived in Sicily it was sent back home again because Leontinoi and Syracuse had managed to settle the dispute themselves.

Nevertheless the Athenians kept an eye on Sicily and planned to return. (See the later section 'Attempting – again! – to take Sicily'.)

Putting up a fight for Pylos

While the Athenians were messing around and interfering with Sicily, almost by accident they struck a blow against Sparta. Incredibly, when a small group of Athenian ships on their way to Sicily passed the harbour of Sparta's ally Pylos in south western Greece, they found it virtually undefended.

The orator Demosthenes was on ship with the Athenian generals because he'd been sent to use his rhetorical skill in Sicily to negotiate terms for help with Leontinoi. He argued that they should take advantage of the situation and was dropped off and left behind with a small force to build a fort at the edge of the bay. The Spartans panicked and sent their army to fight against the Athenians. A land and naval battle ensued, and the Athenians won. Athens established a base at the closest point to Sparta. Also, 420 Spartan hoplites were left marooned on the nearby island of Sphacteria.

The immediate response of the Spartans was to negotiate peace – an offer that the Athenians rejected out of hand. A bit of a mistake really, as the Athenians were never able to really make the most of the advantage that they had gained.

The reaction in Athens was hugely critical; the populace accused the generals of not making the most of things. Chief among the critics was the demagogue Kleon, who claimed that he could've done a better job. In a shock move, one of the chief *strategoi* called Nikias said that Kleon should go and do it then!

Annoyingly, Kleon was quite successful the following year. Taking the experienced Demosthenes with him, Kleon and his men headed for Pylos and managed to capture nearly 300 Spartan prisoners at the battle of Sphacteria, who became a hugely useful bargaining tool for the rest of the war.

Swaying the north-east cities: Brasidas

Although the Athenians had an advantage through the capture of the Spartan prisoners, Sparta had been pursuing another strategy that was proving quite successful. In 424 BC some towns in north-east Greece that had previously been loyal to Athens decided to revolt. With Athens's resources stretched, it must have seemed a good time to try.

Sparta sent a large force to north-east Greece under the command of a leading aristocrat called Brasidas. He went on the equivalent of a PR tour, winning over many of these cities with his personal charm – combined with the presence of around 1,500 heavily armed hoplites.

Thucydides: Warfare's loss is literature's gain

Thucydides was one Athenian who was given command during the action against Brasidas. He was sent to defend the town of Amphipolis and prevent it from going over to Sparta. He failed to keep the city under Athenian influence – more through bad luck than anything else – and on his return to Athens he was sent into exile for an indefinite period as punishment. He resolved to travel around Greece as a result.

At this point in his life, Thucydides began collecting material for *The History of the*

Peloponnesian War, which he spent the rest of his life writing. The book wasn't published until after his death by which point those who had expelled him from Athens had fallen from power. It immediately became a standard work of history that was much admired by other Greeks for its detailed style and focus on accuracy rather than rumour. Just think, if he'd won at Amphipolis, historians probably wouldn't know nearly as much about the war!

Brasidas's campaign was hugely dangerous to Athens because when cities defected from the empire the Athenians lost both their revenues and the opportunity to call on them for military support.

The Athenians set out to stop Brasidas, and the end result was a truce that lasted for one year in 423 BC. Neither side could keep to the truce, however, and in 422 BC, Kleon took a force to the north to attack Brasidas. At a big battle outside the town of Amphipolis, the Athenians were heavily defeated and both Kleon and Brasidas killed.

Brokering a precarious peace deal: Nikias

After nearly ten years of conflict, both Sparta and Athens began to realise that neither side was going to be able to win the war – every victory came at too great a cost for the winning side to be able to take advantage.

Thus, in 421 BC, peace negotiations began, led by the Athenian *strategos* Nikias. The two sides managed to agree to a 50-year peace and also the return of the Spartan prisoners in exchange for Amphipolis. So that was all sorted then, wasn't it? Sadly, no.

Although the peace of Nikias was an excellent deal for Athens and Sparta, it enraged the other cities, including Boiotia and Corinth (see the section 'Initiating a crisis in Kerkyra') that had supported the Spartan side during the years of fighting. As far as these Spartan-supporting states were concerned, the peace deal offered nothing for them – all their grievances against Athens were unresolved.

With so much discontent the peace brokered by Nikias couldn't last.

Complicating the mix: Argos and Alcibiades

The cities that felt hard-done-by in the peace of Nikias deserted Sparta and looked to make a deal with the ancient city of Argos. Argos hadn't been involved in the Peloponnesian War up until this point; the discontented cities believed that an alliance with Argos was in their best interests. But deal-making with Argos added a third potential power to the mix and made a complicated situation even worse.

At the same time Athens was falling under a new and exciting influence in the *ekklesia* – a man called Alcibiades. This young, charming, and apparently immensely handsome aristocrat possessed a tremendous talent for swaying popular opinion. (See Chapter 26 for more on this complicated fellow.)

In 420 BC, Alcibiades managed to convince the *ekklesia* that Athens could profit from what was happening with Argos. He argued that the cities were flocking to join with Argos because Sparta was now their enemy. By logical extension, these discontented states were now Athenian allies. Brilliant!

Alcibiades won the day, and Athens made an alliance with the cities of Argos, Mantineia, and Elis. Although this technically didn't break the peace of Nikias, it certainly strained it.

Of course, confrontation soon happened. In 418 BC, the Spartan king Agis attacked Argos, which the Spartans now saw as their main threat. This attack meant that the allies of Argos had to come to the city's defence – and those allies now included Athens!

The result was a battle outside the town of Mantineia. The Spartans soundly defeated a combined force of Argos and its allies. The victory was a massive confidence boost to the Spartans, reinforcing their reputation for invincibility.

Engaging in siege warfare in Melos

After losing at Mantineia, Athens quickly fell back into the policy that Pericles had proposed – attacking Spartan allies and adding them to its empire. In 416 BC, Athens's focus turned to the island of Melos, part of the Cyclades. The siege wasn't an arduous one, but when Melos finally broke, the Athenians did to Melos what they had threatened to do to Mytilene years before: All the men were put to death and the women and children sold into slavery. (See the earlier section 'Responding to the Mytilenean revolt'.)

The Athenians' actions sound absolutely barbaric today (and have unpleasant echoes of the 'ethnic-cleansing' that took place during the last century). No excuse can justify the barbarous destruction of an entire community, but in the ancient world it wasn't unusual for a siege to end like this.

Laying siege: The waiting game

In Chapter 5, I talk about the infantry battles, cavalry, and naval warfare of ancient Greeks. The other major form of military engagement during this time was the siege. A lot of siege warfare occurred during the Peloponnesian War, and Alexander the Great (see Chapters 10 and 11) was a devil for a siege. In essence, a city that was being attacked had two choices: come out and fight, or lock the gates and try to sit it out. Consequently sieges happened very often.

Generally speaking, laying a siege was a long process. The attacking army blockaded the enemy town and then essentially sat there and waited. The siege came to an end either when the attackers managed to get in, or either party gave up.

In any siege the attacking side needed to be confident that they were able to starve out those inside the city. Thus, the attacker's supply lines needed to be excellent. They had to have enough troops to surround the city and prevent supplies getting in. When laying siege to ports, this blockade activity, known as *circumvallation*, was often done by using a fleet to intercept supply ships and guard the harbour.

Sieges were very time consuming and never guaranteed success. An attacker could waste months on a siege that then had to end because the troops were required elsewhere. The process was also grim, boring work for the attackers, and armies often became ill-disciplined.

Developing new tactics

By the time of the Peloponnesian War, the Greeks had developed some new tactics to go on the offensive. Following are five popular options:

- **Mounds:** This approach was quite simple really. The attackers constructed a very large earth mound with an underlying structure of timber against a wall of the city. The timber ensured that the mound wouldn't be ground down by the thousands of feet pounding on it. The attackers then used the mound as a ramp for mounting infantry charges, bringing archers closer to their targets, and manoeuvring battering rams. Walls could be 25–30 feet high so it was often easier to bash a hole in them than climb over!

- **Towers:** The attackers built siege towers, which were large wooden constructions from which archers provided covering fire to troops attacking the walls. The towers would normally be slightly higher than the walls so that the archers could shoot down onto the defenders (although the height would depend how much timber was available). Check out Chapter 12 for the ultimate siege tower – Demetrius's 'Heliopolis'.

- **Mines:** For this tactic, the attackers literally dug under the other side's protective walls sometimes 10 or 15 feet deep. Digging mines was an incredibly dangerous job because those doing it were liable to be crushed by the mine collapsing or the walls themselves falling on them. The defenders often poured water into the mines, flooding them and drowning the attackers.

- **Battering rams:** This tactic was mostly used in conjunction with mounds. Teams of men continually charged a wall, striking it with a ram made of wood, until the wall fell. Siege towers and archers often provided cover for battering ram teams.

- **Treachery:** By far the simplest way for an attacker to gain victory was to get a message to a traitor *within* the town who then opened the gates. Often these traitorous actions were in return for money or simply the promise that the traitor and their family would be spared when the town was taken. Of course, often the promised safety or compensation didn't happen in the melee that followed.

Following a siege

After a siege broke and a town was in the possession of the enemy, what followed was often terrible. The massacre of all prisoners became increasingly common during the Peloponnesian War, as the war itself became more and more brutal. These killings were often prompted by a shortage of food; limited resources meant keeping prisoners was impossible. On other occasions, the killings were to prevent the town involved from ever seeking revenge.

If a deal could be struck between attacker and the besieged citizens, it often was. For example, the Spartan prisoners taken at Sphacteria by Kleon and Demosthenes (see the previous section 'Putting up a fight for Pylos') were taken only because they were a really useful bargaining tool.

Sometimes the defending city won of course. Laying siege was a lengthy, arduous process and sometimes the attackers ran out of supplies (and energy) first. However, more often than not it was the attackers that won and the defenders who suffered the consequences.

War, like life itself in the ancient world, was a harsh and brutal business. The Athenian plague of 430 BC is a good indication of how death was an ever-present possibility for the ancient Greeks. While the difficulties of just staying alive don't in any way excuse the cold-blooded murders that frequently took place, considering the difficult daily lives of the ancient Greeks does help cast a light on the type of mindset that made the life-or-death decisions on the battlefield.

Attempting – again! – to take Sicily

Soon after the Athenians' brutal siege on Melos they suffered one of the most humiliating defeats ever as part of a failed Sicilian Expedition.

Amazingly, despite his role in the policy that had ended in defeat in Mantineia, Alcibiades (see the previous section 'Complicating the mix: Argos and Alcibiades') was still extremely influential in Athenian politics. When the Sicilian city of Egesta asked for help in a local war with their neighbours Selinous in the winter of 416 BC, Alcibiades enthusiastically championed the cause.

The older statesman Nikias was more circumspect, but because the war with Sparta had eased since Mantineia, the *ekklesia* happily voted to support Egesta. The Athenians also voted that the generals in charge of the fleet would be Nikias, Lamakhos, and Alcibiades himself.

Scandal and drama: Alcibiades

Just as the Athenian fleet was about to leave for Sicily, scandal hit the city. First, people inflicted damage on some *hermai*, which were small statues of the god Hermes that were associated with bringing good luck to travellers. These *hermai* were sculpted with erect penises and vandals had snapped them all off – ouch! The connection between the statues and the upcoming Sicilian Expedition must have been obvious to the Greeks who interpreted it as an attempt to curse the mission by desecrating images of the god of travel. It was both sacrilegious and also considered a bad omen for those going to Sicily, as it proved to be.

At almost the same time, in the *ekklesia* Alcibiades was accused of the crime of mocking the Eleusinian Mysteries (a very strange, sacred ritual that I describe in Chapter 22). Alcibiades's actions seem to have merely been the result of rich, young aristocrats living it up, but the consequences were very serious. Before the Athenian fleet even reached Sicily, a messenger caught up with them to announce that Alcibiades was being recalled to face prosecution. His reaction was to leave the fleet and sail to Sparta where he became an adviser to his ex-enemies! For more on Alcibiades's colourful life, see Chapter 26.

Disaster in Sicily

The Athenian fleet did eventually arrive in Sicily – commanded by Lamakhos and Nikias. Their first move was to lay siege to the great city of Syracuse that was supporting Selinous, the town that had attacked Egesta. Lamakhos was killed in early 414 BC, leaving Nikias in sole control.

Things were progressing well for the Athenians until the Syracusans were relieved by a group of Spartans who'd been sent to Sicily on the advice of – you guessed it – Alcibiades!

The Athenians now found themselves blockaded into the harbour of Syracuse and eventually the Athenian fleet was defeated. The Athenian soldiers tried to retreat across land but were outmanoeuvred and defeated by the Syracusans in 413 BC.

The results of the defeat were catastrophic for Athens. The commanders (including Nikias) were executed and all the remaining prisoners forced to work in the stone quarries of Syracuse. The existence was appalling with death coming as a merciful release. Altogether, about 7,000 Athenian soldiers and sailors were lost to death or slavery.

Thucydides firmly believed that the failure of the Sicilian Expedition was probably the biggest catastrophe that Athens had ever suffered:

> . . . for they were utterly and entirely defeated; their sufferings were on an enormous scale; their losses were, as they say, total; army, navy, everything was destroyed, and, out of many, only few returned.

Pondering the end of Athens

The defeat in Sicily was a real turning point in the Peloponnesian War. From 413 BC onwards, the war ceased to be a struggle between Athens and Sparta and became an opportunity for others to get involved and get rich pickings.

The fat (Athenian) lady hadn't sung yet, but she was certainly warming up. However, in the end Athens's final defeat was really prompted from within – as I explain in Chapter 9.

Chapter 9

Losing Their Way: The End of Classical Greece

As the Peloponnesian War dragged on toward a finish (see Chapter 8), the era that historians consider 'Classical Greece' was also drawing to a close. The dominance of the Greek city-states like Athens, Sparta, Thebes, and Corinth didn't have long to run. By around 350 BC, a new power emerged in the north – Macedonia – and the Greek world was never the same.

In this chapter, I look at what happened at the end of the Peloponnesian War and the chaos that followed. The end of Classical Greece is a complicated – but fascinating – period of ancient Greek history!

Weathering Tough Times: Athens

The failure of the Sicilian expedition in 413 BC (see Chapter 8) was almost a mortal blow for Athens in its long battle with Sparta and its allies, which had lasted decades. At a stroke, Athens lost several thousand fighting men, three of its leading generals and a large portion of its fleet. But although Athens was down, it certainly wasn't out.

Preying on Athens: Another round of Persian intrigue

The rest of the Mediterranean was watching, including the Persians who'd waged a brutal on/off war against Greece from 490 to 478 BC. (See Chapter 6 for all the gory details.)

Unsurprisingly, the Spartans were the first to take advantage of Athens's weakened stature. In 413 BC, the Spartans actually occupied Attica by making a permanent fort outside the town of Dekeleia. The Spartans also began constructing a new fleet.

Elsewhere, Athens's empire was breaking up. Several places such as the island of Lesbos revolted, knowing that the Athenians were unlikely to be able to do anything about it.

Over-extending itself: Athens pesters Persia

At a time like this, you may be thinking that the last thing that the Athenians wanted was to get involved in another foreign war – but that's exactly what happened. They threw their support behind the rebel Amorges who were trying to bring Karia away from Persian control.

Lending support to Amorges raised Persian awareness of Athens's troubles, and the Persians began to negotiate with Sparta. In return for Spartan support, Persia made large financial contributions to help build the new Spartan fleet.

Staging a coup in Athens

By 411 BC Persia wasn't the only power that was trying to benefit from Athens's diminished status. While some of the Athenian fleet was moored at Samos, its commanders were contacted by good old Alcibiades (see Chapter 8). After doing a bunk to Sparta, Alcibiades became (unsurprisingly) unpopular with the Spartans and travelled to the Greek cities in Asia Minor, ending up as a paid advisor at the court of a Persian *satrap* (regional governor) called Tissaphernes. However, Alcibiades had his eye on returning to Athens – but on his own terms.

Alcibiades knew that returning to Athens was going to be immensely difficult. He was still technically on the run and had previously collaborated with Sparta, Athens's prime enemy. So he tried to convince the generals sent to support Amorges to go back to Athens and represent him by stirring up trouble against the current Athenian government. Alcibiades was effectively proposing that Athens stage a revolution so that he could return. He would gain support from the new regime from Persia. Say what you like about Alcibiades, but he must have been some talker!

Many of the Athenian generals rejected Alcibiades's proposal and stayed on Samos, forming a pro-democracy group, but one general called Peisandros headed back to Athens and began agitating for revolt. A mixture of violence and intimidation led to a coup taking place in Athens. A number of leading members of the *ekklesia* were killed and others were forced to flee for their safety – many of them went to the island of Samos.

A new body of 400 was established, made up of 40 men (mostly aristocrats) from each of Athens's ten tribes. (See Chapter 7 for more on the composition of Athens's legislative bodies.) These new leaders made a pledge to divert all financial resources to furthering the war against Sparta. In addition, 5,000 of the wealthiest citizens agreed to pay for their own hoplite armour (see Chapter 5) and form a fighting force.

That's the way the 'coup' crumbles

But like so many political pledges the promise initiated in the coup was never fulfilled. Vast numbers of the wealthier citizens left Athens, and the 400 new aristocrats were unable to raise the money that they needed to fund more fighting. Alcibiades fell out with Tissaphernes, so the promised Persian support never materialised either. In the end, Alcibiades ended up offering advice to the exiled democrats that had fled to Samos from Athens after the coup!

By September 411 BC the Athenians had run out of patience with the 400 new political leaders who'd failed to bring about anything in particular. The democrats that remained, led by a man called Cleophon, re-established democracy, known as the 'rule of 5,000'. It was so named because rule had been handed back to the people, rather than 400 people ruling. It wasn't that 5,000 people seized control!

By the way, Cleophon was known as the 'lyremaker' because he came, like Kleon, from an artisan background.

Thucydides passes the torch to Xenophon

Around time of the Athenian coup (411 BC), Thucydides's historical narrative *History of the Peloponnesian War* runs out. Fortunately, readers have another history that picks up almost directly after, written by a man called Xenophon.

Xenophon was a gentleman farmer from Attica who had an eventful life (see the section

'Mounting Problems in the Persian Empire' later in this chapter). In his retirement, Xenophon wrote an extensive account of Greek history during his lifetime. He is also one of the best sources that we have for the philosopher Socrates. Xenophon wrote many essays and works of philosophy based around his method of argument (see Chapter 23).

The whole coup didn't achieve much, but it did prove two things:

- ✔ Athens's devotion to democracy was surviving – even while engaged in a long war with Sparta.

- ✔ The divide between Athenian aristocrats and 'new men' (see Chapter 8) was still carrying on.

Wrapping Up the Peloponnesian War

With the return of democracy, Athens started doing rather well again. Several naval victories occurred between 410 and 407 BC – some of them involving Alcibiades (see the earlier section 'Staging a coup in Athens') who had thrown in his lot with the democrats who'd fled into exile on Samos and returned to Athens with them.

Alcibiades's success didn't last. Sparta entered into another deal with Persia. This time Cyrus, the youngest son of King Darius (who had invaded Greece in 479 BC – refer to Chapter 6), agreed to finance the Spartan fleet, and the new Spartan ships won a famous victory off the coast of Asia Minor in 406 BC. Alcibiades wasn't present at the battle but was blamed for the defeat, so he went into exile again, this time to Thrace.

Enduring great losses at Arginoussai

Athens's boost was ultimately short-lived. In 406 BC, during what had been a successful battle with the Spartan fleet near the Arginoussai islands, 13 Athenian ships were lost and 12 damaged. The two captains, or *trierarchs,* in charge were unable to pick up the survivors due to a terrible storm. Around 3,000 Athenians were left to drown.

Waiting in the wings: Going into exile

As you might have noticed, exile was a very popular punishment in ancient Greece. In essence it meant being sent away from your city of origin and losing your rights as a citizen. Exile was rarely permanent (due mostly to the fractious nature of Greek politics!) and was an obviously preferable alternative to being put to death. Finding somewhere to be exiled could be a problem because most exiles tended to be aristocrats or leading politicians, so tended to be wealthy and/or well connected. Aristocratic exiles might stay with friends in another city or set themselves up in a new town at their own expense. People must have found it frustrating to lose the opportunity to participate in the political games in their native city, but they were usually back in action again pretty soon. Two of the most famous (and frequent) exiles were Alcibiades and Pausanius; check out Chapter 27 for the full story on both of them.

Six of the *strategoi* (generals) who were in charge of the campaign were put on trial in Athens and executed. Athens could ill-afford the loss of some of its most senior military minds and the decision proved a very unpopular one.

Running out of options

The following year Athens's defeat was final. The Athenian fleet was beached at the Hellespont (between Thrace and Asia Minor) when the Spartan commander Lysander initiated a surprise attack. Almost the entire Athenian fleet was captured with only nine ships escaping. The 26-year-long Peloponnesian War was effectively over. With no fleet to protect Athens, Sparta and her allies seemed likely to lay siege to the city.

Xenophon paints a vivid picture of what it was like in Athens on the evening the lone ship *Paralos* brought news of defeat to the city:

> It was at night when the Paralos arrived at Athens. As the news of the disaster was told, one man passed it to another, and a sound of wailing arose and extended first from Piraeus, then along the long walls until it reached the city. That night no one slept. They mourned for the lost, but more still for their own fate.

Bowing to the Spartans: Athens after the war

After the crushing final naval defeats, Athens expected the worst from Sparta. As I explain in Chapter 8, cities that resisted siege attacks typically suffered heavily after they were finally defeated. Also, Sparta and her allies had 25 years' worth of grudges to avenge.

Socrates: Victim of a shifting society

One famous victim of the new regime in Athens was the philosopher Socrates. Many Athenian aristocrats didn't trust Socrates, and he'd refused to cooperate with the 30 tyrants. The new democracy in Athens was distrustful of anything different or against tradition. Socrates held no official post but was one of the leading intellectuals in Athens and had developed a system of philosophical argument that involved him challenging people's assumptions and questioning their beliefs. Usually this was about moral and ethical questions but he was also interested in justice and the way that the state ran. He famously said, 'All that I know is that I know nothing' meaning that he didn't claim to know any answers himself.

In 399 BC, he was put on trial for not respecting the gods and corrupting the youth of the city. These charges were trumped-up, and he was most certainly framed – nevertheless he was found guilty and sentenced to death. He died by drinking hemlock – his own choice. This was a relatively quick death but still a very painful one because a person's body would go very cold before being gripped by a seizure. It was a sad end for a great man in human history.

Living under Spartan conditions

In the end, Athens wasn't destroyed nor its population enslaved. After the best part of a year in negotiation, Athens finally agreed to Sparta's surrender terms, which included the following:

- All territories that had previously been part of the Athenian empire were set free of any obligations to Athens. They no longer had to pay tribute or supply men for military service when asked.

- Athens's fleet was to be limited to 12 ships. This number would be just about enough to guard their harbours and was a dramatic reduction of the fleet of over 100 that Athens had once enjoyed.

- The protective 'long walls' of the city (see Chapter 7) were to be demolished.

- All Athenian exiles had to be recalled.

- Athens was now a Spartan territory under Spartan control.

The surrender was a huge blow to a city that only 30 years before was the dominant force in the Mediterranean world.

Establishing the rule of the Thirty

The Spartans forced Athens to break up its democracy and go back to oligarchic rule (oligarchy means 'rule of the few'). In 404 BC, the Spartan general Lysander forced the Athenians to establish a new committee of

30 individuals to run the city (under Spartan supervision, or course). Many of 'the Thirty' were formerly exiled aristocrats who'd been involved in the oligarchic coup in 411 BC (see the earlier section 'Staging a coup in Athens') and had only recently returned to the city. The Thirty's authority was backed up by 700 Spartan troops who served as a garrison in the city.

Unsurprisingly, the Thirty had a few scores to settle in Athens, and they used their new authority to take full advantage. In his book *Politics,* the philosopher Aristotle describes what happened when the Thirty came to power:

> *But when they had firmer control of the city, they spared none of the citizens, but put to death those who were noted for their property, family, and reputation, because this removed their own fear and they wanted to appropriate their property; and in a short space of time they had done away with no less than 1,500 . . .*

No honour among thieves

So the 30 newly instated tyrants began turning on each other – and trials and executions followed. At the same time democrats who'd left when the Spartans arrived were trying to find support in other cities such as Thebes (see the later section 'Waging the Corinthian War'). Eventually, the democrats returned to Athens in force in early 403 BC. The Thirty and their supporters fought a battle against the democrats during which several of the tyrants were killed.

The Spartan king Pausanias arrived to try and sort out the mess. Rather than continue to force the oligarchy on Athens, he allowed a limited form of democracy to return. The tyrants and their supporters were allowed to leave and lived in exile in the town of Eleusis. Democracy was back but an atmosphere of distrust and plotting continued.

Winning at a cost: Sparta

Presumably the Spartans were relishing the fact that they'd won a crushing victory against their old enemy after a 26-year war? Well, not really. Victory in the Peloponnesian War proved to be almost as devastating for Sparta as defeat was for Athens.

The first mistake that the Spartans made at the end of the war was the way they dealt with the Athenian empire. Now that they controlled Athens the Spartans were technically the rulers of all the territories that had been a part of the Athenian empire. As a result the Spartans forced many Greek towns and cities to adopt new oligarchic systems of government like that in Athens.

Many of these towns had never directly opposed Sparta during the war, so they now resented the harsh treatment they were receiving. Equally resentful were Sparta's allies in the former Peloponnesian League (see Chapter 8). None of Sparta's former allies got any reward at all when Sparta took control of Athens despite the help that they'd given during the war.

Because the Spartans kept all the spoils, cities such as Thebes were happy to shelter the pro-democracy exiles who fled from Athens during the time of the rule of the Thirty. Sparta had almost become Thebes's and Athens's mutual enemy.

Mounting Problems in the Persian Empire

At the same time as Athens and Sparta's woes, trouble was brewing in the Persian empire – and it had big consequences for Sparta and the rest of Greece.

Marching through the desert with Cyrus

The Persian king Darius died in 404 BC and was succeeded by his son Artaxerxes. Artaxerxes's younger brother Cyrus decided to try and steal the crown and set about recruiting an army.

Cyrus's first port of call was Sparta, which he had helped greatly in the Peloponnesian War (see the preceding section 'Wrapping Up the Peloponnesian War'). The Spartans were pretty much obliged to help Cyrus, and they did so by sending an unofficial force to join up with the Greek mercenary army that Cyrus was putting together.

The expedition didn't go well. Cyrus was defeated and killed in a massive battle at a place called Cunaxa near the Persian city of Babylon. His army of Greek mercenaries was left stranded and leaderless in the middle of the Persian desert!

Among Cyrus's mercenary soldiers was Xenophon who'd signed up after the Peloponnesian War ended (see the sidebar 'Thucydides passes the torch to Xenophon'). Xenophon and the other officers embarked on an incredible march back through Persia and Asia Minor at the head of a force of 10,000 men. Xenophon wrote a book about the experience called the *Anabasis,* or 'march up country', which reads like a daily journal. The narrative's details are said to be so accurate that Alexander the Great used it as a travel guide when he made the journey heading in the opposite direction 75 years later. Reading these details, it's easy to see why:

On this march the army ran short of corn and it was impossible to buy any except in the Lydian market . . . where one could get a capithe of wheat flour or pearl barley for four sigli. The siglus is worth seven and a half attic obols, and the capithe is equal to three pints.

Xenophon and the other generals superbly brought 10,000 men all the way back to Greek territory (in Asia Minor), but Xenophon didn't get any thanks for it. When he returned to Athens, Xenophon was put on trial. The charge was that he commanded Spartan troops – which was true – but he was also seen as a radical and was a known associate of Socrates.

Xenophon was eventually sent into exile. Bad news for him but good for historians because during this time of enforced retirement he started writing history! He lived in Olympia for a while and then Corinth before returning to Athens shortly before he died around 360 BC.

Seeking support from Sparta

After the failure of Cyrus's campaign, many of the Greek cities in Asia Minor that had supported him worried they would be punished by the Persian king Artaxerxes. The cities appealed to Sparta for help because the Spartans had supported Cyrus and were now the dominant Greek state.

The Spartans didn't let them down, fighting a series of campaigns to defend the cities in Asia Minor. The Spartan king Agesilaos led the biggest of these campaigns in 396 BC.

Unfortunately, the Spartans were about to learn that while taking responsibility for Greeks abroad, they left the back door open at home . . .

Waging the Corinthian War

While the Spartans engaged in events in Asia Minor, the other Greek states took advantage. The main players were the Thebans who were still sore about events of a few years before when they felt they hadn't been adequately compensated by Sparta for their support during the Peloponnesian War.

Forging an alliance with Thebes

In 395 BC, Thebes made a treaty with Athens to join forces against Sparta. The partnership was a success, and they inflicted a heavy defeat on the Spartans in a battle near Haliartos during which the Spartan commander Lysander was killed. The Theban victory encouraged the other Greek states, and by the end of 395 BC, Corinth and Argos had joined the partnership too.

This new powerful alliance set about the attack of Sparta. Due to the fact that most of the action took place around the Isthmus of Corinth, the attack was known as the Corinthian War.

Everybody fighting everybody else

The few years following 395 BC were a blur of battles in Greece and abroad with the Corinthian War and Sparta still involved with Persia. In 394 BC the Spartans were very successful against their Greek enemies, and the Spartan king Agesilaos was recalled to help finish the job.

Having suffered some heavy defeats, the other Greek cities avoided open battles with the Spartans, preferring to carry out spoiling attacks on Spartan territories. At the same time the Spartan fleet was almost completely destroyed by the Persians near Knidos.

With the Spartans unable to stop them, the Persians sailed all round the western Mediterranean, kicking out Spartan garrisons from the former Athenian allies that Sparta had taken over at the end of the Peloponnesian War (see the preceding section 'Bowing to the Spartans: Athens after the war'). The Spartan hold on much of Greece and the surrounding areas had lasted just eight years.

Portending a dim future: Defeat at Lekhaion

The era of the Greek city-states was nearing an end – partly because their continual wars were weakening them all! A particularly bleak omen of the future came in 390 BC when a large Spartan force was defeated by a Greek mercenary army at Lekhaion, near the city of Corinth. Once the greatest and most feared army in the Mediterranean, the Spartans were humbled by men fighting in a different way – as lightly-armed *peltastai* (see Chapter 5). And by 338 BC, the whole of Greece came under control of new fighters from the north – the Macedonians (see Chapter 10).

Taking a breather – the King's Peace (386 BC)

The Corinthian War rumbled on throughout the next decade with neither side ever seeming likely to win a victory. (As Athens and Sparta found out before, winning a war in mainland Greece was very difficult!) In the end, diplomacy won out. In 386 BC, the Persian king Artaxerxes intervened and brokered a major peace treaty. In the so-called King's Peace:

✔ The Greeks agreed to allow Persia to control all the Greek cities in Asia Minor.

✔ All the other Greek cities were allowed to rule themselves and be free from any kind of control by another state.

✔ Any country that broke these terms faced attack by the Persian forces.

In a way, Artaxerxes was trying to put an end to all the empire building that had been going on for the past century. The idea was brave – and good for Persia too – but it was never going to last.

Forming the Athenian League

The Spartans first broke the truce set down by King Artaxerxes. Although avoiding any interference in the Greek islands, for the next ten years Sparta continually attacked the Greek towns in the Peloponnese.

The King's Peace had been designed to stop the many Greek towns from ganging up together, but in the end it had the opposite effect. In 378 BC, Athens and Thebes entered into another alliance. Others joined and the new group of allies took the name of the *Athenian League*.

This new league was very different from the Delian League (see Chapter 7). Athens's weakened position meant that the new league was a group with common interests rather than an empire. Athens took no tribute from its allies – it was a group of equals.

The Athenian League made war on Sparta for the best part of the next ten years. The Persians did nothing, despite the fact that these attacks clearly broke the terms of the King's Peace. In reality, the Persian king was perfectly happy for the Greeks to fight among themselves – they were less of a problem for him.

Figuring out the Battle of Leuktra: Greece versus Sparta – and Thebes wins!

The ensuing war between the Athenian League and Sparta – surprise! – followed the pattern of nearly all the other campaigns of the past 50 years. (The real winners appeared to be the Thebans who were building up their territory and revenues from successful battles.)

Playing in the Sacred Band

Thebes's ascent was partly due to the flexible tactics that it had shown at Leuktra, but key to its success were its new elite soldiers.

Although they sound like a Christian rock group, the 'Sacred Band' was actually 300 elite troops from Thebes trained by a man called Pelopidas. These soldiers were called 'sacred' because they were originally created to guard the sacred citadel of the city (an area like the Acropolis in Athens).

What made the Sacred Band even more unusual was that each man was paired with another who was both his companion in the battle line and his lover. The idea was that each man would be inspired to fight even harder with his lover next to him. Homosexuality wasn't thought unusual in Greece (see Chapter 15), but this was still a radical idea.

As the war ground on, Athens found the fighting a real financial burden and struggled to impose new taxes on the citizens to pay for it. The Athenians organised a peace conference at which Sparta and Thebes fell out over who would control the territories of Boiotia.

Before long Sparta and some of her allies (including Corinth which had swapped sides) met the Thebans in battle outside the village of Leuktra in Boiotia. Sparta and her allies easily outnumbered the Thebans and an easy victory was expected.

Only it didn't turn out like that. The Thebans won a stunning victory over Sparta and the Spartan king Kleombrotos was killed, along with more than 400 of Sparta's crack troops, the Spartiates.

The Thebans won the Battle of Leuktra fair and square by lining up their phalanx in a wedged formation. Traditionally, the phalanx was 12 lines deep, but the Thebans lined up 50 deep on the left to make a kind of triangle, like a wedge of cheese. This formation meant their strongest troops (on the left) heavily attacked the Spartans' right (their strongest point) before the weaker Theban troops had even joined the battle.

The Spartans reacted to the defeat in a typically strange way. According to Xenophon:

> Also, while [the Spartans] gave the names of all the dead to the relatives concerned they told them to bear their suffering in silence and avoid any cries of lamentation. And so on the following day you could see those whose relatives had been killed going about in public looking bright and happy, while those whose relatives had been reported living . . . were walking about looking gloomy and sorry for themselves.

Celebrating the Hegemony of Thebes

For a brief time Thebes became the dominant city in Greece, and this period from 371 to 362 BC became known as the 'Hegemony of Thebes'.

Dismantling the Athenian League

As Sparta declined, Athens used its now-restored fleet to try the same trick that it had with the Delian League (see Chapter 7). Athenian ships began sailing to islands in the Mediterranean and asking for tribute money; eventually, allies became territories.

In contrast to the era under the Delian League, Athens wasn't powerful enough to sustain this kind of policy. By 357 BC, members of the Athenian League who were refused permission to leave went into open revolt and a small war followed until 355 BC. The Athenian League eventually broke up as members drifted away.

Signalling the end of classical Greece

By the middle of the fourth century BC, the once proud city-states of Greece were in trouble. A new power, Macedonia, was developing in the north and soon its king, Philip II, had most of southern Greece under his control. Imagine – the Greek city-states that only 150 years earlier had combined to beat Persia were now about to become insignificant.

Xenophon ends his history *Hellenica* with a description of the battle of Mantineia in 362 BC. At this battle, the Thebans beat a collection of other cities, including both Athens and Sparta. He concludes by pointing out that yet another big battle had really solved nothing:

> *Both sides claimed the victory, but it cannot be said that . . . either side was any better off after the battle than before it. In fact, there was even more uncertainty and confusion in Greece after the battle than there had been previously.*

Xenophon gives a pretty good summary of everything that happened to the Greek city-states since the start of the Peloponnesian War in 431 BC. Unfortunately, the Greek city-states had nobody to blame but themselves. After all that had happened – all the wars, treaties, small empires, leagues, and broken promises – the once-great city-states were at the mercy of another foreign invader, the Macedonians, which I cover in Chapter 10.

Chapter 10

Rising Quickly to the Top: Macedonia

*B*asically, by 360 BC the Greek city-states had blown it. The constant infighting and deal breaking among Athens, Sparta, and the rest had opened the door to foreign enemies. And so, during the fourth century BC, a new power emerged – Macedonia.

In a little over 50 years, the Macedonians went from being thought of as simple, barbarous hill people to being the dominant force in Greece and beyond. This amazing ascent came down to two men: Philip II and his son Alexander the Great. Their story, as well as the history of this fascinating culture, starts here.

Meeting the Macedonians

Macedonia was (and is) the territory to the north of Greece formed by the north and north-west ends of the Thermaic Gulf. Macedonia is a hard and rugged country, and throughout its earliest history it had always existed as a tribal society. The Macedonians were Greek in origin, and they spoke a broader, rougher version of the Greek language that was related to the traditional version spoken in Athens (Chapter 1 has more on the intricacies of the ancient Greek language).

Have you seen the film *Alexander* (2004)? It's an entertaining depiction of Alexander the Great's life with some fantastically shot battle sequences. However, one element of the film that people and reviewers criticised was actor Colin Farrell's accent. Farrell spoke in his natural Irish accent throughout the movie. Viewers missed the point: The difference between Farrell's regional accent and an English accent is a really good way of showing the contrast between the ancient Macedonian and Greek cultures. I'm not so sure about Angelina Jolie's accent though. . . .

Growing very good at war

Throughout much of its early history Macedonia was a tribal society made up of a large number of competing groups who spent most of their time at war with each other. The lives most Macedonians led were quite simple – hunting and fighting, and then drinking long into the night to celebrate success in either.

The Macedonians were also excellent warriors. By the fourth century BC, they had extended their territory to the borders of Illyria in the west and Paeonia in the north.

The trouble was, as I said earlier, much like the Greek city-states during the same time period; the tribes of Macedonia were always fighting among themselves. For this reason, the country was very inward looking during much of its early history and only really interacted with other Greek states through a limited amount of trade.

Crowning a new kind of king: Philip II

The Macedonian kings traditionally ruled from a fortress in a town called Aegae. The Macedonian king didn't have absolute power over his subjects:

- ✔ The king had to observe Macedonian law and make decisions that were in keeping with it. This law had been set down generations earlier by previous tribal leaders and decisions were debated within a council of tribal leaders.
- ✔ The king's title wasn't hereditary. When the king died, the tribal leaders chose his successor although often they chose the son of the previous king.

The big change to Macedonia and its governing processes came with the death of King Perdiccas in 359 BC. Perdiccas's son Amyntas was only a child at the time of his father's death and his uncle Philip became his protector. As guardian to the heir, Philip also became temporary ruler of the kingdom until a decision was made about who should succeed. However, he didn't stay temporary for long.

Despite being only 24 years old, Philip made an immediate impact. He utterly rejected established laws and tradition and sought to establish himself as king through violence. Philip attacked in battle or murdered any other rival for the throne, and he set about securing the borders of Macedonia from the rebellious tribes of Illyria. As soon as that was done, he turned his ambitious eye to the south and Greece.

Considering Macedonian warfare

Prior to 350 BC, the Macedonians weren't really too much of a threat to the inhabitants of southern Greece. So what changed?

Building a different army

The new way in which Philip II made war on his enemies was a huge change – and a huge threat to the southern city-states. Philip II created a unique fighting force that the traditional Greek hoplite phalanx (see Chapter 5) found difficult to deal with.

Following are some of the main tricks and tactics of the Macedonian forces under Philip II:

- ✔ **Shock cavalry:** Philip's army was very large and *mixed,* meaning it contained a heavy infantry phalanx as well as cavalry and light troops. Unlike in traditional Greek armies, the Macedonians used their cavalry to charge and break the enemy line. Therefore the cavalry became the Macedonian's main offensive weapon.

- ✔ **The *sarissa*:** The Macedonian infantry was armed differently to its southern Greek neighbours. Rather than the short spear or javelin used by the southern Greeks the Macedonian's main offensive weapon was a 4.5-metre (15-foot) thrusting spear called a *sarissa.* This weapon made getting anywhere near the infantry line very difficult, particularly because the Macedonian phalanx was so well drilled it could form half a dozen different formations very quickly. See Figure 10-1 for some formation examples.

- ✔ **The *hypaspists*:** The Macedonians had their own special troops called the *hypaspists* who were used for special missions that required different tactics to a standard infantry battle. The *hypaspists* were famously fearless and took on all kinds of ludicrously dangerous tasks such as climbing cliffs to attack towns and assaulting cities at night. They were more lightly armed than the phalanx and, as such, much more mobile.

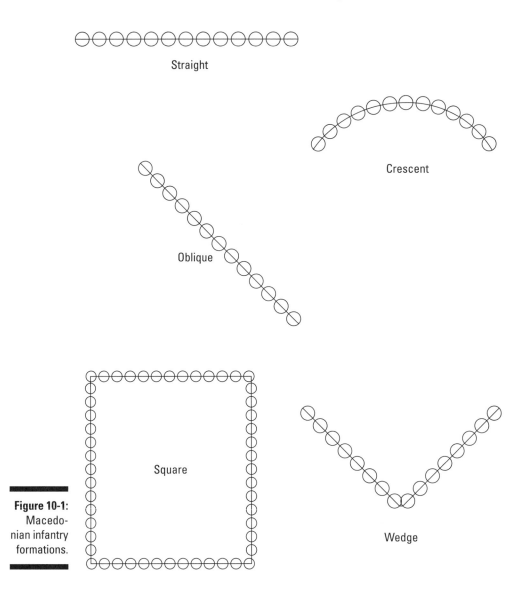

Straight

Crescent

Oblique

Square

Figure 10-1: Macedonian infantry formations.

Wedge

Revealing the secret weapon – camaraderie

Despite all the advances and adaptations of its army, the main reason that Macedonia became so powerful so quickly was the personality of Philip II himself.

The Macedonians had always been a warrior people but had spent generations fighting each other. Philip's personality, political intelligence, and ruthlessness brought the warring tribal leaders together and focused their bravery and skill on mutual enemies.

Philip kept up a culture of hard work and hard play that involved drinking long into the night to celebrate victories. The hard work must have been exhausting – but it worked.

Taking Over: Philip's Successes

During the 350s BC, Philip II and a now professionalised Macedonian army began to seize control of large parts of Greece. In 357 BC, Philip captured the city of Amphipolis (which Athens had long thought its own), and by 352 BC virtually the whole of Thessaly in Northern Greece was under his control. The Thessalians were famous for using their heavily armed cavalry troops in a battle, and Philip quickly incorporated them into his army.

Another notable success occurred around this same time. Throughout his reign Philip regularly conducted dynastic marriages within the cities and territories he conquered. In 356 BC, he and Olympias of Epirus had a baby son whom Philip called Alexander. (Ever heard of him?) You can read a lot more about him in the section 'Taking Over the Family Business: The Rise of Alexander the Great' and in Chapter 11.

Continuing despite criticism

During the 350s BC the rest of Greece was too stunned by Philip's success to really challenge him and the Macedonian forces. The main opposition came from a new Athenian statesman called Demosthenes. Demosthenes was a great speech writer and orator – and almost the exact opposite of Philip. Like Kleon (see Chapters 8 and 9), Demosthenes came from a trade background. His father had owned a business that made cutlery and so his nickname was the 'cutler'.

Demosthenes delivered many great speeches in the Athenian *ekklesia* urging all Greeks to rise up against Philip. These orations became known as *Philippics*, a term people still use to this day to describe a character assassination delivered in the form of a speech. Indeed, 400 years after Demosthenes when the Roman orator Cicero was haranguing Mark Anthony, Cicero's speeches were called philippics.

Philip carried on with his conquest plans, regardless of Demosthenes's speeches, by making war in the north-west as far as Thrace. By 348 BC the Macedonians had destroyed the town of Olynthos and sold its population into slavery. Philip found some Athenians in town and kept them as hostages to use as a bargaining tool. He recognised that it wouldn't be long before he came into conflict with Athens and the hostages would prove useful.

Agreeing to peace (sort of)

Athens had a problem. Despite all the urging of Demosthenes, Athens couldn't afford to fight a war with Philip, and it didn't have the manpower either.

In 346 BC, a peace conference was proposed and an Athenian called Philokrates led the negotiations. Philip eventually agreed to a non-aggression treaty with Athens.

Soon after the peace conference, Philip took advantage of trouble in southern Greece where the town of Phocis had seized the sacred town of Delphi. (Turn to Chapter 22 for more on this prophecy-rich city.) The Macedonians quickly marched south, kicked out the Phocians, and earned the thanks of Delphi. Thereafter Philip tried to portray himself as a kind of peacekeeper who'd intervene if necessary to settle disputes. It's doubtful that people truly believed this but they weren't really in a position to argue with him.

Invading everywhere except Athens

Philip wasn't actually that bothered with Athens or much of southern Greece. He had other fish to fry: He had an eye on an amazingly ambitious invasion of Asia Minor.

Philip spent the years after the peace agreement concentrating on areas north-east of Athens, laying siege to the port of Byzantium on the Bosphorus. Of course, Athens viewed this attack as a threat to the cities in southern Greece because a great deal of grain came from there. The political intrigue against Philip continued in Athens which eventually spurred him into seizing the grain ships in 340 BC.

When Philip seized the ships he finally gave Demosthenes what his critic was looking for – the excuse for Athens to declare war on the Macedonians, which they duly did. The Athenians had support from some of the other major cities, such as Corinth and Thebes – all which feared Philip and felt that as rich, powerful cities, they'd be next on his hit-list.

Battling in Chaeronea (338 BC)

The Battle of Chaeronea was one of the biggest in Greek history and the last real stand of the old Greek states against the new Macedonian power from the north. The world was never the same again after this brutal fight.

The two sides – the Macedonians and the allied southern Greek city-states – met outside the town of Chaeronea in Boeotia.

The allies had a large force of more than 35,000 men from Athens, Corinth, Euboea, Megara, and Thebes, among others. Philip's forces numbered a little less at about 30,000, but he had 1,800 cavalry (see the earlier section 'Considering Macedonian warfare'), which was under the command of his then 18-year-old son Alexander.

The battle was a tough struggle, but in the end the Athenians blew it for themselves. After the two infantry lines came together, Philip's *hypaspists* feigned a withdrawal. The Athenians on the left end of the allied line bought the ruse hook, line, and sinker, and chased after the Macedonians. The allied forces' attack created a massive hole in their line, which Alexander exploited and drove the Macedonian cavalry through. Alexander was then able to surround the Thebans who were the most feared allied fighters. Game over.

Thousands of the Greek allies lost their lives at Chaeronea, and Philip took several thousand more prisoners. The famous Sacred Band was almost completely destroyed with 254 of the 300 killed. A permanent memorial was set up to honour them in the form of a large statue of a lion that still exists today.

Philip's victory was complete. Several Greek towns including Thebes were garrisoned with Macedonian troops. As far as Philip was concerned, the job was done. In terms of his own lifetime he was correct but his son Alexander would have to finish the job after Philip's death.

Enjoying Prosperity at Pella

Philip was an incredible soldier, and he also made great strides to turn Macedonia into what he considered to be a civilised power. One of his first moves was the confirmation of the second city of Pella as the base of his royal court, setting up residence there and meeting with the tribal chiefs. The city's new status meant that tribal leaders from Macedonia and beyond flocked to the city because they wanted to be close to the king and the wealth and success that he'd generated.

Not much of the city survives today. Archaeologists have found the remains of a royal palace which could well have been developed from the one used by Philip. Evidence exists of a massive *agora* (town square) that would have been filled during the fourth century by all the visitors to the city.

Along with Pella's new prominence, a new elite class soon emerged. All the sons of the Macedonian tribal leaders lived and were educated in the city. Chief among them was Philip's son Alexander. The group of young nobles who grew up with Alexander became known as his 'Companions'. They became a new generation who were both highly educated and skilled in war – a new warrior elite. Young men such as Ptolemy and Hephaestion grew up to share the amazing adventures of Alexander's adult life. See the later section 'Following in his father's footsteps' for more.

Pella became a magnet for artists and intellectuals who, like Renaissance painters, were keen to seek employment and patronage of the royal court where high fees would be paid for their skills. Some also worked as tutors to the 'Companions'. This process had already begun under previous Macedonian kings – for example, the playwright Euripides spent time in Macedonia during the beginning of the fourth century BC – but the city's stature increased tenfold under Philip.

Philip himself had no great interest in intellectual affairs, but he was happy to sponsor them because he recognised that if Macedonia was to become a truly international power its new generation of leaders would need to become more worldly. Philip had grand ambitions for Macedonia and ultimately he wanted to test its military power against the might of the Persian Empire.

In particular, he employed the Greek philosopher Aristotle (see Chapter 23) as one of Alexander's tutors.

The Greek biographer Plutarch wrote an entertaining life of Alexander in which he quotes a letter from the young prince to Aristotle. Alexander complains that Aristotle has written a book describing some of the philosophical ideas that his tutor had shared with him:

> *What advantage shall I have over other men if these theories in which I have been trained are to be made common property?*

The court at Pella gave Alexander a great training in all aspects of Greek knowledge. Combined with his obvious aptitude and first-hand experience of warfare on his father's campaigns, he grew into an amazingly confident and authoritative young man.

Taking Over the Family Business: The Rise of Alexander the Great

All things change, and in 336 BC, when Philip was at the height of his power, he suddenly and suspiciously died. His death could have been the end of a brief moment of Macedonian supremacy; instead it heralded the beginning of an era of even greater success under his son Alexander.

Slaying Philip

In 337 BC Philip had received a Greek delegation that wanted to sue for peace. The delegation ended up awarding him the title of *hegemon* ('dominant leader') of all the Greek armies. This title basically gave Philip the authority he needed to attack Persia because he would be doing so in the name of all Greece – on the premise of liberating the Greek cities in Asia Minor. (Yes, *that* old excuse again!)

In the summer of 336 BC, Philip was in Pella celebrating the marriage of his daughter when he was assassinated by one of his bodyguards. Suspicion immediately fell on his wife Olympias who'd recently been sent into exile after Philip had married again. The assassin was killed in the struggle by Alexander before he could be questioned – a fact that many people interpreted as an attempt to hush things up. Philip's death certainly had benefits for Olympias – her son Alexander became king at the age of 20.

In *Alexander* (2004), Olympias is blamed as being behind the scheme and Alexander an innocent bystander. However, I find it difficult to believe that he didn't know anything. What do you think?

Separating the man and the myth

Alexander the Great is a fascinating historical figure. He achieved incredible things in an amazingly short time. No one like him has ever existed before him – or after him. The problem with somebody like this is that he can become a magnet for all kinds of myths and stories. What Alexander did isn't really in dispute, but *how* he did it and what he was like as a person always will be.

Alexander was also quite happy to make up his own myth. As a boy and throughout his adult life he was fascinated by Homer's *The Iliad* and the heroes like Achilles and Hector that feature in it (see Chapter 21). Alexander thought of himself in the same terms and contended that he was actually descended from Achilles.

A horse and his boy

One of the most famous larger-than-life stories about Alexander concerns how he came to own Bucephalas ('Ox-Head'), the massive warhorse that he rode for most of his life.

Apparently, a trader from Thessaly brought the huge black horse to show Philip. Nobody could calm the creature enough to ride it. Alexander asked whether Philip would buy the horse for him if Alexander were able to train it, and Philip agreed. Within a few minutes Alexander was happily riding Bucephalas. Alexander had noticed that the horse was scared of its own shadow and turned him toward the sun so he couldn't see it any longer.

This story is a great example of a historical event that's probably exaggerated. Still, this story is simple and highlights Alexander's most obvious and admired characteristics – confidence, bravery, and intelligence – were present at an early age.

His mother didn't help. From an early age Olympias had told Alexander that his real father was not Philip but Zeus, the king of the gods and that various prophecies had foretold his birth. (Philip and Olympias's marriage was a less than ideal relationship, with him regularly accusing her of adultery. To be honest the family would've been perfect for *Jerry Springer.*)

As a result of this kind of upbringing, Alexander was a bit different. His family and early life explain a great deal about him – particularly his tremendous courage and drive. And his background also explains some of the strange decisions that he later made (see Chapter 11).

Following in his father's footsteps

When he assumed power, Alexander immediately began planning to do exactly what his father had intended – invade Asia Minor and attack the Persian Empire. Alexander had two distinct advantages:

- ✔ Alexander had all his father's old generals – men like Parmenion, Antipater, and Cleitus – around to help and advise him. Alexander spent hours on the eve of a battle planning strategy with these generals, confident that they would carry out all manoeuvres to the letter.

- ✔ Alexander was also part of an exceptional group of young Macedonian men who became known as the 'Companions'. As I mention in the section 'Enjoying Prosperity at Pella', these friends and peers – including Hephaestion, Ptolemy, Cassander, Nearchus, and others – had grown up with Alexander. The Companions fought alongside Alexander now; many of them riding in his companion cavalry.

Alexander, however, had a significant problem: As a new king, city-states with a grudge against Macedonia were going to try their luck against the new leadership. Before Alexander ventured off on his grand adventure to the east, he had to deal with problems closer to home.

Quieting Illyria and Thrace

The first areas to give Alexander trouble were the border regions in Illyria and Thrace. Times were tense because neither side yet knew whether the new young king would effectively take over after his father.

Alexander soon proved the doubters wrong. Within three months he invaded Thrace and utterly destroyed any opposition. While he was there, news came that the Illyrian tribes were now massing on the border with Macedonia and preparing to invade. Once again Alexander dealt extremely well with a difficult campaign.

After two difficult tests, Alexander was probably due a break – but he didn't get one. As he was finishing off the Illyrians, news came of a revolt in Thebes.

Squelching the Theban revolt

After Thebes rebelled against Philip II (see the section 'Battling in Chaeronea'), Philip left a Macedonian garrison in the city to keep an eye on the Thebans. However, while Alexander was campaigning in Illyria, a rumour began to circulate that he had been killed. Where had this rumour come from? Unsurprisingly, the source was dear old Demosthenes (see the section 'Continuing despite criticism') who produced an eyewitness who swore that Alexander had been killed. Demosthenes didn't stop there; he urged Greece to revolt and write to Persia for support.

The Greek cities saw this as a great opportunity. If Alexander was dead Macedonia would be leaderless and it would be the perfect time to strike back. In Thebes two Macedonian officers were killed and the rest of the garrison were forced to go into hiding in the citadel.

In his biography of Demosthenes, Plutarch records his opinion of the young Alexander:

> *Demosthenes now completely dominated the Athenian assembly and he wrote letters to the Persian generals in Asia inciting them to declare war on Alexander, whom he referred to as a boy, and compared to Margites.*

The 'Margites' that Plutarch mentions was a character in a comic story of the day who never really grew up and thought he knew much more than he actually did. Demosthenes and the rest of Greece were about to find out how wrong that comparison was.

Alexander's response to the Theban revolt was swift and brutal. In 335 BC, he marched quickly south, surrounded the city, and took it with little effort. The walls of the city and many of its significant buildings were burned down. Alexander's men massacred thousands of the population and sold those that survived into slavery. The city of Thebes effectively ceased to exist from this point on. Although many buildings were rebuilt, Thebes was never again a leading city.

Alexander had sent a harsh message to the ancient world: Any revolt or betrayal against Macedonia would be dealt with severely. Alexander needed to ensure that when he left for Persia he wouldn't come under attack at home.

However, Alexander made some noteworthy exceptions in his destruction of Thebes. All the temples within Thebes were left alone, as were the houses of the descendants of the poet Pindar whom Alexander much admired. These exceptions illustrate the complex character of Alexander: fierce brutality mixed with an appreciation of architecture and literature.

After dealing with the Thebans, Alexander moved south. The Athenians, especially Demosthenes, must've been seriously worried that they were about to receive the same treatment the Thebans had. A hurried meeting of the *ekklesia* was arranged, and Athens voted to send an embassy congratulating Alexander on his recent victories in the north and celebrate the just way that he'd dealt with the Thebans!

Initially, Alexander demanded that Demosthenes and the other anti-Macedonian agitators be handed over to him, but Demosthenes, as ever, managed to argue his way out of the situation. Athens received no further punishment, but Alexander ensured that an eye was kept on it.

By 334 BC, Alexander managed to get Greece back into the position it was in before his father's death. He was acknowledged as the hegemon of the Greek cities and the general of their armies. With the borders of Macedonia secure, he now needed to complete his father's project – the invasion of the Persian Empire.

Although Philip's intention (and main excuse) for attacking the Persians had been the liberation of the Greek cities in Asia Minor, Alexander ended up taking his campaign so much farther – to India and back. This incredible story is what Chapter 11 is all about!

Chapter 11

Crowning the Undefeated Champion of the World: Alexander the Great

It is my belief that there was in those days no nation, no city, no single individual beyond the reach of Alexander's name; never in all the world was there another like him, and therefore I cannot help but feel that some power more than human was concerned in his birth.

–Arrian, The Campaigns of Alexander

Arrian, a Greek who became a general in the Roman army in the second century AD, wrote the above words about Alexander's skill as a general in his book – which is still in print today. Arrian was a sober, reflective man, not given to making fanciful statements, so his assessment of Alexander is quite compelling.

Indeed, Alexander the Great was an extraordinary individual – visionary, brilliant, cruel, vengeful, and probably more than a little insane. Alexander was 20 years old when he became king of Macedonia. By the time he died, 12 years later, he'd changed the Mediterranean world. This chapter charts his incredible course.

Popping In on the Persian Empire

The Persian Empire had changed a huge amount in the 150 years after the Persian Wars (see Chapter 6 for more). By 334 BC the king very loosely ruled the massive territories that made up the empire, and local rulers or *satraps* effectively ran the show in their own territories. Central control had relaxed considerably since the days of the invasion under Xerxes in 490 BC.

During Alexander's reign, the Persian king was Darius III, who seized the throne in 335 BC after helping to instigate the assassination of his predecessor. He was a weak king, but he had the huge wealth of the Persian Empire and its massive manpower at his disposal.

Although the Persian army was huge, it did have a problem. In many ways, the Persians were the complete opposite of the unified, well-drilled, and professional Macedonian army (see Chapter 10).

With the exception of Darius's personal troops, the Persian army was drawn from throughout the empire and thrown together when needed. Many of the troops didn't speak the same language. In many cases, they had very little to fight for and were basically forced to do so.

Spin versus Reality: The Reasons for Invasion

So why did Alexander want to go to Persia? The real reason was the desire for adventure, conquest, and glory that underpinned his whole life. The idea of invading Asia Minor was originally that of his father, Philip II, who wanted the wealth that the Persian-controlled cities possessed.

The official reasons were very different. The Macedonians were seeking to 'liberate' the Greek cities under Persian control and gain revenge for the Persian invasions of Greece in the fifth century BC.

Overwhelming Persia at the battle of the Granicus River

Alexander's first real confrontation with the Persian army came at the battle of the Granicus River in 334 BC.

The Persian army that came to meet Alexander at the Granicus was made up of large numbers of troops from the most westerly parts of the Persian Empire. Darius wasn't present at the battle and the Persians were commanded by the western satraps. The Persians camped at the bottom of a hill across the river Granicus from Alexander's camp.

Alexander had to cross the river to attack with his Companion cavalry (refer to Chapter 10), breaking a hole in the Persian line. The weakened Persian line gave the Macedonian *sarissa*-wielding infantry and *hypaspists* a chance to get over and engage the centre. Fighting furiously, the Macedonians managed to surround the Persian infantry, and the other Persian troops fled the field. It was an amazing victory that owed a lot to the incredible charge by Alexander and the cavalry.

Considering a controversy

But was Alexander's attack and victory that simple? The battle of Granicus River is very controversial because the sources disagree on whether Alexander crossed the river at night to surprise the Persians with an attack in the morning, or rode straight across it in the morning as the battle began.

You may think that the time of the attack doesn't really matter, but depending on when it happened, the Granicus was either a great 'surprise attack' by Alexander or an amazing example of fighting a standard infantry battle from a situation of great disadvantage. Either is impressive but it would be great to know which it was! This discrepancy is an excellent example of how careful historians have to be when dealing with a quasi-mythical figure like Alexander.

Doling out harsh punishment

The Persian army defeated at the battle of Granicus contained a lot of Greek mercenaries. Alexander dealt harshly with them. Many thousands were killed and the rest sent back to Macedonia in chains to work in the mines. (The Athenians on the Sicilian Expedition – see Chapter 8 – suffered a similarly grim fate under Alexander's father.)

Liberating the Greeks

I mention in Chapter 10 that Alexander's main reason for attacking Persia was to liberate the Greek cities in Asia Minor. Whether they needed liberating was a bit of an open question.

The Greek cities were locally ruled by Persian *satraps*, but they were pretty autonomous and their only obligation was to pay taxes to their *satraps*. Still, the Greek cities' attitude seemed to be 'Anything for a quiet life', and they threw in their lot with Alexander as he marched south-east through Asia Minor, liberating them as he went.

A knotty problem

In 333 BC, during Alexander's trip through Asia Minor, a famous, semi-historical event happened that's a great example of the kind of mythologised stories that attach themselves to him. When Alexander arrived at the Greek town of Gordium, he was shown the famous 'Gordian Knot' that fastened a chariot to a tree. Supposedly, the chariot had been tied to the tree for hundreds of years and locals believed the man that could untie it would become the ruler of the whole world.

Based on accounts of the day and later mythologising, Alexander had a quick look, decided it was a bit tricky, and cut the knot in two with his sword. It was a logical solution that was typical of Alexander: the quickest and most expedient way to solve the problem that disregarded the traditional approach. It didn't seem to matter that he didn't untie it either – he still went on to conquer Asia and beyond.

Slipping by at the battle at Issus

After the Battle of the Granicus River, the next big confrontation between Alexander and the Persian Empire came when Alexander headed south from Asia Minor into what's known as the Levantine coast. This stretch of land includes Syria and the Holy Land and links the near Middle East with Egypt, as Figure 11-1 shows.

Alexander and his troops had been on the road for a year. Having successfully liberated many Greek cities, Alexander decided to press on into the heartlands of the Persian Empire and defeat the Persian king Darius.

However, by 333 BC, Alexander had travelled so far south that Darius now appeared to the north of the Macedonian army outside the town of Issus – cutting off Alexander from the way that he'd come. Alexander had to fight the Persians in order to protect the supply lines that he'd established in the towns and cities that he'd already passed through.

Although the Persians never defeated Alexander, the battle of Issus was a dodgy one. It was fought on a plain in between the sea (to Alexander's left) and some hilly ground (on his right). The Persians outnumbered Alexander by two to one, but many of the Persian troops had been pressed into service against their will (see the section 'Popping In on the Persian Empire').

A fierce battle raged and the Persians fell back across the river Pandarus. The Macedonian infantry really struggled against the Persians' superior numbers and the difficult terrain. In a decisive manoeuvre, Alexander took his cavalry up into the hills before veering left and charging for Darius's chariot. This was an inspired move but also a highly dangerous one – a great example of what Alexander was like. Darius wisely did a runner – and before long so did much of the Persian army.

Issus was a great victory for Alexander but not a total one. Darius was still alive and Alexander knew he'd probably face even greater numbers of Persians the next time they met.

Getting Tyre'd out

Throughout 333 BC, Alexander continued to move south down the Levantine coast. As he went, cities either welcomed him or he forced them to.

Alexander had a particularly tricky time at the siege of the ancient city of Tyre (refer to Figure 11-1). Here, the people had fled to the sanctuary of the citadel, which was on an island just under a kilometre off the coast.

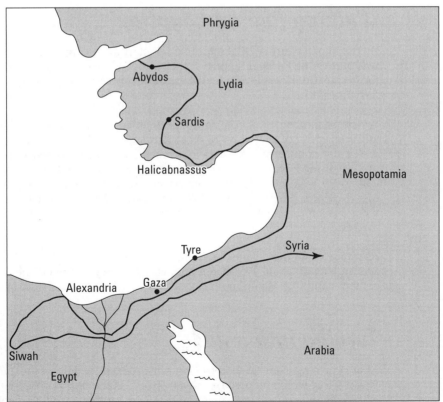

Figure 11-1: Alexander's journey south.

Alexander's solution was to build a *mole,* or causeway, out to the island. The siege required seven months of continual attacks on the island before it fell. In the end, only a combined infantry and naval assault on all four sides of the island enabled Alexander to defeat the incredibly resistant Tyrenians. More than 30,000 citizens were sold into slavery as punishment. Finally, in July 332 BC, Alexander was able to leave.

Taking a Surprising Turn: Alexander in Egypt

Given the fact that Darius was still at large and that he'd spent so long at Tyre (see the preceding section), Alexander's next step was quite surprising – he chose to head toward Egypt.

Walking like an Egyptian

By the fourth century BC, Egypt had fallen from its centuries of greatness and was part of the Persian Empire. Check out *The Ancient Egyptians For Dummies* (Wiley) by Charlotte Booth for all the details of the rise and fall of this amazing culture.

By far the most ancient civilisation in the Mediterranean world, Egypt was still something of a mystery to most Greeks – and there was no way Alexander could resist it. Alexander received a rapturous welcome when he arrived at the Egyptian town of Pelusium in 332 BC. The Egyptians saw him as a liberator who'd freed them from Darius. To show their thanks, they made him their new pharaoh. Up to this point Egypt had been under the control of a Persian *satrap* called Mazaces who surrendered as soon as Alexander arrived.

As pharaoh, all the palaces of Egypt and its immense wealth were now at Alexander's disposal. He set out on a voyage down the river Nile to visit the ancient capital of Memphis.

Turning into a god

After returning from his visit to Memphis, Alexander set out for the ancient Siwah oasis, which involved a huge trek across the desert. The journey was extremely difficult – even today the trip is incredibly hard if you go across the desert the way that Alexander did.

Alexander's reason for going to the oasis was to consult its famous oracle and, allegedly, discover whether he was the son of a god. The story goes that the oracle identified him as being the son of the Egyptian god Ammon who Greeks equated with their own god Zeus. This, of course, fitted quite nicely with what his mother Olympias had always told him (see Chapter 10) – so Alexander wasn't inclined to argue.

The events at the Siwah oasis were very controversial to the Greek mind, which clearly delineated between men and gods (see Part IV for the low-down.) Later on, this proved a problem for Alexander and his Macedonian followers (see the section 'Going Persian'). But the notion of Alexander as a god in human form was entirely acceptable to both the Egyptian and Persian systems of belief – indeed, kings and rulers in these cultures were worshipped as gods.

Founding the first Alexandria

While in Egypt, Alexander spent a lot of time reorganising its government and appointing his own men as officials to oversee the running of his new territories. These efforts were nothing new; he'd been doing so all the way down from Asia Minor. But in Egypt he also decided to found a new city.

Choosing a spot at the mouth of the Nile, Alexander declared that it would be his new capital – called Alexandria. He recognised that the location would be a tremendous port and would link his territories in the east with those in the west.

Having drawn up a plan for the city itself, Alexander left others to build it for him. He would never return to see it completed. (For more on how the city turned out, see Chapter 12.) Never one to stop when he had a good thing going, Alexander went on to found many other Alexandrias on his travels – possibly as many as 12 spread out over the whole of the Persian Empire and as far afield as India. Only the original city was referred to purely as Alexandria; the rest were given a second name that emphasised their location such as 'Alexandria in the Caucuses'.

Hunting Down Darius

With fun time in Egypt over, Alexander returned to the hunt for Darius, and a final showdown loomed. Alexander headed west, and by the end of September 331 BC, he and his troops (around 40,000 men) were into the heartlands of Mesopotamia.

Going into the Battle of Gaugamela

Darius's and Alexander's armies met on the plain of Gaugamela in 331 BC. Darius had spent the two years since the battle of Issus building up his army. The Persians took the field with a force of well over 100,000 men and probably 15 elephants. Some sources quote up to 250,000 Persian combatants! However, such a big force faced the familiar problems of communication, commitment, and training that I mention in the section 'Popping In on the Persian Empire'.

The film *Alexander* (2004) features a brilliant depiction of the Battle of Gaugamela in all its bloody brutality. Even better though is the scene of the evening before the battle where Alexander and his generals discuss the tactics that they'll use the next day. That's exactly what they would've been doing in 331 BC.

Darius chose the spot for the showdown with Alexander with great care. In fact, he levelled out the ground so he could use his chariots. Alexander used his troops in a wedge formation. His plan was to follow a similar attack as at Issus and use the *cavalry punch tactic.* For this tactic, Alexander and the Companions rode a long way to the right of the battlefield, forcing the Persians on their left to follow. Suddenly turning back left, the Macedonians charged at the weaker Persian line, and after fierce fighting they broke through.

While this was going on, the Macedonian left was desperately holding on against the huge Persian numbers. Alexander led a charge toward Darius, and even went as far as throwing a javelin that just missed the Persian king.

Darius turned and fled again taking only a tiny fraction of his army with him. Alexander was unable to chase him because the Persians had broken through against the Macedonian left, and Alexander and his Companions had to return to support. However, as soon as news of Darius's flight spread, the Persian army followed.

Alexander had won an amazing victory against overwhelming odds. Darius was still alive – but on the run with no army. There was effectively nobody to pull together an organised response and challenge Alexander's supremacy and he and his victorious troops moved south to the city of Babylon.

Meanwhile, back at home . . .

While Alexander was away, various things were going on back in Greece and Macedonia. Alexander had left the general Antipater in charge while he was away. As you may expect, Antipater was very, very busy putting down uprisings from the Greek city-states. Even less surprisingly, Sparta, under King Agis, was the city-state that caused most of the trouble (see Chapters 5 and 8).

Burning down the house

Alexander's visit to the ancient religious capital of Persepolis in 330 BC was less successful than his time spent in Babylon. During an evening of heavy drinking, the story goes that a conversation began about the fact that the Persian king Xerxes (who built the palace that Alexander and his men were in) had burned the temples of Greece when the Persians attacked 250 years before. In revenge, Alexander set fire to the Persepolis palace. Apparently, the following morning he was very sorry. Whether or not the story is completely true isn't certain, but the palace was certainly damaged by a huge fire at that time and it seems like the sort of impulsive thing that Alexander would've done.

Things came to a head in the Battle of Megalopolis in 331 BC where Antipater crushed Sparta and her allies. King Agis died in the battle, and it was the last revolt against Macedonian control.

Moving on to Babylon

To the victor goes the spoils. With Darius defeated at Gaugamela (see the earlier section 'Going into the Battle of Gaugamela'), Alexander was free to take possession of the major cities of the Persian Empire: Babylon, Susa, and Persepolis.

Alexander was welcomed into Babylon as the new Persian king and immediately took possession of its wealth, its palaces and, among other things, Darius's harem.

The incredible wealth and opulence of Babylon must've amazed the Macedonians. It was the biggest city that any of them had ever seen. Plutarch describes Alexander's own reaction to the city's riches:

> *[Alexander] observed the magnificence of the dining-couches, the tables and the banquet which had been set out for him. He turned to his companions and remarked, 'So this, it seems, is what it is to be a king.'*

Pressing further east

By the summer of 330 BC, Alexander had a decision to make: Stay in Babylon and be content to rule his new empire from a glorious city or go farther? Unsurprisingly, he went for the latter option. His excuse was that he needed to hunt down Darius because, while Darius lived, Alexander wasn't the true king of Persia.

In fact, Darius was hunted down quite quickly; some of his own supporters had already killed him but Alexander wasn't aware of it until some scouts from his army found the body of the Persian king unceremoniously dumped onto a cart. Nevertheless, Alexander spent the next three years tearing around the mountainous regions of Bactria and Sogdiana in the north-east of the Persian Empire subduing every tribe he encountered. It was hard work, fighting guerrilla battles against fast-moving enemies in mountainous terrain.

Going Persian

Alexander experienced another difficulty during this time. Now that he was Persian king, he began to adopt certain Persian customs that his Macedonian comrades found difficult to accept.

For example, Alexander began wearing trousers and make-up – both unusual practices for Macedonians. But the custom that caused the most fuss was *proskynesis*. This traditional Persian practice required all those who met and addressed the great king to prostrate themselves before him. Although Alexander didn't ask it of them, the old generals who fought with Philip II found this new and foreign practice difficult to accept.

Unhappy campers

The mood in the Macedonian camp was further soured by the deaths of two notable Companions – Parmenion and Cleitus. (See Chapter 10 for more on the Companions.) Parmenion was killed on the orders of Alexander after an alleged plot involving Parmenion's son Philotas, and Alexander killed Cleitus after a drunken argument about, of all things, *proskynesis.*

Camaraderie had been a vital strength of the Macedonian army and culture; now it was beginning to break apart.

Taking a new queen

Alexander made another surprising decision in 327 BC. After defeating the tribal chief Oxyartes in Sogdiana, he married Oxyartes's daughter Roxanne.

The sexuality of Alexander the Great continues to fascinate people to this day. In modern terms he was probably bisexual. Alexander's relationship with his companion Hephaestion was probably sexual, and several historical writers such as his biographer Plutarch said that he also loved a Persian eunuch called Bagoas. This relationship features in the film *Alexander* (2004) and caused a furore in the final edit when much of it was cut. It's worth seeing *Alexander Revisited* (2007), Oliver Stone's second 'cut' of the film that restores much lost material.

To the end of the world and back again

Some historians believe that Alexander planned to march through India to what he thought was the edge of the world and then build a fleet. Using this, he would then sail back around the 'bottom' of the world (where India was joined to Ethiopia), find the source of the Nile, and then travel back up it to Alexandria!

It was a brilliant and fantastical idea on Alexander's part – but the geography was all wrong. Regardless of the seriousness of this plan, Alexander and the Greeks didn't know that China lay beyond India. But that was just the first of their problems. . . .

Alexander probably did find women attractive too, but it seems likely that he married Roxanne mostly because he felt it was time to father an heir to his new empire.

Alexander took a second wife, Statira, the daughter of Darius, when he returned to Babylon in 324 BC. Neither marriage was a love match, but some ancient writers allege that he took many mistresses over the course of his life.

Making a passage to India

In 327 BC, Alexander went farther than any Greek had before – through the Hindu Kush and into India itself. In doing so, he followed in the footsteps of the mythological figures Heracles and Dionysus who were said to have travelled there (see Chapter 21). Alexander was travelling toward what he believed was the edge of the world.

Having entered India, Alexander made his way to the Hydaspes (now Jhelum) River in 326 BC. He fought a furious and very difficult battle with the local king Porus, which involved his troops tackling jungle warfare for the first time.

The battle was a real struggle with great losses on both sides. (The elephants got scared and ran amok, killing scores of Porus's own men.) But Alexander was very impressed with how bravely Porus had fought. As a result, he made Porus governor of his new province of India!

Suffering a defeat – and returning home

Alexander planned to go even farther across the Indian desert, toward the Ganges River and from there to the edge of the world (see the nearby sidebar 'To the end of the world and back again'). But he suffered a revolt from his own troops who refused to go any farther.

By 325 BC, Alexander had been on campaign for nearly ten years, and many of the men in his infantry had served with Philip II for many years before that. These men were absolutely exhausted from fighting. Reluctantly, Alexander agreed to their demands.

The journey home was incredibly arduous. Alexander sent part of his army back to Persia along the land route that they had travelled a few years earlier. He also used the huge amount of timber available to construct a new fleet. With this, he sailed down the Indus River to its mouth in the Indian Ocean. To Alexander, this was the southern edge of the world.

Alexander then led the rest of his troops in a march across the Gedrosian desert. It was an appalling journey with terrible heat and a lack of food. Thousands of men and all the pack animals died before they eventually met up with the fleet, under Nearchus, on the Persian Gulf.

Returning to Babylon and Ruling the Empire

On his return to Babylon in 324 BC, Alexander set about ruling the empire he had created. He was now technically the ruler of Macedonia, Egypt, all the territories in the Persian Empire, and western India, and he was commander of all the Greeks.

Of course, such a massive area proved impossible to manage. News regularly came to his court of corrupt practices among the governors that he appointed as well as revolts by the tribes in Bactria and Sogdiana.

Creating a new master race

Alexander seems to have been well aware of the wider problems associated with ruling such a large empire. For some time he'd been incorporating young Persian men into his army and training them as replacements in the phalanx for some of his father's veterans who'd retired. After he was back in Babylon, he took this training a stage further.

Various cities that Alexander had founded from Egypt to India were already filled with a mixture of European (Greek/Macedonian) and Asiatic (Egyptian/Persian/Indian) settlers. Alexander now decided to try and settle some Asiatics in Greece and Macedonia.

Getting hitched

To realise his plans, he arranged marriages between almost the whole of his Macedonian high command and aristocratic Persian brides. Alexander himself married Statira, the daughter of Darius III. Following Alexander's lead, up to 10,000 Macedonian soldiers took Persian brides.

Plutarch describes the massive, magnificent joint wedding, which cost a fortune and certainly would've made the pages of *Hello!* these days!

> *We are told that 9,000 guests attended this feast and each of them was given a gold cup for their libations. The whole entertainment was carried out on a grand-scale and Alexander went as far as to discharge [pay off] the debts owed by any of his guests: the outlay for the occasion amounted to 9,870 talents.*

To put this in perspective, the total cost of the wedding festivities was equivalent to 97,536 kilograms of gold. Even Elton John may struggle to match that!

Boyz 2 men

Alexander had also recruited the best part of 30,000 young Persian boys when he visited Babylon in 331 BC. These males had spent the six years that Alexander was away being trained and educated in the fashion of Alexander and his Companions (see Chapter 10), and they were now ready to become the bulk of Alexander's expedition army.

Historical accounts indicate that Alexander planned future campaigns to Arabia (in the south) and even possibly to the western Mediterranean. These men would have made up his new army.

Contemplating the death of a god

Despite the great festivities and exciting new plans, Alexander's time in Babylon wasn't happy. He was constantly dealing with unrest and revolt in the empire and his loyal Macedonians reacted badly to the new Persian recruits. The death of Hephaestion in early 323 BC left Alexander stricken with grief, and he held a suitably lavish funeral with a 30-metre high pyre.

In June of 323 BC, Alexander was about to leave for his expedition to Arabia when, following a banquet to honour one of his Companions, Nearchus, he fell ill. He struggled against a high fever for a week before becoming bedridden. Finally, on 13th June 323 BC, Alexander died. He was 32 years old.

Death – or murder?

Alexander's death – by catching a fever and then dying – wasn't unusual. Alexander's companion Hephaestion died of something similar only a few weeks before. Yet rumours persist that Alexander was murdered, and several recent books have been written on exactly this subject. These books point to the unhappiness of the Macedonians at Alexander adopting 'Persian behaviour' (see the section 'Going Persian'), and his troops' unwillingness to go on another campaign now that they were fantastically wealthy in Babylon.

Others argue that Alexander had suffered a severe chest wound during one of his last battles in India. The effects of this wound, coupled with the march across the Gedrosian desert shortly afterwards, would have been severe.

It seems quite appropriate that a life so full of myth, adventure, and amazing tales should finish with death in mysterious circumstances. I still can't decide whether Alexander was murdered or not. What do you think?

Alexander's life and activities brought the world to a very different place by the time of his death:

- ✔ The traditional powers of Athens, Sparta, Thebes, and even the Persian Empire had lost their dominance.

- ✔ The continents of Europe and Asia were closer together than ever before. The old barriers between the Greek world and the Persian Empire never really existed again.

- ✔ The Mediterranean world was left in the hands of Alexander's former generals who carried out a vicious struggle for power. Chapter 12 looks at this *Hellenistic world,* as it became known.

- ✔ Almost every other dictator that's followed, from Julius Caesar to Napoleon, has regarded Alexander as a role model.

These were impressive accomplishments indeed for a mere ten years in power. In the words of the Greek general Arrian:

> *Anyone who belittles Alexander has no right to do so . . . But let such a person, if blackguard [berate or criticise] Alexander he must, first compare himself with the object of his abuse: himself, so mean and obscure, and, confronting him, the great king, with his unparalleled worldly success, the undisputed monarch of two continents, who spread the power of his name all over the earth.*

Chapter 12

What Happened Next?

Ancient Greece was never the same again after the death of Alexander the Great. In fact, historians call the period of Alexander's life (356 to 323 BC) until about 150 BC the *Hellenistic* period (meaning 'relating to Greece') because of the spread of Greek influence around the Mediterranean that happened as a result of Alexander's travelling (see Chapter 11 for all the details) and the population movements that followed. Notably, the various cities named Alexandria that Alexander founded put the Greeks in positions of power throughout the Mediterranean world and far beyond. But as this chapter explains, this prominence didn't last. Within 150 years the Greek world was effectively under the control of the Roman Empire, and that's why this period of ancient Greek history doesn't get as much space in this book as other periods do.

Still, the Hellenistic period is full of characters and events that are well worth looking into. After all, don't you want to know how the story of ancient Greece ends? Read on.

Having a Bad Heir Day: Alexander's Successors

Alexander the Great was very good at many things (see Chapter 11), but detailed planning for the future wasn't one of them. When he died in June 323 BC, he hadn't clearly stated whom he wanted to act as his successor.

The situation was complex:

- ✔ Alexander left at least one child from his marriage to Roxanne, and Alexander's mother Olympias still lived (see Chapter 11) – but neither of these women had any hope of taking over the empire because they didn't command the respect of the army and any successor would have to fight to protect their position.

- ✔ Alexander and Roxanne's small boy was named Alexander IV and was born shortly after his father's death.

- ✔ Alexander also left a half-brother in Babylon, one of Philip II's other children (see Chapter 10). Known as Philip III, this half-brother was an unfortunate man who suffered from severe mental disabilities and lived in an almost childlike state.

Auctioning off an empire

Because none of Alexander's closest relatives were capable of ruling the vast territory that he acquired during his life, a regent was required and there was precedent for this in Macedonian tradition. The general Perdiccas (one of Alexander's 'Companions') took the job and the rest of Alexander's generals divided up the empire between them.

Before long, Perdiccas was murdered along with several others. Eventually, the empire was divided up into five parts and leaders assigned:

- ✔ **Asia Minor:**   Antigonus
- ✔ **Egypt:**   Ptolemy
- ✔ **Eastern territories:**   Seleucus
- ✔ **Macedonia and Greece:** Antipater
- ✔ **Thrace:**   Lysimachus

Although these territories changed hands regularly over the next century or so, they effectively made up what became known as the *Hellenistic kingdoms*. See the section 'Raising Hell: The Hellenistic Kingdoms' for more information.

Revolting (again) in southern Greece

Here's a real shocker: Virtually as soon as Alexander had died, the southern Greeks revolted against Macedonia. Athens formed part of the revolt, and the movement was initially quite successful.

Ptolemy the body snatcher!

Ptolemy, the leader of Egypt, managed to secure his own kingdom following the death of Alexander. Alexander's body rested in Babylon for a while until the transfer to Macedonia began. The body travelled in state in a massive mobile tomb known as a *'catafalque'*. It was about 13 feet wide by 20 feet long and constructed like a mini Ionic temple (see Chapter 18) with full decoration in gold and marble. As the tomb moved through Syria, Ptolemy and his men took control of it and transported it to Memphis in Egypt. After Ptolemy and Alexander's body arrived, Ptolemy kicked out the *satrap* appointed by Alexander and declared himself ruler. Ptolemy later moved to Alexandria to supervise the city's completion and installed Alexander's body in a permanent mausoleum in Alexandria. Body snatching – so much simpler than negotiation, don't you think?

Alexander's tomb has now been lost and debate continues to this day about where it might be located.

In late 323 BC, Antipater, the Macedonian in charge of the region, marched south to meet the Greek allies and was initially forced back and besieged in the town of Lamia. However, by the summer of 322 BC, Macedonian reinforcements arrived, and Antipater was able to take on the Greek allies in a pitched battle near the town of Krannon. The Macedonian victory wasn't crushing, but the Greeks were forced to make terms – because they couldn't agree among themselves how to continue the war!

Ending democracy in Athens (322 BC)

If you've read any of the preceding chapters, you won't be surprised to find out that Antipater had to arrange peace terms separately with each city because none of the Greek allies trusted the others enough to negotiate a general peace.

As part of Antipater's peace settlement, the Athenians were required to house a Macedonian garrison that supervised a new government run by Athenian aristocrats who the Macedonians had hand-picked.

The unpleasant squabbling after the revolt and during the peace process brought democracy in Athens to an end. Nearly 200 years of democratic rule – one of ancient Greece's greatest achievements – was over, as was Athens's role as a military power.

Raising Hell: The Hellenistic Kingdoms

After the final blow to Athens, the newly established Hellenistic kingdoms (see Figure 12-1) spent about 170 years bashing each other in the hope of making some territorial gains. Nothing much ever really changed and any gains that were made were usually lost fairly soon afterwards.

Thrace
Lysimachus I

Thessaly & Macedonia
Cassander I

Asia Minor & Levantine Coast
Antigonus I

The Eastern Kingdoms
Kingdom of
Seleucus I

Egypt & Libya
Ptolemy I

Figure 12-1: The Hellenistic kingdoms.

Developing dynastic struggles

The Hellenistic kingdoms were all individually powerful, but none was powerful enough to dominate the others. Throughout the third century BC the sons of Alexander's generals fought with each other for territorial gains throughout the Mediterranean. This squabbling was very similar to the way that Greek city-states had continually fought each other throughout the century before (refer to Chapter 9).

One thing that the Hellenistic rulers did manage to achieve was the creation of dynasties that saw their descendants running the various kingdoms. The dynastic tradition was particularly true of Ptolemaic Egypt where descendants of Alexander's commander ruled all the way until Cleopatra (along with Mark Antony) was defeated at the battle of Actium in 31 BC. See the section 'Attending the greatest show on earth: Alexandria' for more on the exploits of Ptolemaic Egypt.

Laying siege on Rhodes: Demetrius

One of the more interesting successors to Alexander was Demetrius, the son of Antigonus who ruled in Asia Minor. Demetrius was known as *Poliorcetes* or 'The Besieger', although he seems to have spent more of his time eating and getting drunk.

In 304 BC, Demetrius laid siege to the island of Rhodes in a bid to expand his territory. Demetrius's main tactic was to build a massive siege tower called *Helepolis*, which was as close as the Greeks got to developing a tank. This contraption was 43 metres (140 feet) high and made up of nine storeys. Each storey contained catapults and other siege machinery operated by hundreds of men. For protection, *Helepolis* was covered with iron plates on three sides. Weighing around 150 tons, it needed more than 3,000 specially trained men to pull it.

Impressive, huh? Well, the only problem was, it didn't work. The citizens of Rhodes resisted the siege, and Demetrius left the *Helepolis* behind along with all his other siege equipment when he sailed home. The people of Rhodes celebrated Demetrius's retreat by melting down the *Helepolis* and using it to build the famous statue known as the Colossus of Rhodes, one of the original Seven Wonders of the World (and covered in Chapter 18). A much more prof-itable end to a bad idea. You can read more about Demetrius in Chapter 26.

The activities of Demetrius are a good example of what the Hellenistic period was like. Demetrius had no real reason to attack Rhodes other than empire building. Treaties proved meaningless as successive generations broke them and carried on fighting.

Attending the greatest show on earth: Alexandria

For all the fighting that went on throughout the Hellenistic kingdoms, Ptolemaic Egypt was relatively stable, and the new city of Alexandria thrived as a result.

City planning panache

Alexandria was ideally placed to gather the revenues from trade all across the Mediterranean, and Egypt itself was hugely wealthy due to the fertile lands surrounding the Nile. *The Ancient Egyptians For Dummies* (Wiley) by Charlotte Booth offers more insight into this exceptional city.

A gift that keeps on giving

The library at Alexandria is hugely important to historians today because the work begun centuries ago to catalogue and preserve texts started a tradition that has carried on through the medieval period and the Renaissance. This tradition is solely responsible for the fact that you and I can still read the works of Homer, Sophocles, Thucydides, and others – and that I'm able to write a book like this. Thanks, Ptolemy!

Alexandria was unusual because it was built from scratch to a definite plan for the location and design of all the major public buildings. A huge amount of money was spent on a large earth work that helped to form a double harbour and the construction of the mighty *pharos* (lighthouse) that dominated the skyline.

Checking out the library

One of the most famous public buildings in Alexandria was the library . The library was actually part of the museum of Alexandria. For the ancient Greeks, a *museum* was literally 'a sanctuary of the muses'. (The muses were Greek goddesses associated with all areas of learning; see Chapter 20 for more on these lovely ladies.)

The library of Alexandria was founded by Ptolemy and thrived throughout the Ptolemaic period. It became the new centre of learning in the Mediterranean, replacing Athens in the process. Scholars travelled from all around to work and study there. Historians believe that at its height it contained 500,000 scrolls, which catalogued nearly everything that had ever been written in the Greek language at the time.

The library flourished throughout the Hellenistic period and beyond until it suffered a terrible fire in 47 BC when Julius Caesar was laying siege to the city. Several Roman emperors subsequently lavished money and attention on the library and attempted to replace its stock, but it may have been finally destroyed during the Byzantine period when the emperor Theodosius demanded the destruction of all pagan temples in AD 391.

The museum and library weren't just about preserving things, but also about new discoveries. The Hellenistic period saw breakthroughs in science (see Chapter 26) and a new, more realistic style in art and sculpture (see Chapter 18). This new community also saw great developments in literature and distinctive poetry produced by men like Apollonius of Rhodes and Theocritus.

A cosmopolitan metropolis

One of the other great new developments in Alexandria was the cosmopolitan nature of its population. Alexandria's new ruling class was Greek and Macedonian, but many other people came to live there.

In this way, Alexandria was rather different to the other major cities of the Greek world. In Athens and Sparta, for example, citizenship and the right to reside were zealously guarded. Alexandria was much more the kind of city that Rome became later, a large metropolis with a real cosmopolitan feel where people came from far and wide to live and work.

The Greek historian Polybius became a Roman citizen and was sent as an envoy to Alexandria in 180 BC. Here he describes the city's population:

> *It is inhabited by three classes of people: first the native Egyptians, a volatile group, hard to control; secondly by the mercenaries [foreign soldiers from all over the Mediterranean resident in the city]; thirdly there are the Alexandrians themselves, a people not genuinely civilised . . . for though they are mixed they come from a Greek stock and have not forgotten Greek customs.*

Clearly, the cosmopolitan city wasn't to Polybius's taste! Alexandria must have been an amazing place to be, because despite the multinational feel the city was very firmly under the control of its Ptolemaic rulers.

Fading Away: The End of Ancient Greece

Greek influence on the Mediterranean during the Hellenistic period had never been stronger. But ironically, this period was exactly the same time that the Greek world began to lose its independence and get swallowed up by the emerging Roman Empire.

Meeting the Romans

The Roman Empire was the successor to the Greek world and carried on for the best part of 650 years. The Romans themselves came from what was originally a small market town in Umbria that, according to myths, was originally populated by criminals and runaway slaves. By the third century BC the Romans had come to dominate the whole of Italy and were at war with the mighty Carthaginian civilisation based at Carthage in north Africa.

Death by old lady

Pyrrhus carried on his life of adventure, and by 272 BC he was fighting in Argos. During a street battle an old woman standing on the roof of her house saw Pyrrhus attack her son. She picked up a tile from the roof and flung it at him. It knocked him unconscious and he fell from his horse and was killed in the melee. Quite an appropriate end to the life of somebody who was characterised by heroic failure.

Although Rome's rise was all going on in the western Mediterranean, the Greek world felt the impact through the Roman conquest of Sicily in 241 BC. It wasn't long before the Romans began to look east.

Tangling with the Romans: Pyrrhus of Epirus

One of the first contacts between Greece and Rome came at the beginning of the third century BC. The Romans were beginning to expand their interests and the people of Tarentum in southern Italy appealed for help against them.

Their appeal was answered by Pyrrhus, an aristocrat originally from Epirus. Pyrrhus was the joint ruler of Macedonia after driving out Demetrius (of *Helepolis* fame) – see the earlier section 'Laying siege on Rhodes: Demetrius'. But Pyrrhus had then been forced out by his co-ruler Lysimachus.

As something of a military adventurer, Pyrrhus was happy to try and further his ambitions in the west, and he landed at Tarentum in 282 BC. He brought a large army with him, including traditional Macedonian infantry with *sarissas* and about 30 elephants. Over the next three years, he fought a series of campaigns against Rome, heavily defeating the Romans on several occasions.

The problem that Pyrrhus faced was that every time he won a victory, the Romans, with all their available reinforcements, came back stronger, but Pyrrhus's own forces diminished. Despite his victories, Pyrrhus eventually lost the war, leaving to fight in Sicily in 278 BC.

His campaigns are the source of the modern expression 'a pyrrhic victory' – winning the battle but not the war.

Clashing cultures: The Battle of Cynoscephalae

In 197 BC, the Macedonian king Philip V (no relation to Philip II) became engaged with the Romans. Philip was a bit of a chancer and had spent many years fighting small territorial wars against his Hellenistic counterparts. However, in 197 BC, Philip bit off more than he could chew.

During the Second Punic War between Rome and Carthage (218 to 201 BC), Philip supported the Carthaginians and thus made himself an enemy of Rome.

The Romans used their friendship with Ptolemaic Egypt (see the section 'Developing dynastic struggles') as a reason to attack because Philip had recently helped the Seleucid king Antiochus against them. The Romans sailed across the Adriatic Sea and met Philip's forces at Cynoscephalae in Thessaly.

The battle was a real test of military strategies with new, lightly armed, and mobile Roman legions set against the formidable and old school Macedonian phalanx. In the end, the Romans won the day. They surrounded the relatively slow-moving Macedonian phalanx. When the Macedonians lifted their pikes in surrender, the Romans failed to understand the gesture and cut them down. Philip's army was destroyed, and his allies fled.

Becoming a Roman province

Commitments elsewhere meant the Romans were unable to finish the job they began against Philip V, but in 168 BC, they defeated the Macedonians again at Pydna. This time there was no coming back.

Roman forces split Macedonia into four tribal republics and placed a Roman governor in control in each region. After further trouble, the republics were eventually done away with in 146 BC. The country that had produced Philip II and Alexander the Great was made a Roman province.

Generally, the Romans were quite content to allow the Greek cities to rule themselves. The Roman governor in Macedonia kept an eye on things and (as ever!) the Greek cities were too busy squabbling among themselves to ever mount a serious threat against the Romans.

The last Greek hurrah

Following the Roman annexation of Macedonia in 146 BC, several Greek cities formed a coalition called the *Achaean Confederacy,* which rose up in revolt again Rome. Of course, the gesture was futile. The small army that the confederacy mustered never stood a chance against the professional Roman army. The confederacy was easily defeated and the city of Corinth destroyed in the process.

After the revolt, Rome more closely monitored the Greek cities from Macedonia, and in some cases, Roman garrisons were installed. Finally, in 46 BC a large part of southern Greece turned into the Roman province of Achaia. The ancient Greeks never really ruled themselves again.

Living On: Rome and Beyond

Although the Greeks as a powerful entity were no more by 46 BC, Greek civilisation thrived for hundreds of years after. The Romans and subsequent civilisations adopted many elements of Greek life:

- ✔ The Roman gods were broadly similar to Greek gods, even though they had different names.

- ✔ Greek art, architecture, literature, philosophy, and all manner of other elements of Greek society were incorporated into Roman and Byzantine life, and then rediscovered and reintegrated into Europe during the Renaissance.

Even today you're reading a book about the ancient Greeks. So the Greeks never really went away; they just stopped existing in Greece!

Part III
Living a Greek Life

The 5th Wave   By Rich Tennant

EXTRA VIRGIN OLIVE OIL:
ANCIENT ATTEMPTS

Okay - bring in
the extra virgin!

In this part . . .

With all the fighting they did it's a wonder that the Greeks ever found time for anything else. In this part I look at the nature of everyday life in ancient Greece. I cover what people did in their working lives and leisure time; what they ate and drank; and the art and architecture that they enjoyed. This great cultural life is one of the things that the Greeks are most famous for, and I reveal why . . .

Chapter 13

Out in the Fields: Farming, Herding, and Travelling

In This Chapter

▶ Farming and winemaking

▶ Herding livestock

▶ Getting around in ancient Greece by land and sea

*T*hroughout its 2,000-year history, ancient Greece was an *agrarian society*, which means huge numbers of people spent nearly every day working the soil or tending livestock. Most Greek towns and cities started off as farming communities, and many of them remained so throughout the entire ancient Greek period. Many Greeks were involved in industry or trade (see Chapters 14 and 15 for more on city life), but the vast majority of people derived their income and kept themselves alive by what they and their animals produced.

In this chapter, I discuss what was involved in making a living from the land. I also look at how the Greeks travelled and transported things by land and sea. As you may guess, living a successful life – in the seemingly idyllic Greek countryside – demanded a lot of very hard work!

Scratching a Living

Working the land was tough in the ancient world. People worked from the moment that the sun was up until it set. In the Mediterranean, this schedule meant a 14-hour day most of the time – and they didn't even have weekends to look forward to for time off (although they did have a lot of festivals and public holidays).

The typical ancient Greek farmer worked a relatively small patch of land; a house with perhaps two or three acres that would usually have been in his family for generations.

Richer farmers owned estates that incorporated several pieces of land, sometimes in various locations. Larger farms used slaves and serfs. Serfs were paid workers tied to working on the estate, which was also their accommodation.

Working a farm was exceptionally hard work, and people were only a bad storm or a dry season away from ruin. Furthermore, if a man was called up for military service (see Chapter 5) and his relatives were unable to manage the farm during his absence, he could lose everything.

Growing crops

The basic farming traditions in ancient Greece were similar to those everywhere else in the Mediterranean at the time and they hadn't changed for a very long time. Specifically:

- ✔ Nearly all smallholding farmers grew two basic staple crops, which were the mainstays of the Greek diet:

  - • **Wheat:** The most common type of wheat was basic emmer wheat, also known as farro wheat. Farmers grew other types of wheat elsewhere in the Mediterranean, and these crops were sometimes exported abroad. Wheat was ground and made into bread.

  - • **Barley:** Barley was a lower grade wheat alternative that was easier to grow and was turned into a hard bread or small cakes. Generally speaking, poorer people ate barley bread because the better lands (worked by the wealthier farmers) could grow wheat rather than barley. Barley was also grown a lot in Egypt where it was used to make beer (the Greeks didn't drink beer).

- ✔ Greek farmers also grew grapes (see the later section 'Growing grapes and making wine'), olives, and vegetables (mainly pulses and beans).

- ✔ Farmers grew crops using *dry farming methods*, meaning that they were able to grow without irrigation. This was very important because of the relatively low rainfall in Greece. See the section 'Working the land' for more info.

  The ancient Greeks had no knowledge of wet-farming (using irrigation) techniques used to grow crops such as rice. However, wet-farming was practised in the near east from as early as 1500 BC, and Alexander the Great and his men probably passed through rice fields on their travels.

- ✔ Farmers usually sowed crops in autumn (September in modern terms) because the rainy season in Greece was between autumn and spring. This schedule meant that the summer was usually festival time for celebrating the harvest (June/July). The harvest needed to be successful, too, because it had to sustain the farmers all the way through until next summer.

Chapter 15 discusses more exotic foods and meal preparation.

Going underground: Persephone and Demeter

The myth of Persephone is an interesting story. The daughter of Zeus and Demeter, she was chosen by Hades (the god of the dead) to be his wife. This meant that she was taken from the living to the underworld where Hades lived. Demeter was shocked by her daughter's disappearance and searched the world for her, withholding her blessings from men. This turned the world barren and caused widespread famine. Eventually she discovered where Persephone was and whisked her away from Hades's clutches. However, Zeus ruled that Persephone would have to spend six months of the year with Hades and six with her mother. The Greeks interpreted this as the reason why the world is cold during autumn and winter when Persephone is in the underworld, and warm in spring and summer when she's returned. This is a great example of a myth being used to explain a natural phenomenon.

Honouring Demeter, the friend of the farmer

Several of the Greek gods had associations with farming and fertility, but the most relevant one was the goddess Demeter. Her main association was with wheat, and her name effectively means 'god-mother'. In myth she had a daughter called Persephone, and mother and daughter became known as 'the two goddesses' or sometimes 'the Holy Twain'.

The ancient Greek religious calendar was closely aligned with the farming year, so most celebrations of Demeter coincided with ploughing or harvesting. One of the most famous celebrations was the Thesmophoria, which occurred during sowing time. The festival was for women only; men were strictly banned from it (Chapter 21 has more details). This exclusivity was due to the fact that the Greeks saw fertility on the farm as being closely related to a woman's capacity for child bearing. This rationale is also part of the reason why Demeter was called 'god-mother'. For more on ancient Greek religious customs, see Chapter 22.

Working the land

The techniques used to work the land in ancient Greece were fairly straightforward. If they were able, farmers used the traditional method of 'half and half', which involved ploughing and working half their land every year while leaving the other half *fallow,* or unused. The following year the farmer worked the other portion, so some land always got a break and the soil was able to replenish its natural nutrients.

Unfortunately, some smallholders weren't able to rotate their field because they needed to work every scrap of land. Over time their soil became less and less fertile.

Ploughing

Given the crops the Greeks were growing (see the section 'Growing crops'), ploughing was a major farming activity. The methods for ploughing were very straightforward:

- On bigger farms, two oxen pulled a simple wooden plough. Sometimes the implement was tipped with iron to allow for more accurate ploughing.

- On smaller farms, ploughing was done by hand, which was back-breaking work. This form of ploughing didn't generally turn the soil, only broke it to allow for planting.

Sowing and growing

Similarly, sowing would have been done mostly by hand although on larger estates the number of serfs meant that the work was more evenly spread out. On a small farm the whole family would have been involved.

As I mentioned, the Greeks were dry farmers so watering and irrigation weren't really an issue. They did use manure and most farms would have had an evil-smelling dung heap that it was wise to steer clear of.

Harvesting

After the crops had grown, they were reaped with a simple curved sickle, heaped in a basket, and taken to be threshed. Farmers carried out *threshing* – separating the buds from the main plant – on a threshing floor; a cleared patch of dry ground. Sometimes they used a sled drawn by animals. Barley collecting and wheat 'winnowing' were typically done by hand with a small shovel and a basket. Not a fun job.

Crops were stored in small outbuildings. The Greeks had no refrigeration techniques so things were kept and used for as long as possible until they eventually spoiled.

Following the herd

Most ancient Greek farm estates weren't very big, so the majority of farmers didn't keep many animals. Grazing land was at a premium, so a few pigs, sheep, or goats alongside a pair of oxen were all the livestock most farms supported.

IN THEIR WORDS

Pan: Friend of the farmer – and the soldier?

The Greek god associated with farm life was Pan. His name means 'guardian of the flocks', and he is always depicted as a young man with pipes who tends a herd of goats. However, because he was said to lead a fairly hermit-like existence, he was also associated with the unfortunate soldiers who had to perform guard duty on isolated borders. Several ancient writers suggest that he appeared in the Athenian ranks at the battle of Marathon (refer to Chapter 6). Quite handy to have a god on your side. No wonder the Athenians won!

The female Hellenistic poet Anyte, who was born in Tegea in Arcadia, not far from where Pan was supposed to have come from, writes of Pan:

Why, country Pan, sitting still among the lonely shades of the thick-set wood, do you shrill on your sweet reed?

So that the heifers may pasture on these dewy mountains, cropping the long-haired heads of the grass.

The type of animals that larger farms kept very much depended on the terrain involved. Generally, larger animals, such as cattle and oxen, tended to be kept in the north of Greece and Macedonia because these regions were wetter and more grazing land was available. In the Peloponnese and the south, sheep and goats were better choices because the land was rockier.

Goats and sheep were particularly useful to the ancient Greeks because they were used to produce milk, cheese, wool, and meat – all things that farmers could trade for other commodities at the market in town. Goats and sheep were also useful because farmers could sell or use them in sacrifice; healthy, well-kept animals fetched a very good price for religious purposes.

Hunting high and low

The other method of living off the land was the original one – hunting game. Hunting was a big part of Greek myth with boar being the most popular animal for heroes to hunt. Hunting itself was seen as an activity that helped to sharpen skills for war. These heroes usually hunted with either a spear or a bow, but everyday hunting was rather different and mostly for game such as hares using traps and snares. This was often an activity carried out by young boys.

Farming by the book

Manuals and books about farming weren't really available to the ancient Greeks (although they were developed later in the Roman Empire). Instead, many Greeks referred to a long poem first composed by the poet Hesiod around 700 BC called *Works and Days*. It's full of advice in poetic form for individuals intent on running a farm and relies on mythological examples of what could go wrong if farmers didn't follow Hesiod's advice.

Hesiod was particularly scathing about whether or not a farmer needed a wife, suggesting that a female slave might be better:

First of all you should acquire a house and a woman and an ox for the plough . . . A female slave, not a wife, who can follow the oxen as well.

Hesiod was no great fan of women in general. Later in the poem, he warns that women are not to be trusted as they are likely to want to 'steal your barn'. Clearly, he just never met the right woman.

Boar hunting did go on using hounds and (when done by the rich) on horseback in large groups. Boar hunting was still seen as a noble art and one that a man of action should be proficient in.

Growing Grapes and Making Wine

People drank a great deal of wine in ancient Greece. Grapes were relatively easy to grow because of the climate and soil, so most farms and estates included some vines.

Evidence indicates that the forerunners of the ancient Greeks, the Mycenaeans (see Chapter 2), grew grape vines and made wine, so viticulture (the growing of grapes to make wine) was fairly well established by the last millennium BC.

Despite the region's long history of wine making, little is known about the processes, and no books on the subject survive. However, historians do know that the beverage was usually mixed with water, and the alcohol content wasn't as high as with wine today.

Different varieties of red and white wine were available. Usually, the geography and climate of the region dictated what type of grape farmers grew and the sort of wine they produced. For example, the island of Ceos produced three specific types:

'High on the hill sat a lonely goatherd . . .'

Spending time tending goats day in and day out may not sound like the most romantic of jobs, but the occupation became very popular in ancient Greek art and literature – and beyond.

The idea of the Greek goatherd – and, in particular, one pining for a lost love – became a traditional feature in classical art and poetry.

Over a thousand years after the ancient Greeks, the goatherd became popular again, and during the Renaissance the idea of 'pastoral' was born. Everything from the paintings of Titian to the Symphony No. 6 'Pastoral' by Beethoven trace back to the old goatherds of ancient Greece.

- ✔ *Austeros*: A dry wine
- ✔ *Glukazon*: A sweet wine
- ✔ *Autokratos*: A variety somewhere between the two – a medium-dry, if you like.

These varieties from Ceos were established and known all over Greece (see the sidebar 'An early marketing effort'), and other cities and regions had similar specialties.

Wine was a vital part of Greek life and people drank it for a huge variety of reasons including religious celebration. See Chapter 15 and also Chapter 20, where I look at the god associated with wine and generally having a good time – Dionysus.

Getting Around in Ancient Greece

Like just about everything else in ancient times, travelling throughout ancient Greece was seriously hard work. If you were on dry land, you either travelled by horse, cart, or your own feet. On water, you had the option of riding in boats, but these vehicles weren't plain sailing (see the later section 'Venturing into Poseidon's realm: Travelling by sea').

The concept of travel for its own sake or of going on holiday wasn't really a part of Greek life. Certainly, only the very rich could've afforded the time away from work, let alone the expense of the journey. Generally speaking, the ancient Greeks travelled only if they had to. Traders, for example, were almost constantly on the move between market towns, buying local produce and selling it in the next town.

Occasionally, the ancient Greek people made massive journeys to move and set up in another place. See Chapters 3 and 4 for more on colonisation in early Greek history.

An early marketing effort

Greeks were very proud of their local vintages and had an easy system for identifying where wine came from. Each town had its own slightly different type of double-headed jug, known as an *amphora*, that exclusively held its wines. (In fact, the people of the island of Ceos were so proud of their wine that they used the symbol of their *amphora* on their coinage.) The distinctive shapes have been extremely helpful to archaeologists trying to work out where various pieces of unearthed pottery originally came from.

Going by horse

If you were able to afford a horse, riding it or using it to draw a cart was the preferred mode of transportation throughout ancient Greece. A horse was expensive – essentially another mouth to feed. Being able to maintain and equip a horse was a sign that you were financially well off. (Chapter 4 discusses the social classes in Athens.) Furthermore, riding equipment was rudimentary; stirrups didn't appear in Europe until around the ninth century AD. Add the lack of decent roads to the situation and you can see how difficult riding must have been.

Wild horses were rare in most parts of Greece with the exception of Thessaly, where large numbers of horses were tamed and bred. The Thessalians became famous for their formidable cavalry (see Chapter 11).

For those less well off an ass or a donkey was an acceptable substitute. Unlike finely bred, expensive horses, the life of a donkey wasn't happy. They were worked extremely hard as an all-purpose animal, as this little poem by Palladas suggests. Palladas was a Greek writing during the Roman era (around AD 350) but the experience of the donkey would have been exactly the same even then!

> *Poor little donkey! It's no joke being a pedant's not a rich man's moke [donkey] preened in the palace of the alabarch [official in the Jewish community].*
>
> *Little donkey, stay, stay with me patiently until the day I get my pay.*

Burning sandals

Most people had no transportation option other than to walk to wherever they needed to go. Consequently, people tried to limit journeys to when they were absolutely necessary.

A good example of a typical journey was the walk between Athens and the port at Piraeus, a journey of about 7 kilometres (4 miles). It would take a large part of the day to walk there and back, but some people made the trip every day, such as small farmers or people trekking in to attend the jury courts. Rich Athenian merchants often kept small houses or apartments in the port for when they needed to conduct business there before returning to their main home in the city.

Venturing into Poseidon's realm: Travelling by sea

Some journeys were only possible on the 'Great Green', as the Egyptians and Greeks called the Mediterranean Sea. The Greeks were capable and experienced sailors, and Chapters 6 and 7 describe many of their successes in naval warfare.

The Greek god of the sea was Poseidon (although many other gods and deities were associated with it). Poseidon was a violent god, and the Greeks attributed storms, earthquakes, and mishaps at sea to his rage. Making offerings to him before a voyage was seen as essential and a wise move upon returning from a successful trip.

The following passage from Homer's *Iliad* gives a great idea of how the Greeks viewed Poseidon:

> *Down Poseidon dove and yoked his bronze-hoofed horses onto his battle-car . . . skimming the waves, and over the swells they came, dolphins leaving their lairs to sport across his wake, leaping left and right – well they knew their lord. And the sea heaved in joy, cleaving a path for him.*

Another real danger in sea travel was falling overboard. Most people in ancient Greece couldn't swim. Many sailors felt that it was unlucky to learn to swim because it tempted fate and caused your vessel to be shipwrecked. Also, swimming itself wasn't a leisure activity in the way that it is now. If you were a city dweller on a sea voyage and you fell overboard, you had to hope that one of the crew swam!

Ships for trade and transport

Most military vessels were long, sleek, and powered by oars (see Chapter 5), but ships used for trade and transport were very different. Generally, they were much larger with a far greater draft (meaning they sat much lower in the water with more of the ship under the waterline) and looked a little more rounded. These larger transporters were nearly always powered by sail alone.

Pytheas: Boldly going where no Greek had been before

Despite the sea being so perilous, some Greeks attempted long journeys of discovery. The most famous of these was a man named Pytheas who in around 320 BC claimed to have sailed from the Mediterranean around Spain, into the Atlantic Ocean, around the British Isles, and even farther – almost to the Arctic Circle. When he returned home, he wrote a book about the expedition called *On the Ocean*. Nobody believed him at the time but many modern commentators think he was telling the truth.

Sails were made of linen. They were often painted and decorated with designs indicating where the ship came from or the type of cargo that it was carrying. With a decent wind behind it, one of these ships could travel at about 7 to 10 kilometres per hour (about 4 to 6 knots).

Although the dimensions and power source of trade ships meant they offered far more room for carrying cargo and passengers, the vessels were also entirely at the mercy of the weather and were also far less manoeuvrable than their military cousins.

Shipbuilding

The building of ships was a highly skilled trade that was passed down through families. Great examples of shipbuilding appear in mythology, like the construction of Jason's ship the *Argo,* which Homer's *Odyssey* describes in detail. Amazingly, the construction methods that Homer describes in around 750 BC were still being used during the Hellenistic period 600 years later.

The construction method Homer describes is known as the 'shell first' technique, where the ship begins as just a keel on to which planking and other frames are added later. This method was quite fast; ships could be built relatively quickly. Depending on how many people were involved, a ship could be put together in about a month.

Navigating

Travel by sea was highly dangerous. The sailing season was usually confined to between March and October because during the winter months the weather was too unpredictable.

The Greeks didn't have the ability to navigate by using charts, so as much as possible they stayed close to the coast or used individual islands to judge distance. Some navigation by the stars was possible on clear nights, but sailors didn't rely on this method.

The pirates of the Mediterranean

Assuming you survived bad navigation, terrible storms, drowning, or the wrath of Poseidon, you also had to watch out for pirates! Piracy was a big problem with sea travel. The ancient Greek myths are full of episodes that can be interpreted as piracy:

- ✔ Jason and the Argonauts sail to the Black Sea and steal the Golden Fleece, an obvious act of piracy.

- ✔ Many of the events in Homer's *Odyssey* are piracy, but they go unpunished and aren't criticised.

Pirates thrived because nobody (until Roman times) was able to crack down on them. Also, during wars like the Peloponnesian War (see Chapter 8), telling the difference between an act of war and an act of piracy was very difficult.

In general, pirates operated on popular trade routes using hideaways on small islands. The area around Rhodes (see the map on the Cheat Sheet) in particular was known to be a hotbed of piracy with the five harbours on the island providing rich pickings.

These navigation limitations meant that sailors only really knew a small number of local journeys and routes because they had to have specialist knowledge of local currents and how they affected the journey. So if you wanted to travel between Athens and Asia Minor you had to make a number of small journeys, hopping between islands, rather than one long trip. And you were at the mercy of the trade routes and whether somebody was going your way.

Fishing

Just like hunting on dry land, fishing was a way of getting food from the sea. Fishing was an important industry in ancient Greece, although probably not as big as you may think. Predicting the movements of heavy shoals was very difficult for Greek fishermen without the aid of modern technology, and the Mediterranean isn't as well stocked with fish as the larger oceans.

Most fishing took place close to shore with large nets. (Only the very brave fished farther out in the open sea due to navigation limitations; see the section 'Navigating'). However, the varieties of fish available in deeper, open waters were very highly prized and fetched higher prices.

The Greeks loved fish and it was a staple part of the diet for those who could afford it. For more on fish and how the Greeks ate it, see Chapter 15.

Chapter 14

Home and Family

*P*arts I and II of this book cover some of the most brutal battles in all history, but this chapter looks at something you may find just as shocking – the everyday interactions of ancient Greek families. So prepare yourself: Ancient Greek attitudes about women, sex, death, and violence were very different to those held today.

This chapter (as well as Chapter 15) looks at what life was like in Greek towns and cities. For the most part, I concentrate on Athens because it was the biggest and most successful city at the time, and because of the huge amount of archaeological and documentary evidence it's the one that historians know most about.

Much of what I describe in this chapter is what you can call *social standards*. Ancient Greek social standards were very high, and an awful lot of people did not – indeed, *could not* – live up to them the whole time. You discover the Greeks' frame of mind and how they viewed the world. In a perfect world these are the standards that people expected themselves and others to live up to. However, comic plays and novels from ancient Greece indicate that people lived their lives far beneath the standards of what was supposedly acceptable. Think of it this way: Nowadays most people consider speaking with your mouth full to be rude – but many people still do it!

Appreciating the Household: The Oikos

The *oikos* was the basic unit of Greek society. In modern terms, *oikos* would probably translate to 'household', but the word meant much more than just your home. The *oikos* included:

An Ithacan's *oikos* is his castle

In *The Odyssey* by Homer, Odysseus is delayed on his return home to the island of Ithaca from the war at Troy (see Chapter 21 for more on Homer). While Odysseus is away, various local nobles turn up at his house and try to persuade his wife, Penelope, to marry them, claiming that her husband is obviously dead. Penelope is no doubt very attractive, but what these would-be suitors really want is Odysseus's land and property – his *oikos* – that come with Penelope's hand in marriage.

In the recent TV adaptation of *The Odyssey* (2000), Odysseus returns home and kills the suitors who invaded his house. He justifies killing them by saying, 'They tried to steal my world.' That's a great way of expressing what the *oikos* really meant.

- ✔ The physical building itself (see the following section 'Touring the typical Greek house').

- ✔ The people within it (see the later section 'Meeting the extended family').

- ✔ All property associated with the family and building.

The Greeks considered the *oikos* to be one entity, like a very small version of the *polis* or 'state' (see Chapter 4). Best to keep your hands off another man's *oikos*, or big trouble lay ahead.

Touring the typical Greek house

As Figure 14-1 shows, the average house in an ancient Greek town wasn't very big. Floor plans were simple and similar:

- ✔ All the rooms opened onto a rectangular courtyard, which featured a doorway to the street on one side.

- ✔ Each house had a main living room where family members spent most of the day.

- ✔ A secondary room, called the *andron* (which literally means the 'men's room') was used to receive visitors. As the name implies, this room was primarily the domain of men. Men slept in quarters adjacent to the *andron*.

- ✔ Women's quarters were located elsewhere in the house – usually well away from the *andron*, often on the upper level. The women would work and sleep here.

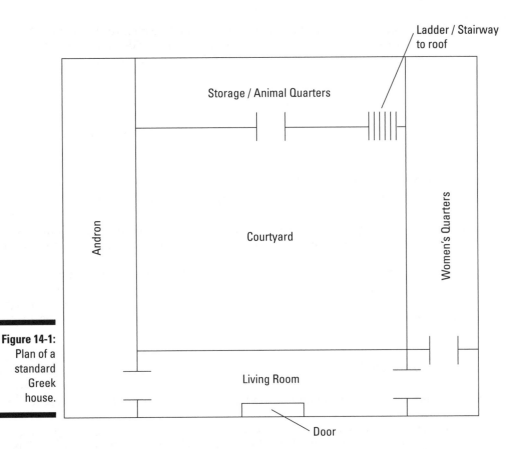

Ladder / Stairway to roof

Storage / Animal Quarters

Andron

Courtyard

Women's Quarters

Figure 14-1:
Plan of a
standard
Greek
house.

Living Room

Door

The building itself was fairly basic with walls made of mud brick or rubble and the floors most likely of beaten earth. Houses usually included a ladder (or an external stairway in wealthier houses) that family members used to access the roof, which they used as another living space.

A Greek house didn't have a specific bathroom or kitchen. Cooking would often be done outside. Washing was done with cold water in the privacy of the sleeping quarters.

No matter how much money you had, the style of house would be mostly the same. Luxury was represented by the size of the property and the quality of decoration or finish.

Meeting the extended family

In general, the concept of family was very strong. A lot of people lived within the small space of a Greek house. In addition to the modern 'nuclear family' (man, woman, and probably between two and five children), other relatives often formed part of the household. Unmarried or widowed females lived under the protection of their nearest male relatives, and grandmothers, nieces, and sisters were often legally obliged to seek shelter in an already busy household. Add to this mix several slaves, and the average household usually numbered between 9 and 12 people.

But within the family, however, equality didn't exist. Men were the absolute rulers, and women had very little status at all.

Kurios: Man about the house

The dominant male in the *oikos* was its absolute ruler. He was known as the *kurios*, which means 'the man in charge'. The *kurios* literally had the power of life and death over everybody within, including his wife and children. A man who killed his wife could be legally challenged by her relations but if she was proved to have been unfaithful he had acted legally. He carried out all the financial and legal transactions of the *oikos*. Nobody else interacted with the *oikos* in any way without his consent. A husband in a new home would automatically become *kurios* and stay in this position until he died, although in some households the eldest son would take charge if the father became too old or ill to cope.

Beyond oikos

Although the *oikos* itself was an independent unit, the concept of family was very strong and extended beyond the *oikos* to other groups:

- ✔ The *ankhisteia* was a wider network of relatives to which Greek families belonged. This network usually went as far as second cousins and comprised people's wider family.

  If a woman was widowed, her first move was to look for a new husband within the *ankhisteia*. This group also played a very big role in the inheritance process. Inheritance law was hideously complex but basically followed the rule that the nearest male relative inherited. If there wasn't an obvious heir then a male relative from the *ankhisteia* would step in and marry the widow, so inheriting the property.

- ✔ The *phratiai* were religious associations that are probably best described as brotherhoods because all the members were male, representing their *oikos*. Although the members may not have all been related, their families normally had some kind of association through marriage or business in the past.

Like the *oikos*, these other associations were very powerful. Men were expected to give absolute loyalty to them. If a man fell out with either his ankhisteia or phratiai, he was shunned by the rest and open to attack.

With all these loyalties life could become very complicated. A man's ultimate loyalty would be to his *oikos* and then his *ankhisteia* but the *phratiai* interests were strong too because they usually had a strong business or financial element. Fortunately the interests of these groups wouldn't really clash because they were all representing the same thing – the furtherance of the *oikos* and those involved in it on a wider basis.

Spending Time with the Women of Ancient Greece

Ancient Greek women were second-class citizens at best – or even less in many cities. For example, Athenian women didn't count as citizens; they were instead classed as 'Women of Attica' (Attica was the region of eastern Greece that Athens belonged to). The point was to separate the women from the city – they were associated with it but not part of its ruling class.

Women had very little liberty in ancient Greece. They were expected to spend the vast majority of their time within the *oikos* (see the section 'Appreciating the Household: The Oikos' earlier in the chapter) and were discouraged from interacting with anybody else. For example, if male guests came to the home and visited the *andron*, women were unlikely to be asked to join them. In more traditional households if women were invited, they were required to wear a veil at all times or even to sit behind a screen.

The poet – and marital advice-giver – Hesiod (see Chapter 13) had a bit of a downer on women. In his long poem *Works and Days* he's scathing about the problems that women can bring:

> *For a man acquires nothing better than a wife – a good one, but there is nothing more miserable than a bad one, a parasite, who even if her husband is strong singes him with the torch and brings him to a raw old age.*

The ancient Greeks saw women as something to be controlled and they limited the type and amount of property a woman could own. For example:

- Women weren't technically allowed to own property above the value of one *medimnos* of barley, which was about as much as it cost to feed a family for a week.
- Any property that a woman used, like clothes or jewellery, was part of the *oikos* and as such belonged to her husband.

Even when her husband died a woman wouldn't hold on to the family property – she needed to swiftly remarry (preferably to a member of the *ankhisteia*) so that the property could be taken on by another male.

Mythical monsters

Women in Greek myth and tragic plays have a hard time. Most are portrayed as untrustworthy and temperamental. Examples include:

✔ **Clytemnestra:** Wife of Agamemnon. She murdered her husband when he returned home from the Trojan War.

✔ **Medea:** The wife of Jason from the Argonauts story (told in Chapter 20). When he left her for another woman, she murdered their new children and his new bride.

✔ **Pandora:** The first ever woman. She was responsible for bringing all the ills into the world.

Of course, things aren't quite that simple and most men behave appallingly in myths too. But these images of women in myth affected the ancient Greeks. Men were suspicious and tried to keep women under close control.

Although restrictive, the position women were expected to adopt in ancient Greek society was somewhat manageable in wealthy households where numerous slaves ran the *oikos*. Women from poorer families, however, had to be much more active because they carried out all the tasks necessary to keep the household going. Some women even worked alongside their husbands in the family trade or at the market. Despite their hard work, women were still tied to and financially dependent on men. The only women who were financially independent were some of the more exclusive prostitutes, who I talk about in Chapter 15.

Marrying and Divorcing

Part of the reason why ancient Greek society controlled women so tightly was so as not to damage their chances of securing good marriages. Marriage was the main event of a woman's life – something that she spent her young life preparing for.

Girls married at a young age, usually about 14, to men who were considerably older, probably 25 to 30 years old. Often, women married much older men, if the men had been recently widowed.

The poet Theognis describes the challenges of marrying a young bride, particularly when the husband is older:

> *'A young wife is not suitable for an elderly husband*
>
> *For she is a boat that does not obey the rudder.*

Nor do anchors hold her; and she breaks her mooring cables,

Often at night to find another harbour.'

Getting hitched: It's all about the money

Weddings were complicated things to organise because they centred largely on property transfers. When a bride moved in with her new husband, she brought a *dowry* with her. The dowry was typically a large sum of money that represented a portion of her father's property because giving up the land itself would be very complicated. The wife didn't own her dowry and it immediately became the property of her husband – even though he may have to return it if they divorced.

Marriage took place in two stages: the betrothal (when the union was announced) and the actual (and completely unromantic) wedding itself.

The betrothal

The first part of the marriage was called the *eggue*, which is similar to the modern notion of betrothal – although the term really means something more like 'pledge'.

The coming marriage was announced publicly (read out in front of members of the *ankhisteia*) so others were able to witness both the size of the dowry the bride's father was offering and to make assurances that the girl was still a virgin. A betrothal often took place very early in a girl's life when she was still a child of maybe 5 or 6.

A young man picked his wife on the basis of status and family connections usually as a result of intensive negotiations within the *ankhisteia* carried out by his father. The couple probably never met each other before the betrothal. Romance didn't even come into the picture. The entire process was a business transaction, pure and simple.

The wedding – or moving day

The actual marriage itself was very straightforward. The girl simply entered the *oikos* of her new husband and began living with him. The couple went through a small formal ceremony to bless the union, but it was all very private. You didn't need a marriage licence because marriage was a private transaction between the two *kurioi*.

A wedding feast usually took place afterwards and sometimes went on for two or three days. All the members of the *ankhestia* would attend with the women all gathered with the bride in the women's quarters of the house. It was usually a good natured revel with much eating, drinking, and dancing – not too different from the average wedding reception today.

Packing up and moving on

Ancient Greek divorce, like marriage, was pretty straightforward: The bride simply moved out. She went back to the house of her father, if he was still alive, or to the home of the nearest male relative.

Either side of a couple could ask for divorce, but more often than not men sought divorce following an allegation of adultery. (Men commonly slept with other women and prostitutes, but wives were supposed to be entirely faithful.) Typically public proclamations were made about unfaithful wives, and the women were totally humiliated.

The other major reason for divorce was so that men could make other, more socially attractive and financially beneficial marriages. Having been married before was no barrier to marrying again – for a man or a woman – but a man had much more choice in whom he married the second or third time. Unlike other ancient cultures only one spouse was allowed at the same time!

Of course, some marriages took place that didn't conform to these well-defined social structures. The poorer and lower classes also married but without the elaborate preparations and negotiations involved in more moneyed households. Many more of these marriages would have been for love; unfortunately historians don't know too much about them because all of the evidence relates to the moneyed literate classes.

Starting Out in Life: Children

In general, the ancient Greek attitude toward children was very harsh. Some of the things that I talk about in this section are quite upsetting – so be warned.

Ancient Greek men were pretty paranoid about adultery and it partly explains their distrust and restriction of women. Part of their concern was because of the possibility of illegitimate children. Greek law around inheritance was very strict and the emergence of any illegitimate children could really complicate a situation and result in lengthy legal cases.

Clearing a difficult first hurdle: Birth

Ancient Greece had no scientific methods of contraception so women often fell pregnant. Women would be expected to give birth a number of times during their life and because they married quite young (age 14 or 15) would have had many fertile years ahead of them. Four or five children in a family wouldn't be unusual.

Oedipus: A case in point

Probably the most famous Greek play is *Oedipus Tyrannus* by Sophocles. The drama centres around the fact that, after receiving an unfavourable prophecy, Oedipus's father gives his son as an infant to be exposed. The shepherd asked to expose the child takes sympathy on Oedipus and gives him away to be adopted, starting one of the most famously tragic cycle of events ever.

The fifth-century BC audience that watched this play originally wouldn't have been shocked by the decision of Oedipus's father because they were familiar and comfortable with the ultimate power that a man had over his *oikos*. You can read more about the play in Chapter 16.

Delivery

In the vast majority of cases, birth was an all-female affair. Either experienced midwives or female friends delivered babies. Male doctors were called in only for the most difficult of cases. (See Chapter 15 for more on ancient Greek medical practices.) Birth took place in the household where the woman would have spent her entire term.

The risks to the woman giving birth were as high as they were for the child. The potential loss of blood and complications in delivery that would be manageable today were potentially fatal in ancient Greece. In many cases, one or other didn't survive the experience.

Infanticide

Although appalling, *infanticide* (the killing or leaving to die of small children) wasn't uncommon in ancient Greece. Most Athenian men wanted sons because a male was able to work in the family business and provided an heir for the *oikos*. (The poet Hesiod in his *Works and Days* poem advises that it's best to have only one son and no daughters at all.) Daughters were considered problems. They were expensive to keep and cost a lot in dowries when they married.

The Greek solution was appalling but simple. If the *kurios* of an *oikos* decided that he already had enough children, then subsequent children, especially girls, were exposed. This horrific practice involved leaving the infant out in the countryside where he or she either starved or was taken by animals.

I'm not excusing the appalling practice of infanticide, but as I mention when I discuss warfare (see Chapter 5), the everyday presence and possibility of death and disease hardened the ancient Greek people. Also, although exposure of babies is terrible, you need to bear in mind that life expectancy in ancient Greece was only around 30 years. Of course, loads of people lived to be much older than 30, but the average was brought down by the huge number of infant mortalities. Death and the loss of loved ones was a common experience, although that wouldn't make the pain of losing somebody any easier.

Getting an education

If you managed to make it through early childhood, the next stage of life was your education. This varied hugely depending on whether you were a boy or a girl.

School for boys

No age requirement existed for schooling. Many boys received some kind of formal education from 5 or 6 all the way through to adulthood (16).

Ancient Greece didn't have a state-sponsored education system. All classes were paid for by a boy's *kurios* or guardian. Wealthier families provided tutors who lived and worked in the home, giving lessons to a number of children.

Boys experienced three main strands of education:

- *Grammatistes* taught formal subjects like mathematics, reading, and writing. Boys spent a lot of their time memorising the works of Homer and other poets. The Greeks felt that the great works of literature provided moral training via the conduct of the characters in the stories.

- *Kitharistes* taught music and poetry. Boys learned how to play the lyre and perform songs and poetry.

- *Paidotribes* taught gymnastics and fitness training, most probably at the *palaestra*, or training ground. For more on this sort of training see Chapter 16.

A boy usually had lessons from all these tutors every day (apart from festival days), often travelling to different places for classes.

For the wealthy, further study was available when boys became men. Men could obtain individual tuition in a specific area or subject from teachers called *sophists* who hired themselves out for the purpose. By the beginning of the fourth century BC, Plato's Academy, and later Aristotle's Lyceum, became established as official schools of higher education. I talk more about all this in Chapter 23.

Education for the poor

Education was expensive. For families without money, education meant working in the family business or on the family farm. This education was vocational so that children could take over the business from their parents. Girls would also be involved in this work until they reached an age where they might marry. Many poorer people would have been illiterate.

Girls: They don't need no education!

Like so many things in ancient Greece, education was different for girls. It was very unusual for a father to spend money on his daughter's education. Boys were educated because they were taught the skills they needed in order to succeed in public life. Girls, by contrast, were expected to be domestic and were taught the skills of needlework and how to run a home.

Some women were highly educated and nothing stopped them learning later in life, but these more learned women were very much in the minority and never had a public role to showcase their talents.

Examining Slavery

In addition to the family members themselves, an *oikos* included the slaves within the household. Slavery formed a big part of Greek society, and ancient Athens included a huge number of slaves. Modern writers have estimated that at the beginning of the Peloponnesian War in 431 BC (see Chapter 8), about 50,000 male citizens resided in Athens. At the same time, about 100,000 slaves also lived in the city. If you consider women and children, historians contend that the total population of Athens was split about 50:50 between slaves and non-slaves. Both men and women were slaves although they fulfilled different roles, women being mostly confined to maid duties and childcare.

Defining a slave

Slaves were the property of the *oikos* and had no legal rights whatsoever. Technically and legally, a slave was exactly the same as a pot or a sheep. Whoever owned slaves had the power of life and death over them and could do whatever they wanted. If a man regularly beat and even killed his slaves, he wasn't thought of as unreasonably cruel.

As well as fighting wars and writing history Xenophon also wrote books about philosophy (see Chapter 9). In his book *Memorabilia* he recreates a conversation where Socrates discusses the appropriate punishments for slaves who are lazy and misbehave. The treatment he describes was probably quite commonplace:

Socrates: Do they not control their lecherousness by starving them? Prevent them stealing by locking up anything they might steal from? Stop them running away by putting them in fetters? Drive out their laziness with beatings?

Some people were born into slavery (as the children of slaves), but the vast majority were sold into it, mostly as a result of warfare. For example, Alexander the Great (see Chapters 10 and 11) sold the entire populations of several cities into slavery. He could only have done that if the market were thriving.

Establishing the going rate for a slave

Slave markets regularly took place in most cities, and Athens was no exception. The individuals for sale mostly came from the north in Thrace and Dalmatia but also from Asia Minor across the Mediterranean (see the map on the Cheat Sheet in the front of this book).

Following are some prices for slaves from an auction that took place in 415 BC:

- A Thracian woman: 165 drachmas
- A Syrian man: 240 drachmas
- A Scythian man: 144 drachmas
- A Carian child: 72 drachmas

To make some sense of the prices, 1 drachma was the average daily wage of a skilled worker (think of about £25 or $50). Young men were most valuable (and hence expensive) because they could be worked harder for longer and there was no risk of them falling pregnant. Older people could be expensive if they were well educated, and they were often bought to serve as tutors.

Dividing up the labour

After a slave owner bought a slave, the slave had several possible destinations and roles:

- Most households had at least one *oiketes*, or basic domestic slave.
- Some better skilled slaves were set up to work in businesses by their masters, working as potters or other types of craftsmen.
- The Athenian state also owned slaves called *demosioi* who performed official functions, such as working with coinage or serving as clerks in the courts. The Athenian 'police force' was also made up of Scythian slaves often referred to as 'Scythian Archers'.

Legal responsibilities

One of the most unpleasant aspects of being a slave was their legal position. If slaves were required to give evidence in legal cases (see Chapter 7), only statements given under torture were considered valid because it was felt that they would otherwise lie to protect themselves (being poor they were considered easy to corrupt with bribes and inducements).

Both parties in a legal case agreed to the form of torture in advance and to the compensation should the slave be disabled as a result. Typical tortures included the rack, beating, and having vinegar poured up the nose.

In general, slaves were best off claiming that they hadn't seen anything.

- ✔ Many slaves worked outside the cities on the farms owned by citizens. Some became trusted to run elements of the farm.

- ✔ The most unfortunate slaves worked in the silver mines at Laureion near Athens. Their work was hard and remorseless, and death was the only thing to look forward to.

The huge number of slaves in Athens and in Attica generally did an enormous amount of work. Their efforts made it possible for male citizens to spend so much of their time involved in the political process (see Chapter 7). It's kind of ironic that one of the major reasons that the Athenians were able to develop democracy was their system of subjugating and stripping the rights from hundreds of thousands of people.

Buying your freedom

Slaves were technically able to either buy or be given their freedom by their master, a process called *manumission.* Gaining freedom from slavery wasn't as common as in some other civilisations (like the Roman Empire, for example).

And freedom had its issues. Freed slaves were in awkward positions because they weren't able to gain Athenian citizenship and had to become *metoikoi* or *metics* (resident foreigners) instead.

Connecting with Alien Life: Metics

In addition to family and slave, the Athens *oikos* had one other possible household member: legal aliens, known as *metoikoi* or *metics.*

Metoikoi were foreigners who resided in Athens but weren't granted citizen status. Their status was slightly different to that of normal visitors to the city because *metoikoi* paid a special tax and needed to have patrons who guaranteed them while they stayed in the city. Often, guaranteeing included providing accommodation to the *metoikoi*.

Metics sometimes worked as tutors in the houses of their patrons. Several famous characters went through this process, including the following:

- ✔ The historian and traveller Herodotus performed his work for several years in Athens and was very popular, but he left when the city refused to grant him citizen status.

- ✔ The great philosopher Aristotle spent years in Athens living in a house just outside the city walls. As a *metoikos* he wasn't allowed to buy property in the city and was forced to build a house outside it.

Chapter 15

Going About Daily Life in Ancient Greece

*L*ike much of the ancient Greek experience, many things seem very close to how people live today, whereas other aspects seem very strange. In this chapter (and Chapter 16), I examine how people lived their lives on a day-to-day basis. After shedding some light on how the ancient Greeks kept track of their days, this chapter focuses on three staple elements of daily human existence: eating, drinking, and procreation. Along the way, I also touch on two other essentials: money and medicine.

Biding Their Time: The Greek Calendar and Clock

As I mention in Chapter 1, people in the ancient world most commonly dated things by events rather than an actual year. For example, they probably said 'In the year Pericles died' or 'the year after the battle of Marathon', rather than 429 BC or 479 BC, respectively.

Although this convention is very straightforward, the actual Greek calendar was really complex. The following sections cover the basics.

Figuring out the day

Part of the challenge of working with ancient Greek dates is that the region didn't operate under a single calendar. Although every city based its calendar on the lunar cycle, they named individual months and fixed dates after local gods and religious festivals.

In fact, not only did every town or city have a different name for each month, but each possibly used a different date for the start of a new year. So if you were celebrating the New Year in Athens, folks in Thebes may still be in the previous one. The dissimilarities weren't vast and probably didn't make that much difference. In the time it took to travel from Athens to Thebes it would be new year when you got there anyway!

Exploring the Athenian calendar

Because this chapter, as well as most of Part III, focuses on Athens, this city's calendar is worth examining in detail. Table 15-1 outlines the Athenian calendar.

Table 15-1	The Months of the Athenian Calendar	
Summer		
1	Hekatombaion	June / July
2	Metageitnion	July / August
3	Boedromion	August / September
Autumn		
4	Pyanepsion	September / October
5	Maimakterion	October / November
6	Poseidon	November / December
Winter		
7	Gamelion	December / January
8	Anthesterion	January / February
9	Elaphebolion	February / March

Spring		
10	Mounichion	March / April
11	Thargelion	April / May
12	Skirophorion	May / June

Each of Athens's 12 months was either 29 or 30 days long, meaning that a year usually added up to about 354 days. Except the system wasn't actually that simple. The *arkhons* designated some years as leap years and added a whole extra month. Leap years sometimes involved just repeating an already existing month, and mostly the *ekklesia* chose to have another month of Poseideon. This curious custom meant that a leap year was up to 384 days in length.

Although this was a lunar calendar and the Greeks were using the moon to calculate it, this wasn't the main reason for making changes. More often than not the changes were used to create extra time. In 271 BC the Athenians added four extra days to the month of Elaphebolion to allow more time to prepare for the City Dionysia festival (see Chapter 16). It's probably fair to assume that other cities did the same sort of thing.

What day is it again?

The days within each month were even more complicated. The Athenians didn't name the day (Monday, Tuesday, and so on) – instead, they numbered them. But even this convention wasn't as straightforward as it may seem.

A month started with the new moon and the Athenians then divided it into three parts: waxing, full, and waning. The first two parts counted forward the next 21 days. However, at the 22nd day things changed. As the moon began to wane, the Athenians counted backwards from 10 until the end of the month, finishing at day 1. This last day was known as the 'old and new' day.

So, despite having a 30-day month, the last day of Poseideon, for example, was actually the 1st. It's very confusing. It confused me when I was writing about it.

Additional calendars

Incredibly, time keeping was actually even more complicated. In addition to the calendar conventions I describe in the preceding section, the ancient Athenians used two other forms of calendar:

- ✔ A calendar for scheduling religious festivals
- ✔ Another calendar to date political documents and legislation

Phew, that was a long week!

If you read through the details of the section 'Exploring the Athenian calendar', you may wonder how the numbering system left any room for weekends. Well, it didn't. There weren't formal days of 'non-work' apart from festivals and when you worked depended on what you did. For many people, if they didn't work they didn't eat. Other wealthier farmers or business people would be able to choose what they did and when. At certain times there was more to do, particularly in seasonal work like farming.

In Athens pretty much every day was a work day except when they held religious festivals. Athenians spent about 60 days in festivals every year, and probably about another 20 days were other specified non-work days for those taking part: citizens, women of Attica, and in some cases *metics*. Slaves were mostly excluded.

With the current two-day weekend, modern folks get about 20 extra days off each year compared with the ancient Greeks – but then again, they also had thousands of slaves to do a lot of the work for them!

The various calendars were mapped against each other, and on many occasions people must have needed to be told what day it was! The public slaves, or *demosioi* (see Chapter 14), were put in charge of keeping dates and records straight.

Working from dawn till dusk

The average Athenian day began at dawn, or just before, and carried on until last light (probably an average of about 15 hours). Because most jobs and activities required light, they usually ceased by the evening, when it was time for eating, drinking, and socialising – if you were male. See the later sections for more on these good-time activities.

However, like keeping track of the specific day, telling the time in ancient Greece was tricky. The Greeks only really worked on the basis of the hour rather than minutes. The two main methods were:

  ✔ **Sundial:** The Greeks found out about the sundial from Babylon in Persia where the device was developed, and first started using their own less refined versions in the sixth century BC. The Greek instruments weren't terribly accurate until the third century BC when Hellenistic scholars (see Chapter 12) worked out the mathematic formula that made sundials work properly.

> ✔ **Water-clock:** At night and when no sunlight was available, some people
> turned to crude water-clocks that used the flow of water as a timing
> device. Again, these devices weren't very accurate, and the Hellenistic
> scholar, Ctesibius of Alexandria, refined the mechanism in the third
> century BC.

Greeks referred to time by using dawn, midday, and dusk as reference points
and then adding hours, such as 'in the third hour after dawn'.

After you got up in the morning, what you actually did for the rest of the
day was pretty dependent on who you were. Ancient Athens didn't include a
wide range of occupations: farmer, artisan, labourer, or slave were the most
common. For these people, most days were very similar and very hard.

More interesting are the lives of those people who were wealthy enough to
be able to afford not to work every day. For them life in the city – particularly
Athens – held other attractions like the *ekklesia* (see Chapter 7), the jury-
courts, the gymnasium, and the theatre (see Chapter 16). The pleasures of
wine, women, and song were also popular as the later section
'Acknowledging the oldest profession' explains.

Managing Your Money

Just like today, ancient Greeks had to pay to run a household and to buy
products at the market, and the Greeks were the first people in the
Mediterranean to introduce the actual concept of money.

Money started off as a measure for assessing how rich in possessions people
were. By 800 BC the Greeks had introduced small wooden sticks called *obeloi*,
meaning 'spits'. These sticks were a measure of an amount of wealth, like a
modern-day cheque or a note.

Within a couple of hundred years, the Greeks moved on to using actual coins
of which the main basic unit of currency was known as the *obol*. Greek coins,
as shown in Figure 15-1, were made from gold, silver, or copper alloy. Their
weight determined the value of the coins so this was closely regulated by
officials appointed by the governing council. This caused a new trade to
develop, that of the money changer who would swap coins for a hefty com-
mission when you visited a city.

Coins were illustrated with an image on each side that indicated where they
came from. Most often the coin represented a god or local deity. Demeter was
very popular because she was the goddess of crops and fertility, and she
was often represented by an ear of barley. (Refer to Chapter 13 for more on
Demeter.)

Figure 15-1:
Example of
Greek coins.

Dining and Delighting

Some of the first written descriptions of meals in Greek literature appear in Homer's *The Iliad* and *The Odyssey*. Both poems feature multiple scenes that involve a sacrifice and a subsequent meal. The description is repeated whenever the heroes make a sacrifice and then sit down to a meal. In *The Odyssey* it's often when Odysseus and his men set down their ships on an island – think of them doing this on the beach!

> *Once they'd prayed, slaughtered and skinned the cattle, they cut the thighbones out and then wrapped them round in fat. . . once they'd burned the bones and tasted the organs they hacked the rest into pieces, piercing them with spits.*

That's right – Odysseus and his men were making beef shish kebabs!

The people of ancient Athens loved to eat, and in the fifth century BC, when Athens was a rich and successful port, a range of food was readily available. In this section, I look at what everyone ate – from basic everyday foods to the splendid feasts that took place as part of a symposium.

Putting your money where your mouth is

One of the more remarkable stories about the ancient Athenians was that they carried their small change in their mouths. Because people mostly wore clothes without pockets, your mouth was seen as a way of keeping your money safe and out of the reach of thieves. This practice gives a good guide as to how small Greek coins were. You had to be careful though – if you swallowed at the wrong time, you had to wait a day or so until you got your change!

Enjoying a simple meal

Depending on who you were in ancient Athens, most meals were pretty basic. As I write in Chapter 13, the staple of the Greek diet was cereal crops like barley and wheat. That meant that most meals involved bread in combination with other things. The Greeks described anything that was eaten with bread (perhaps cheese, honey, or another accompaniment such as being dipped in spiced wine) as *opson*.

A breakfast snack may be just some bread dipped in olive oil. A more sub-stantial meal usually included beans, peas, lentils, or chick-peas – again with bread. A typical midday meal included honey or cheese as the *opson* – rather like a Ploughman's lunch. A huge variety of cheeses were available, the most traditional being goats 'feta' cheese but, like wine, regions had their own specialities.The ancient Greeks kept lunch simple because work continued in the afternoon.

The big meal of the day was in the evening after work. At this meal a greater variety of food was available (especially at more formal meals like a sympo-sium – see the later section 'Sipping at a symposium'). Fish was usually on the menu. Beef, pork, and even poultry were less popular and eaten less often – people usually ate meat after sacrifices and saw it as something of a luxury food.

Favouring fish

The Athenians loved fish. The Greek word *osophegos* meant 'fish eater'. As I mention in Chapter 13, fish were quite difficult to catch in the ancient Mediterranean because the fishermen lacked modern deep sea fishing techniques. As a result, fish were highly sought after.

Greek literature is full of references to fish and where different specialities came from. Eels from Boeotia and dog-fish from Rhodes are quoted as being real delicacies. If you visit Athens today, you still find a large number of fish restaurants offering these delicacies!

In addition to fresh fish, pickled fish and fish sauce were highly prized delicacies. Often fish was used to flavour other foods, and the most expensive type of sauce, which later became known as *garum,* was popular throughout the Greek and then Roman world.

Hedylos was a Hellenistic poet from Samos who wrote mainly about food and drink. In the following poem, he describes the excitement over a special fish dinner. He also references the myth about Zeus turning himself into a shower of gold so that he could fit through the keyhole and have sex with Danae whose father had locked her away!

> *Our prize fish is done! Now jam the door-pin in Proteus! Agis the fancier of fishes might come in. He'll be fire and water, anything he wants. So lock it up . . . but maybe he'll arrive turned into Zeus and shower gold upon this Danae of a dish!*

Sampling side orders

The ancient Greek diet wasn't all just bread and fish. Some of the feasts put together for expensive formal dinners included all kinds of ingredients. A lot of vegetables supplemented main courses but people didn't usually eat veggies on their own. Vegetarians did exist but they were thought of as unusual people.

The most popular veggies were onions, turnips, leeks, and celery. (The potato hadn't been discovered yet.) Fruit was available, but mostly only grapes, apples, and figs. The Greeks didn't have bananas or citrus fruits, and they didn't have tomatoes either.

Cooking up a storm

Although not as advanced as today, the Greeks did use some cooking techniques. Baking was common practice, with bread being a staple part of the diet. Cooks usually boiled vegetables and beans, and heated other foods on a brazier (small portable stove), which was hot, sweaty work. In good weather cooking would be done outside and the food then taken in to eat.

Cooking skill was all about how a cook used sauces and spices to flavour the food. People whom the Greeks considered knowledgeable about food and cooking were those who understood the process of flavouring rather than cooking itself. Cooks often used wine to enhance the flavour of a dish, along with olive oil and the stock produced from cooking meat and fish. Marinating was a secret technique for boosting the flavour of ordinary ingredients.

Celebrity chefs

The life of a cook in ancient Greece was varied. Many cooks worked like caterers for hire to individual households, but some richer Greeks had their own cooks who were part of their domestic staff.

Some people even wrote about food and cooking. Fragments of two of the most famous cookbooks – *Gastronomy* by Archestratus and *The Art of Cookery* by Heracleides of Syracuse – still exist.

Shopping for ingredients

Most Athenians did their food shopping in the market that was located in the centre of the city. The farmers of Attica held monthly markets, bringing their wares to the city and selling them to the market traders.

Markets in Athens and elsewhere were made up of individual tables (*trapezai*) and booths rather than actual shops. The closest thing to shops were the workshops of specific artisans like potters or smiths who also did business there.

Sometimes, Athenians would travel a good distance to buy goods direct from the supplier. Fish lovers often made the half a day's walk to Piraeus to buy fresh fish from the fishing boats.

Drinking It Up

The most important accompaniment to food was drink, and drinking was a big part of Greek life. Wine was, of course, the main drink (see Chapter 13 for more on wine and viticulture), although the Greeks knew about beer because people drank it in Egypt, Syria, and the east.

Greeks drank a lot of wine, but they mixed it with water. The Macedonians were considered vulgar because they drank their wine without mixing it. The wine wasn't as alcoholic as modern wine, but ancient Greeks still got drunk and sometimes drank with the intention of doing so.

Imbibing publically – and privately

The most famous drinking sessions took place at symposiums (see the following section 'Sipping at a symposium'), but plenty of other places existed where you could sink a few. The most popular spot was a tavern or *kapeleion*.

These establishments were pretty basic places that sold only wine and their managers were called *kapeloi* – men who ran the business, mixed the wine, and dealt with any troublemakers, much like modern pub landlords.

The Greeks had an interesting take on drunkenness. In private (such as in the symposium), intoxication was entirely permissible and even encouraged. In fact, drunkenness formed a large part of many religious festivals (see Chapter 22). Public drunkenness, however, was regarded as uncouth and unpleasant.

Sipping at a symposium

Simply put, a *symposium* was a posh drinking party for men only with a bit of philosophical chat and some flute girls. Women did meet with each other but it was very rare that they attended a symposium. The only women usually present were the flute girls and possibly prostitutes. Held in the *andron* of a private household (see Chapter 14), a symposium was a two-stage evening:

- ✔ The first stage was the *deipnon*, or formal dinner.
- ✔ The following stage was the *symposion*, or session of drinking together.

Usually, a symposium involved 14 to 30 guests who drank from special wine cups, or *craters* as they were known (see Chapter 17 for more on Greek pottery). During a *symposion*, guests discussed philosophical issues. Professional performers such as poets, singers, and actors entertained the guests, and slave boys and sometimes expensive courtesans known as *hetairai* (see the section 'Acknowledging the oldest profession') attended to guests's every need.

The evening ended with a torch-lit procession through the streets known as *komos*, to show the bonding within the group that had taken place.

In one of his poems Hedylos gives a flavour of the *symposion* mood:

> Let's drink up: with wine, what original, what nuanced, what sweet fancy speech I might hit on! Soak me with a jug of Chian, and say, 'Have fun Hedylos.' For I hate wasting time unless I'm high.

Hedylos's boisterous words are probably a good guide to the quality of the philosophical discussion after a few *craters* of wine!

Pondering Sex and the Ancient Greeks

The concepts of love and sex were very different from that of marriage. As I mention in Chapter 14, Greek men commonly had affairs with other women –

and in some cases, younger boys (see the later section 'Contemplating homosexuality').

More often than not, the heterosexual affairs were with prostitutes or other sex workers, and sometimes these relationships were considered love affairs.

Love, sex, and wine were all linked together in the Greek mind. The following poem by Asklepiades from Samos is very evocative in its description of wine and unhappy love.

> *Wine is love's test. Nicagoras told us he had no lover, but the toasts betrayed him. His tears, yes and unhappy eyes, the tight wreath on his bent head slips out of place.*

Acknowledging the oldest profession

Prostitution was legal in Athens. Indeed, it was a thriving business that actually paid tax to the city treasury. The women involved were very unlikely to be Athenian and were most often from Asia Minor.

Although *prostitutes* is the general term used to describe these women, three distinct classes existed:

- ✔ *Pallakai* **(concubines):** These women were 'permanently' attached to a male and may even have lived in his household. Often men set up their *pallakai* in separate houses and apartments within the city and visited them regularly. These women were more like mistresses than prostitutes, although they did receive money and gifts.

- ✔ *Hetairai* **(courtesans):** These ladies were very expensive and exclusive, handpicking their clients. Often highly educated, *hetairai* had more in common with a Japanese geisha than other classes of prostitute. They were employed for their intelligence and conversation as much as their sexual attractiveness.

- ✔ *Pornai* **(prostitutes):** This term covered all types of prostitute from those who worked in brothels to more expensive girls for hire. They include the *aulos* or 'flute girls' who were invited to the *symposia*. The category also included some male prostitutes, although these were unusual.

Contemplating homosexuality

The Greeks regarded homosexuality as nothing unusual. If a man found women attractive, then there was nothing surprising about the fact that he found adolescent boys attractive also and chose to actively pursue them.

Athens does Pericles a favour

A public association with *pallakai* or *hetairai* was seen as nothing unusual in ancient Athens. Pericles, the famous Athenian politician, even went as far as divorcing his Athenian wife so that he could live permanently with a *hetaira* from Miletus called Aspasia. They had a son who couldn't receive citizen rights under Athenian law. However, when Pericles's two sons from his first marriage died of the plague in 430 BC, the *ekklesia* voted that his son with Aspasia be made a full citizen.

The normal situation was that an older man (the *erastes* meaning 'lover') pursued the affections of a younger boy (the *eromenos*, or 'beloved').

The most common place where such liaisons took place was the *palaestra* at the gymnasium where older men watched the young boys exercising. This being the case, only leisured aristocrats with time on their hands probably really engaged in homosexual affairs.

This short poem by Phanias describes his love for a boy who has grown slightly too old to be considered an *eromenos*, and it shows how quickly these relationships were considered to be finished.

> *By Themis and the wine that made me tipsy, your love won't last much longer Pamphilus. Already there's hair on your thigh, down on your cheeks and another lust ahead. But a little of the old spark's still there, so don't be stingy – opportunity is love's friend.*

That's not to say that the Greeks didn't mock homosexuality – the plays of Aristophanes are full of jokes. But their scorn was specifically reserved for men who carried on relationships with each other into middle age and those who showed any sign of effeminacy. Finding young boys attractive was entirely acceptable – a mature man allowing himself to be treated like a woman was not.

Love and sex between two women probably happened regularly in ancient Greece but it was never public and there's very little evidence of it. The most famous association is with the poet Sappho (seventh century BC) who came from the island of Lesbos (giving rise to the term 'lesbian'). Sappho wrote beautiful lyric poems about love and the goddess Aphrodite, many of which could be interpreted as being about both men and women and we know little about her actual life. The Greeks didn't recognise Sappho as being gay; only more modern readers. Sappho's poems are wonderfully evocative of the ancient times she lived in before the Greeks had begun to record their history.

Seeking Medical Assistance

So what did you do if you'd overindulged in food, drink, or sex? Consulting a doctor was relatively easy in ancient Athens, but it was also very expensive – and some of the methods were rather scary.

Doctors were professional people rather like craftsmen or artisans, and as such their methods were equally varied. Doctors travelled throughout Greece, finding work where they could. In big cities like Athens, however, they ran small businesses like a kind of shop and charged high prices.

Turning to the gods

Throughout the whole of Greek history many people believed that anger of the gods caused illness. Many gods had associations with health and wellbeing including Apollo, but the most important of all was Asclepius.

Asclepius was an interesting character who was born a mortal but became a god when he died. As the son of Apollo, he was born with miraculous healing powers, and he travelled far and wide healing the sick. In the end, Asclepius's powers didn't do him much good because, when he tried to resurrect the dead, Zeus killed him with a thunderbolt for trying to act like an immortal! Apollo intervened and Asclepius was made into a god.

Greeks all over the Mediterranean worshipped Asclepius and made offerings to him, hoping to be cured of illness. He had sanctuaries in several places but the most famous was on the island of Cos. Quite an industry built up around the shrine, and people travelled from all over the Mediterranean to visit it. The deal was that if you made an offering to the god Asclepius (such as some money, a piece of art, or the sacrifice of a small animal like a chicken), he may visit you in the night and cure you. And if he didn't? Well you obviously hadn't made a big enough offering!

Some temples offered healing services, but it was unlikely that the priests had any medical training. A large amount of belief was the best that people received.

Meeting the Father of Medicine: Hippocrates

Other people did try to cure illnesses. The most famous and influential of these was a man called Hippocrates of Cos (460–377 BC). His father was a doctor and Hippocrates followed in his footsteps. He eventually left the island of Cos and was in Athens during the Peloponnesian War, where he treated people suffering from the plague.

What made Hippocrates special was that he was one of the first ancient Greeks to argue that illness was caused by natural factors rather than being a punishment from the gods. He was keen on a healthy diet, clean conditions, and the use of herbs and pastes to treat patients. Because of his healthy lifestyle he was rumoured to have lived to be 120 years old – he didn't!

After the Peloponnesian War, Hippocrates returned to Cos and founded his own school of medicine and put together the *Hippocratic Corpus*. This massive book included 60 different essays on good medical practice, including the famous *Hippocratic Oath*.

> *I swear by Apollo Physician and Asclepius and Hygieia and Panaceia and all the gods and goddesses, making them my witnesses, that I will fulfil according to my ability this oath and this covenant.*

The *Hippocratic Oath* was written by Hippocrates as a guide for new doctors about what they should do. It includes promises not to carry out abortions, euthanasia, or any surgery that they haven't trained in, or to have sexual relations with patients. Much of the oath's language and philosophy is very out of date now, but some doctors swear by it even today!

Treating all manner of ills

Most ancient medical treatments involved the use of herbs or spices and some attempted to either cool or heat the body as a way of controlling the illness. Most doctors were keen on the idea of balance in everything and that a lack of it caused illness. So if you were too hot, you needed cooling down, and vice versa.

Surgery was rarely attempted because people knew little about the inner workings of the body. The Greeks considered the examination and dissection of corpses to be sacrilegious, and so opportunities to discover anything further after a patient's passing were slim. For example, most Greeks believed that the heart was in the head and not the body.

For anybody who contracted a serious illness, the chances of recovery were slim. Those injured in battle very often died of their wounds.

Things changed a little when the philosopher Aristotle began his study of the human body (see Chapter 23), but no major advances in medicine occurred until late in the Roman Empire through people like Galen (circa AD 200). The best advice was not to get ill!

Chapter 16

Plays and Pugilism: Enjoying Ancient Greek Entertainment

*W*hen seeking out good times, the ancient Greeks were a contrary bunch. On the one hand, they loved tragic theatre where noble heroes struggled with terrible choices and met with appalling fates. On the other, they loved comic plays chock full of nasty jokes at the expense of some of the audience and ridiculous gags about farting and sex. They also enjoyed hard, gruelling athletics, including an incredibly violent form of boxing where competitors often died.

Even more strangely, the same people enjoyed events that closely connected all these diverse activities. The games and festivals that the Greeks loved combined athletics and theatre – and they considered both endeavours to be equally prestigious.

Theatre and athletics combined a lot of themes: competition, public celebration, honouring the gods, and literature. Entertainment in ancient Greece was for everybody and enjoyed by everybody.

The type of entertainments that I look at in this chapter date from around 600 BC to the end of the Greek era in the first century BC. However, as you'll see, they had roots that went back much further into the past and their influence carries on this day.

Making Art Onstage: Greek Theatre

Going to the theatre in ancient Greece was very different from today's experience of popular long-running shows and entertainment districts with multiple theatres.

Getting in a festive mood

Opportunities to see plays and performances were quite limited in ancient Greece. When productions happened nearly everybody tried to go, because the plays and performances were part of something else, something larger – festivals.

Ancient Greek plays were performed only at certain times of the year, at the same time as specific religious festivals. These plays were massive events that involved the whole community.

The main festivals in Athens were the Lenaia in January and the Great or City Dionysia that was held in March. The dramatic performances were in government-organised competition with each other, and the rivalry was intense. See the later section 'Competing: And the winner is . . .' for more.

Touring the theatre

The key venue for the festivals was the theatre itself. In Athens the main venue was the theatre of Dionysus. The space was large and probably held an audience of about 14,000 people.

The theatre of Dionysus was one of the first permanent theatres built by the Greeks so its design was very influential. The theatre was a major public space located next to the Acropolis. A theatre of Dionysus is still in the same spot now but it's a rebuild of the original carried out by the Romans in the second century AD.

For such an important and well-attended site the actual 'building' was pretty basic. Performances took place in the open air with the audience sitting on very simple benches or sometimes just the bare ground. All the views were excellent and, with the exception of a few special seats at the front that were reserved for *arkhons* and officials involved in the competition, anyone could sit anywhere.

All social classes attended the theatre – much like the Globe Theatre in Elizabethan England where people of all classes met to watch the plays of Shakespeare, Marlowe, and other writers of the day. Entrance was either free or came at a small charge depending upon the nature of the event. It seems quite likely that women attended the theatre but they would have been very much in the minority.

The modern word 'theatre' comes from the Greek word '*theatron*', which means 'viewing place' and refers to the seated area for the audience.

The theatre of Dionysus and other ancient Greek theatres had a roughly semi-circular arrangement. As Figure 16-1 illustrates, theatres included:

- ✔ ***Orchestra***: The large circle at the centre of the theatre was mostly used by the chorus (see the later section 'Dealing with a chorus of disapproval'). The Greeks often referred to it as the 'dancing circle' because the chorus spent most of their time there and their performance was full of movement and dancing compared to that of the main actors.

- ✔ ***Parodoi***: Both the performers and the audience used these two entrances to access the stage and seating areas.

- ✔ ***Skene***: This area was most like a modern stage. Behind the platform stood a long building with a flat roof that was used as both scenery and a place for the actors to change. It was this that was actually called the *skene* although the platform was attached to it.

- ✔ ***Theatron***: These terraces were often just cut into a hill and provided seating for thousands of audience members.

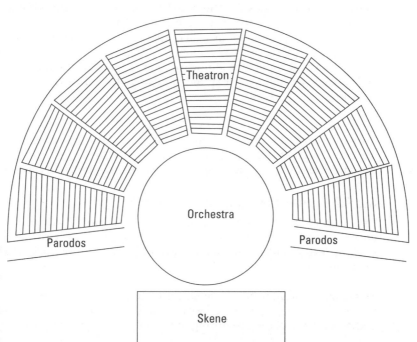

Figure 16-1:
The plan of a typical Greek theatre.

Greek theatres were *not* amphitheatres! The word *amphi* means 'on both sides', like in *amphora*, which was a double-handled jar. Amphitheatres were, therefore, double theatre spaces, making a full circle. Amphitheatres were mostly built during the Roman period (roughly 300 BC to 330 AD) and used for gladiatorial games. A good example is the Colosseum in Rome, which was originally called the Flavian Amphitheatre.

Most of the larger cities would have had a permanent theatre but smaller towns would erect a temporary structure for when performances were put on. Historians have no direct evidence that the theatres were used for other events (when plays weren't on) but given their size it seems likely that they may have been used as meeting places.

Acting up

Acting was a very specific skill in ancient Greece – and an activity that was exclusively male. Women never appeared on stage and men played all the female parts. As a result, the Greeks considered actors to be unusual in that they allowed themselves to appear like women.

Being seen and heard

The acoustics in ancient Greek theatres were tremendous. Members of the audience at the back of the theatre were able to hear every word spoken by the actors onstage, despite the fact that they were separated by around 20 metres across the orchestra and a further 80 metres to the back of the *theatron*. It required tremendous skill on the part of the actors to be audible for the length of a play (probably about 90 minutes). I've been to many Greek theatres and the acoustics still work today – you can stand in the *orchestra* and speak in a relatively clear and loud voice to be heard at the very back. Amazing!

The view was different. With no television projection technology, all the audience saw were the actors in front of the *skene* or in the orchestra. These sight limitations meant that the acting had to be very physical and not particularly realistic. Gestures were most likely large, exaggerated, and obvious.

Getting into costume and wearing masks

To accommodate the large venues, the Greek actors relied on very large costumes and masks. Masks were made of wood, brightly painted with big, obvious features meant to convey two things: the age of the character and their mood.

Masks and costumes helped male actors to play female roles and enabled the actors to swap roles if necessary. These elements minimised subtle and naturalistic acting, requiring the actors to use expansive gestures and elaborate vocalisations to get their points across to the audience. (It's no coincidence that characters in Greek plays are usually introduced and briefly described in the dialogue – it helped the audience even back then to identify who had just appeared on stage!)

Competing: And the winner is . . .

During a festival, all the plays were in competition with each other for the overall prize. First, second, and third prize were awarded to the plays and the winning poets.

The system of judging was rather strange. City officials appointed ten judges from the citizen body and they held a secret ballot at the end of the day's performances. They'd each drop a pebble into a jar, the colour of which corresponded to the poet who they'd chosen. Of these ten votes only the first five were drawn out and counted. It must have led to some very controversial results, although there are no recorded cases of anybody appealing!

As far as we know there were no material prizes; only the honour of winning. However, the winning poets could expect to be asked to perform some of their work at expensive *symposia* (refer to Chapter 15) following a victory so at the very least they'd get some decent dinners out it and would more than likely get paid as well!

The playwrights (the Greeks referred to them as 'poets') submitted their plays to the *arkhons* (see Chapter 7), who then selected three pieces for each competition. During the fifth century BC many poets wrote numerous plays, and competition was fierce. For example, out of the 92 plays written by the great dramatist Euripides, only six won first prize at a festival (although as all the works were submitted in groups of three it means that 6 out of 30 won rather than 6 out of 90). Once every five submissions!

Each poet in the competition was assigned a wealthy citizen, known as a *khoregos*, who paid for the production, including the actors, dancers, and all other expenses. Serving as the patron of a play was considered to be an extremely prestigious honour.

The poet was also assigned by lot his lead actor, whom the Greeks referred to as the *protagonist*. The poet directed the play himself.

At each festival, a poet typically presented three tragic plays and a *satyr play* – a short, comic version of a myth that provided some light relief at the end of the day. The plays weren't necessarily trilogies, although they frequently had similar themes. The audience sat through the whole offering in one day – it probably took the best part of six hours!

The vast majority of plays were produced only once because the poets didn't want to enter them twice for a festival. More popular plays were taken on tour to small rural festivals or sometimes revived many years later. For example, Alexander the Great (see Chapters 10 and 11) had a love of tragedy and regularly asked for his favourites to be performed at festivals, sometimes more than 100 years after these works were first produced.

The plays themselves took two forms: tragedy and comedy. The forms were very different but equally respected.

Delving into tragedy: Tears and fate

Tragedy was the earliest form of Greek theatre. It was probably invented in Athens in as early as 550 BC, growing out of the traditional religious hymns that the Greeks sung at festivals. These hymns known as *dithyramb* were based on a mythological and religious theme and sung solo. Over time a second voice joined the hymn, turning it into a dialogue that eventually became a play. The earliest play that survives is *The Persians* by Aeschylus, which was produced in 472 BC.

The fifth century BC was when tragedy took the form students and scholars still study today. This period is also the time when the three great tragic poets were at work:

- ✔ **Aeschylus (525–456 BC):** Wrote 80 plays of which 7 survive
- ✔ **Euripides (485–406 BC):** Wrote 92 plays of which 19 survive
- ✔ **Sophocles (496–406 BC):** Wrote 120 plays of which 7 survive

The subjects of tragic plays were very familiar to audiences because the stories were nearly all based on Greek myths. This meant that the audience was almost certain to know how a play ended before it even began. For the Greeks, the ideas of plot and suspense weren't very important. Tragic poets were much more concerned about the portrayal of the characters and the ideas that the plays were exploring. It isn't that unusual an idea to us now. Everyone knows how films like *Titanic* are going to end and they're still hugely popular. Theatre performances of *Hamlet* or *Macbeth* end in the same way – but the way that they're performed and interpreted is what the audience finds interesting.

The ancient Greeks didn't really have history as such (see Chapter 21). Nor did they have a religion that set out an ethical code of behaviour (see Chapter 22). Therefore, the myths that had existed for generations filled gaps in their knowledge and beliefs. In the tragic plays, the mythological characters explored ethical and moral issues that were relevant to the way people led their lives, providing something that history and religion didn't.

Tragedy: The Greatest Hits

Quite a few Greek tragedies still survive. Here's a rough guide to some of the best to investigate.

Play	Poet	Plot
Agamemnon	Aeschylus	Agamemnon returns home from the Trojan war and is murdered by his wife Clytemnestra and her lover Aegisthus. Orestes (Agamemnon's exiled son) then returns home and kills his father's murderers before being haunted with guilt. These plays, known as the *Oresteia*, are the only existing complete trilogy of plays.
The Libation Bearers		
The Eumenides		
Oedipus	Sophocles	The classic tragedy. See the later sidebar 'Oedipus: A complex case'.
Antigone		Oedipus's daughter strives for the right to bury her brother who's been killed fighting against their home city.
Philoctetes		Philoctetes, hero in exile, holds the famous bow of Heracles that the Greeks need to win the war in Troy. Odysseus is sent to take it from him at any cost.
Ajax		The great Greek hero Ajax is furious at being denied the armour of the dead Achilles and his anger drives him to the brink of madness.
Medea	Euripides	Cruelly spurned by the Greek hero Jason, who she helped to steal the Golden Fleece, Medea plots to avenge herself.
Trojan Women		The fate of the wives and mothers of Troy's fallen warriors is laid bare in this harrowing play.
The Bacchae		Cadmus, the king of Thebes, offends the god Dionysus and pays a terrible price at the hands of his followers.

Meeting a typical tragic hero

The main method for exploring ethical and moral issues was the role of the *tragic hero*. During the plays, tragic heroes typically underwent philosophical journeys that ended with suffering great loss and often death. Usually, the journeys are the result of mistakes or transgressions that the characters commit. Very often, the heroes are said to have a fatal or tragic flaw.

This play contains strong, bloody violence

The nature of Greek tragedy usually means that hugely unpleasant things took place: murder, suicide, mutilation, and incest, just to start with. However, all these things happened offstage (and are often vividly described by a servant or messenger who unwittingly witnesses the gruesome event) because the idea of them was thought to be terrible enough without enacting the cruel deeds.

As a result, the heroes – and the audience – know more about themselves and recognise their faults and mistakes. The Greeks referred to the process as *pathos* (suffering), *mathos* (understanding), or *anagnorisis* (recognition).

Women were often the lead characters in the plays. Characters such as Medea, Hecuba, Antigone, Clytemnestra, and Electra dominate the plays they appear in and are fascinating multi-layered characters. However, they would have all been played by men!

Dealing with a chorus of disapproval

The chorus delivers most of the commentary on the action in a tragic play. In ancient Greece, these performers generally stayed in the orchestra and commented on the things that the other characters were doing, sometimes providing the back story too. Very often the chorus is in opposition to the main character and his or her actions. Most interactions between the chorus and main actors involved the chorus leader who was the only person that spoke directly to those on the *skene*.

We don't have any evidence of the sort of music played, because none of it has survived. However, if you read a good translation of one of the plays you can see how lyrical the words are and how easily they could be chanted rather than spoken.

Aristotle wrote a book called *The Art of Poetry.* Here he sums up what good tragedy should do:

> *The tragic fear and pity may be aroused by the Spectacle [the onstage action], but they may also be aroused by the very structure and incidents of the play – which is the better way and shows the better poet.*

The gods help out at last!

In many plays a resolution is found to the terrible problems of its human characters by the appearance of one or more of the Olympian gods (which I describe in Chapter 19). Often the gods do something to tie up loose ends that humans could never do. This might seem like a bit of a cop-out but remember that the ideas rather than the plot are the important bit!

Oedipus: A complex case

Probably the most famous Greek tragedy is *Oedipus Tyrannus* (also known as *Oedipus Rex* or *Oedipus the King*) by Sophocles. Aristotle thought the play was the greatest tragedy ever written.

The story of Oedipus, the king of Thebes, goes as follows:

- Prior to the beginning of the play, Oedipus as a young man fled Thebes after a prophecy said that he would murder his father and marry his mother. Eventually, Oedipus returned to Thebes, defeated the fearsome Sphinx, married the widowed queen Jocasta, and became king as his reward.

- As the play opens, Thebes is undergoing a terrible plague. The oracle at Delphi (see Chapter 21) tells Oedipus that he has to punish the man who murdered the previous king Laius. Oedipus determines to do so despite the warnings of various people.

(During these conversations, Oedipus finds out that Laius and Jocasta had a child who was left to be exposed – see Chapter 15 – but was eventually adopted by others.)

- Eventually, Oedipus discovers that he in fact murdered Laius in a roadside argument – and worse, that Laius was his father and the queen, Jocasta, his mother. Grief-stricken, Oedipus blinds himself and says the following famous words:

Ah God, ah God: all come true and be known! Let this be the last time that I see the light of day. Cursed in my parents, cursed in my marriage, cursed in the blood I have shed!

Oedipus Tyrannus proves that human beings cannot escape who they are and that fate is unavoidable. Oedipus's fatal flaw is his pride and arrogance that blinds him to the warnings of others to stop his search before he uncovers the tragic truth.

The appearance of the gods like this gave rise to the expression '*deus ex machina*', Latin for 'god out of a machine' because when the gods appeared they were lowered down on a cradle at the back of the *skene*. The expression is now used to describe any situation where something unlikely happens to sort out a plot!

Considering comedy: Sex and satire

Greek comedy was very different to tragedy (see the preceding section 'Delving into tragedy: Tears and fate') but followed rules in a similar way.

- Comic plays were entered in festival competitions and paid for by a wealthy *khoregos*.
- Ideas were very important in comedy, but spectacle was too. The chorus usually wore impressive costumes and featured loud singing and intricate dancing.

✔ Comic plots are absurd. By mixing fantasy with elements of real life, the Greek comic poets virtually invented satire, the genre that involves poking fun at the establishment and criticising it using comedy. For example, in the surviving Greek comedies, men fly away to live in a land run by birds (*The Birds*), a sausage seller becomes the chief politician in Athens (*Acharnians*), and Euripides and Aeschylus have an imaginary poetry competition in Hades (*The Frogs*).

Aristophanes: Old comic genius

The most famous of Greek comic poets is Aristophanes (447–385 BC) who had an amazingly successful career and won many prizes. Quite a number of his plays still survive today.

The plays are coarse and elaborate fantasies that deal with contemporary issues and very often mock the decisions of Athenian politicians. For example:

✔ In *Lysistrata*, the women of Athens refuse to have sex with their husbands until they stop the Peloponnesian War. (This strategy seems about the only thing Athens didn't try during this long war with neighbouring Sparta; see Chapter 8.)

✔ The Athenian demagogue Kleon (see Chapter 8) tried to prosecute Aristophanes for slandering Athens in his play *Babylonians* in 425 BC. Kleon was unsuccessful, and Aristophanes took his revenge by mercilessly mocking Kleon in his next four plays. Kleon would have been in the audience for every one of them (Chapter 25 has more on this and Kleon)!

The comedies of Aristophanes had a very specific structure with key elements:

✔ The entry of the chorus (*parodos*) was always very spectacular with the actors dancing and singing while wearing extremely elaborate costumes.

✔ The following *agon* was the real meat of the play. Two sides debated issues through songs and speeches.

✔ The final key element was the *parabasis* where the chorus again took centre stage. The chorus leader directly addressed the audience and presented a long speech about the 'big issue' of the play. (The poet also usually left some room for some pleading to the judges to award him victory!)

Following is an excerpt from the *parabasis* in Aristophanes's *Wasps*, a satire on the Athenian jury-courts (see Chapter 7). The chorus leader complains that all the people that collect their jury pay don't contribute to the war effort.

It makes us wild to think that those who've never raised a hand, or risked a single blister to defend their native land can draw their pay with all the rest: I think that the rule should be, that if you haven't got a sting you get no jury fee!

Aristophanes included a lot of sharp political satire, but he also appealed to those looking for cheap laughs. His plays are full of sexual innuendo and jokes at the expense of members of the audience. Some real-world Athenians are mocked for being effeminate, people's wives are slandered, and foreigners are usually portrayed with ludicrous comic accents.

Audiences at a comedy knew what they were coming to see and, in fact, expected to see familiar elements in place. Some characters appear again and again in the plays, in particular the crafty slave. Aristophanes even joked with the audience about this repetition. At the beginning of his play *Frogs*, the slave Xanthias asks his master, 'What about one of the old gags, sir? I can usually get a laugh with those.'

The comedy of Aristophanes provided something for everybody: outrageous spectacle, absurd plots, knowing satire, and jokes about Heracles farting after too much pea soup. What more could you ask for?

Menander: 'Alternative' comedy

Greek comedy didn't stop with the death of Aristophanes but it did change. The foremost comic poet after Aristophanes was Menander (341–291 BC). Menander's comedies dropped much of the satire that was Aristophanes's main thrust and instead were about the lives of ordinary Athenians with plots based around mistaken identity and overheard conversations. The play that survives in full is *Dyskolos*, a witty comedy about a cantankerous old man.

Extending to today: The influence of Greek theatre

The plays that the ancient Greeks enjoyed still have tremendous impact on today's stage entertainment – as well as books, television, and film.

William Shakespeare was well aware of the tragic poets and their impact on what he wrote. The mental crises and unwise actions of characters like Hamlet and Macbeth would have been very recognisable to Aeschylus, Sophocles, and Euripides.

Ancient Greek comedy has stood the test of time too. The broad playing to the audience by the actors and stock characters to be found in Aristophanes's plays carried on through the Roman theatre and the *commedia del arte* plays that were popular during the Renaissance. And satire has become an established comic tradition, showcased every day on late-night comedy shows.

Getting Physical: Athletics and the Olympic Games

Athletics was big news in ancient Greece. Physical training for boys and young men was seen as vital for their personal wellbeing and education (see Chapter 14). And as most Greek cities defended themselves with citizen militias, the bodies of the male citizens had to be kept fighting fit.

For this reason many cities, including Athens, provided a *gymnasion* (exercise area) at public expense so that exercise was available to all male citizens and *metics*. Many other exercise areas were available in the city, including the popular *palaestra*, or wrestling ground.

The *palaestra* were like private gyms where richer citizens met and exercised. They also had other uses: Older Greek men pursued the affections of younger boys and paid court to them (see Chapter 15) and important social meetings often took place, in which Greeks made political and business deals.

Working out at the gym

The modern word *gymnasium* comes from the Greek *gymnasia*. This word is derived from *gumnoi*, which means 'completely naked', because in Greece all exercise was carried out in the nude.

Unsurprisingly, only men attended the *gymnasia*. To the Greeks, athletics was hugely competitive; the word *athlon* itself means 'prize'. Whatever event you were taking part in, it was vital that you did everything for victory.

The activities at the gymnasium were fairly standard (see the later section 'The Olympic schedule') and included running, chariot-racing, boxing, wrestling, and some field events such as throwing. All these activities produced physical abilities that were very useful for fighting in wars.

The Greeks saw athletic achievement as a fitting subject for poetry, and the well-regarded poet Pindar of Boeotia (518–438 BC) wrote a huge amount about it. The following excerpt comes from a poem celebrating the achievement of a man called Timodemus in the *pankration* (an incredibly tough fighting sport) at the Nemean Games in 485 BC. Pindar compares the start of Timodemus's athletic career with the beginning of an epic poem.

Just as the women of Homer, the singers of woven verses, most often begin with Zeus as their prelude, so this man has received a first down-payment of victory in the sacred games by winning in the grove of Nemean Zeus.

The spirit of competition was alive throughout the ancient Greek world, and regular international events were held. Most cities held their own games but the more important international events were the Pythian, Nemean, and Isthmian Games.

Bigger than all these, however, were the games at Olympia – the Olympic Games.

Attending the original Olympic Games

The Olympic Games were hugely influential. They are, arguably, the longest lasting single event from the ancient world. Every four years between 776 BC and AD 395 the greatest athletes in the Mediterranean (and sometimes beyond) gathered together to compete at the town of Olympia.

Like the dramatic festivals (see the earlier section 'Getting into a festive mood'), the games were held in honour of a god – in this case Zeus (see Chapter 20). The games brought huge fortune and fame to Olympia. The town eventually constructed a vast complex of temples, stadiums, and other buildings, the ruins of which you can still visit today (see Chapter 18). Thousands of people would have flocked to Olympia. They were probably wealthy because they needed to be able to afford to be away from work for a lengthy period of time.

 The Greeks were so proud of the Olympic Games that they went as far as using them as a method of historical dating. Records often refer to events as having taken place in 'the year of the 28th Olympiad' rather than in a specific year.

The Olympic schedule

The events at the Olympics were fairly standard from the first games to the last. Although the Greeks added some events over time, the main ones were as follows:

- ✔ **Boxing:** This sport was similar to modern boxing but contestants didn't wear gloves and instead fought with leather strapping on their hands. It was fought until a knockout with no rounds – just one long single bout.

- ✔ **Discus:** This event was a little like the modern shot put because the ancient Greeks used flat, round stones that weighed about 4 kilograms. Whoever threw furthest won.

✔ **Equestrian:** The Olympics also featured some horse-racing events. The chariot races and horse races were most popular, but there was also a mule-cart race that featured very small carts. The Sicilian Greeks probably introduced the mule-cart race (they were good at it because of mining!), but the event wasn't popular and the Greeks dropped it after 14 games.

✔ **Javelin:** This category was an obvious test for a war-related skill, although the athletes used lighter javelins that were designed to travel a long distance rather than penetrate armour. Some sources claim that athletes regularly achieved throws of more than 90 metres.

✔ **Long jump:** This event was much harder than the modern version. Athletes jumped from a standing start holding weights!

✔ **Pankration:** This event was incredibly tough and violent and involved a fight in which any style was allowed. Only two things were barred: biting and eye-gouging. The fights were amazingly fierce, and many participants died.

✔ **Pentathlon:** This event involved the discus, javelin, long jump, running, and wrestling. It was really hard work, but if somebody won the first three events, the authorities cancelled the other two because nobody else could win.

✔ **Running:** Like the modern Olympics, running events were numerous in the original games and included:

- The *stadion,* which was the length of the stadium (about 200 metres)

- The *diaulos,* or 'there and back again', which involved running the length of the stadium and back

- The *dolichos,* which was a full 12 laps of the stadium

- One additional (and odd) foot-race which involved running the standard *stadion* sprint while wearing armour (refer to Chapter 5 for what this armour would have been like).

✔ **Wrestling:** Very different from the WWF today! Wrestling was very formal. The winner was whoever forced his opponent's back, hips, or shoulders to the ground. The successful fighter was known as the *triakter* or 'trebler' because you needed to cause three falls to win the contest.

Jam-packed competition

The Olympic Games themselves took place over only five days with an opening and closing ceremony. Each day featured a different group of events. For example, all the fighting disciplines took place on the fourth day. The final day saw the procession of all the victors to the Temple of Zeus, where they were crowned with wreaths of wild olives and showered with leaves.

Girls just wanna have fun!

Although women were excluded from the *gymnasia* in cities, they did partake in athletics and even had their own festival at the Olympic Games – The Heraea, in honour of Hera, the wife of Zeus (see Chapter 20).

The Heraea featured only one event, a foot race that was 25 metres shorter than the male *stadion*. It seems strange to cut it short in this way but it emphasises the tendency of the Greeks to put limits on opportunities for female achievement.

The inequalities didn't stop there either. Married women were banned from attending the games, in case all the naked flesh tempted them to stray! Curiously, young virgin girls were allowed to attend – perhaps so they could check out future husbands.

The laurel crown was all that the victors won – that and the eternal fame of being an Olympic victor. Sponsors of other non-Olympic events offered material and financial prizes, but nothing was prized as highly as an Olympic victory – rather like an Olympic gold medal today.

Cheats never prosper

Although the fame for winning in the Olympics was unsurpassed, the shame at being caught cheating was equally intense. The games were policed by a group of soldiers called the *alytai*, who publicly flogged anybody caught cheating. Additionally, the names of the winners were inscribed on stone tablets around the Olympic stadium, and so were the names of cheats.

Heralding the new Olympics

The ancient Olympics probably came to an end in around AD 390, when the Byzantine emperor, who was a Christian, banned all pagan festivals. Several attempts were made to revive the games, and athletics carried on elsewhere throughout the region. However, the next official Olympics held in Athens wasn't until 1896. The instigator was a French nobleman called Baron Pierre de Coubertin.

One of the main features and symbols of the Olympics nowadays is the torch and the journey that it goes on to arrive at the games from the last venue to the next (in 2008, Athens to Beijing). Most people think that this is an ancient tradition, but it isn't! The torch was only used in the ancient Olympics as a baton on a six-horse relay race called the *lampadedromia* that took place as part of the opening ceremony. De Coubertin adopted the torch because he thought it was appropriate for the revival of an ancient tradition. Remember that trivia when you're watching the next Olympic opening ceremony!

The greatest Olympian: Milo of Croton

The ancient Olympics featured many great champions, but the greatest of them all was probably Milo of Croton. A great wrestler, he won at five successive Olympic Games (a 20-year period) as well as another 25 at the other festivals.

Milo favoured a method of training that involved carrying around a four-year-old cow for a number of months to build up his shoulder muscles. Apparently, he then ate the animal – in one sitting. Another story says that Milo downed three big jars of wine (about 9 litres!) for a bet.

Unfortunately, Milo died when he attempted to split open a tree trunk with his bare hands and got them stuck. He was trapped there and in the night wild animals attacked and ate him. Whether these stories are true or not, Milo was a phenomenal Olympian and probably the greatest of all time.

Chapter 17

Depicting Men, Women, and Gods in Art

*W*hat is art? It's an eternal question that nobody can ever really answer. Today, art comes in many different forms – painting, sculpture, photography, printing, film, and digital, to name just a few. Each art form offers a way of interpreting the world. Different people find different forms important or moving for different reasons.

In ancient Greece the types of art that existed were rather more formal and subject to rules. They fell into distinct categories, or *mediums*. The most obvious examples of ancient Greek art are sculptures and painted items, including plates, cups, and vases – which I look at in this chapter. Other forms of art existed too – like interior painting – but most of this work has been lost.

Rather than forms and mediums, however, what's most recognisable about Greek art is its subject matter. The sculptures and painted works are dominated by the gods and heroes of Greek mythology (see Chapter 20 for more on this cast of characters). Other themes developed and began to appear later. By the Hellenistic period (see Chapters 10 and 11), artists began to take an interest in the ordinary world around them.

Loads of Greek art survives in hundreds of museums all over the world. In this chapter, I cover the basic forms, techniques, and details that can help you better understand the meaning behind all those 'naked men with broken noses'.

Where did *that* come from?

One weird thing about Greek art is how it changed all of a sudden around about 500 BC. As Figure 17-1 shows, it was almost as if the Greeks had decided to start producing fantastic lifelike sculptures at the drop of a hat between the Archaic and Classical periods!

For years people wondered where this sudden expertise came from. The relatively recent work of scholars and archaeologists, notably Sir Arthur Evans (1851–1941), points to the Mycenaean culture (see Chapter 2). The discovery of the Mycenaean world meant that historians could link an earlier Greek-speaking, art-producing people with the ancient Greeks. Although Mycenaean art was very different, being much less accurate in its portrayal of people and objects, the connection proved that Greek art wasn't just a sudden invention.

Defining Greek Art

The ancient Greeks didn't really have a word that meant 'art'. The closest equivalent was *tekhne,* which was more like 'skill'. So the Greeks didn't think of art as an abstract, inspired thing, more as a craft or technical ability.

In fact, many of the items that modern eyes would classify as Greek art were not really thought of as art objects back in the times when they were created. The Greeks used the plates and bowls that museums now display in glass cases to eat their dinner from, and they used the *craters* (like a cup) for drinking. In a sense, these were everyday objects to the Greeks. (Clearly, some plates are better than others, and the Greeks would've appreciated and paid more money for those with a superior design – just as you do today.)

Scholars classify Greek art into several periods, all of which date from after the Mycenaean period which finished around 1200 BC. Here's a rough guide:

- ✔ **The Geometric period (1100–700 BC):** This earliest form of Greek art consists mostly of pottery with repeated geometric patterns and few representations of people or figures.

- ✔ **The Archaic period (700 BC–480 BC):** This art is heavily influenced by Egypt and Asia. Sculptural representations of people and animals are notably Eastern-looking. See the later section 'Analysing Archaic sculpture: Naked Egyptians'.

- ✔ **The Classical period (480–330 BC):** Art from this period features idealised and beautiful representations of men and gods, very often naked with an emphasis on athletic physiques and postures. See the later section 'Contemplating Classical sculpture: Even better than the real thing'.

> ✔ **The Hellenistic period (330–30 BC):** Greater realism and an interest in ordinary subjects typify art from this period. See the later section 'Surveying Hellenistic sculpture: Art mirrors life'.

Surveying Greek Sculpture: Men with No Noses

Greek sculpture is the most famous form of art from the ancient world. Their big statues of men and gods with bits missing have influenced sculptors and painters for hundreds of years. Here's the story behind one of the ancient Greek's greatest artistic contributions.

Sculpting, old-school style

For the ancient Greeks, sculpting was a definite skill that was handed down through families. It was a full-time job and a very respected trade. Sculptors usually worked on their own although on large projects, such as a big statue for a temple, they might employ other sculptors to work with them.

Greek sculptors worked in two forms – marble and bronze:

> ✔ **Marble sculptures** were cut from large stone blocks. It was incredibly intricate work; with just a few incorrect strokes the sculptor could ruin a complete image.

> ✔ **Cast bronze sculptures** were even trickier than marble ones. The sculptor produced a clay or plaster model into which he poured molten bronze. After the metal cooled, he finished the piece, removing any blemishes and buffing the bronze. The final effect was very bright, shining almost like gold. Bronze statues nowadays look a little dull in colour due to the effects of time. The ancient Greeks, however, kept their bronze pieces polished and glowing. Bronze was much more expensive than marble and many popular bronze pieces were copied in marble.

These large statues were used in many ways. Some were set up in public (such as those of successful athletes); others were privately owned by rich householders. The most common use, however, was to decorate large public buildings like temples (see Chapter 18).

Analysing Archaic sculpture: Naked Egyptians

The earliest examples of ancient Greek sculpture come from the Archaic period (700–480 BC). These early Greek statues were like those the Egyptians produced, but they differed in two crucial respects:

✔ Greek statues were free standing, rather than sculpted onto a wall or column as is typical for Egyptian art of the time.

✔ The Greek figures were completely naked whereas the Egyptians preferred to show male figures wearing a kilt or skirt over their nether regions.

Take a look at the sculpture in Figure 17-1. This *kouros*, which means the naked figure of a male youth, was made around 550 BC. The human form is quite realistic and is about two-thirds the size of an actual human figure. The skill of an ancient Greek sculptor was in his ability to accurately depict the human body, its contours, and its muscles.

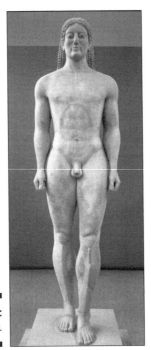

Figure 17-1:
A *kouros*.

What a beautiful fake!

Many of the Greek sculptures that survive aren't actually Greek at all. Very often these sculptures are high-class Roman copies of Greek originals. In particular, surviving marble pieces are frequently Roman versions of bronze Greek sculptures. The originals are usually lost to history as people melted down the bronze pieces to make other things. But because the originals were famous and celebrated, people wanted their own copies. Art lovers today are really fortunate that the Romans loved Greek sculpture, because at least copies exist to look at.

During this period, sculptors also produced female figures known as *korai*. These figures are much the same, apart from the crucial difference that they are fully clothed. This fits with the male Greek view that women should be modest and kept concealed (refer to Chapter 14).

The pose of the *kouros* is very rigid but also very symmetrical. This positioning became the standard pose in the Archaic period. The figure's stance is particularly noteworthy – he looks like he's stepping forward. This is a significant difference from rigid Egyptian sculptures and is an early attempt at portraying movement. The depiction of the face is still very Egyptian though: large eyes and hair in ringlets. Check out *The Ancient Egyptians For Dummies* (Wiley) by Charlotte Booth for more on the Egyptian aesthetic.

Contemplating Classical sculpture: Even better than the real thing

During the Classical period (480–330 BC), the Greeks raced ahead of other ancient civilisations in their ability to portray lifelike figures. The idea of *mimesis*, or imitation of life, became an important ideal. A sculpture was considered a success if it was close to life but also represented an aspirational image of how men and women potentially looked.

The sculpture in Figure 17-2 is a copy of one created around 444 BC by a man called Polyclitus. It's a life-size representation of an athletic young man (a *doryphoros*, or spear bearer). Look at the differences between this and the Archaic kouros. The subject is the same but the treatment is completely different:

✔ Both sculptures convey movement in the pose, but the weight of the entire Classical figure is now carried on one leg.

✔ The muscles on the body of the Classical statue are a lot more defined – the kind of physique that it would take hours in the *gymnasium* to produce!

✔ The Classical sculpture's face is different too. He's more expressive, concentrating on something yet lost in thought. His features are much more Western than those of the *kouros*.

Figure 17-2:
Copy of
Polyclitus's
Doryphorus.

Women in art

Another important development during the Classical Period was that female figures were frequently portrayed naked, like their male counterparts. For the most part, these nude female figures represented Aphrodite, the goddess of sexual love, often shown emerging from a bath.

Other goddesses sculpted during this period (Athena, Demeter, and Hera were popular subjects) are often portrayed wearing clothes. Getting the drapery right was considered a massively important skill on the part of an artist, and the folds in the robes are incredibly realistic on sculptures from the Classical period.

Celebrity artists

During the Classical period sculptures became hugely popular as a way of decorating temples and other public buildings (see Chapter 18), and artists producing the most perfect works became celebrities themselves. Here are the most famous Greek sculptors:

- **Pheidias (circa 460–400 BC):** Probably the most famous of Greek sculptors, Pheidias had a permanent workshop in the sanctuary complex at Olympia for which he made the famous statue of Zeus that sat in the temple dedicated to him. The statue is long gone but Figure 17-3 shows a representation. He also worked on the Parthenon decorations (see Chapter 18). He was killed by the people of Elis who were jealous of his work at Olympia. Rather harsh critics, the Eleans.

- **Polyclitus of Argos (circa 460–410 BC):** Polyclitus worked exclusively in bronze and was most famous for his statues of mortals (like the *Doryphorus* in Figure 17-2). He is credited as being responsible for the creation of the standard form of depicting muscles in movement.

- **Myron (circa 470–420 BC):** Known as the great experimenter, Myron produced figures of gods and mortals in new and unusual poses. Myron was one of the first artists to depict people in actual movement. The best example is the *Discobolus*, or discus thrower, which is shown in Figure 17-4.

Figure 17-3:
Pheidias's
statue of
Zeus.

Bright-eyed and colourful

Two important elements in Greek sculpture of all periods were the use of colour and painted details. These days, when you visit a museum or look at photos of surviving figures, you see faded bronze and marble forms with big, open, sightless eyes. These sculptures were originally very different: Eyeballs and pupils were painted as well as the clothes (drapery) and any weapons or other items. Statues of the gods were meant to be intimidating; in their original painted form they would have been. Covered with red, black, and gold paint the images were meant to emphasise the awesome power of the gods.

  ✔ **Lysippus of Sicyon (circa 370–315):** Lysippus produced a huge variety of pieces at the end of the Classical era and the beginning of the Hellenistic. Mostly, these were new and different versions of gods, but his most famous image is the head of Alexander the Great (Figure 17-5), which ancient sources said was the most lifelike portrayal of the king.

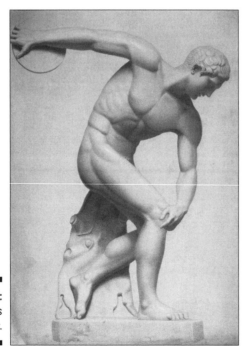

Figure 17-4:
Myron's
Discobolus.

Figure 17-5:
The head of
Alexander
the Great,
by Lysippus.

Surveying Hellenistic sculpture: Art mirrors life

During the Hellenistic period (330–30 BC) a new aesthetic emerged. After Alexander the Great's conquests broadened the horizons of the Greek world, the subjects and representations that sculptors chose changed too. While they still produced images of heroes and gods, they also developed an interest in more human subjects of a different type, such as children and older adults, than the idealised youths of the Classical period.

Although works still reflected an accurate portrayal of the human form, depictions became less stylised and more realistic. One of the most famous Hellenistic sculptures is of a drunken old woman – a subject and treatment that would never have interested earlier sculptors.

Take a look at the bronze sculpture of a boxer in Figure 17-6. This figure was produced in the second century BC. Although he's an athlete, he looks tired after a bout – like you'd expect him to be. His physique is almost over-developed, like a WWF wrestler, and if you look closely you can see his broken nose and damaged 'cauliflower ears'. This sculpture has some of the idea of *mimesis* (see the earlier section 'Contemplating Classical sculpture: Even better than the real thing') without anything aspirational. This is a worn-out, past-his-prime boxer, after one bout too many.

Figure 17-6:
Second
century BC
bronze
sculpture of
a boxer.

Inviting the Gods to Dinner: Greek Vase Painting

Along with bronze and marble sculpture, the other major area of ancient Greek art was the painting of pottery. Clay was one of the biggest natural resources in Greece, used for roof-tiles, small sculpted figures, and house bricks. The quality of the clay varied depending on where you were in ancient Greece but the skill in using the potting wheel and correctly firing the pot was more influential on the quality of the finished product than the clay itself.

The trade of pottery was one of the most prevalent practices and the closest that the Greeks had to a modern manufacturing industry. Greek pottery was exported all over the Mediterranean. Different regions developed their own individual styles, some of which were quite sought after. Some of the vase-painters became renowned, although never as much as the sculptors because sculpture was perceived as being a much higher art form. In most cases painters also made the pots themselves.

Getting into shape

Although the patterns and designs on pottery varied, the actual objects themselves took the following forms:

- ✔ *Amphora*: This was the standard type of big vessel used to transport large quantities of wine or oil. The name came from its distinctive double-handle design.

- ✔ *Crater*: This vessel looked like a large cup, but the Greeks used it as a mixing bowl where water was combined with wine.

- ✔ *Skyphos*: This standard cup form usually featured a handle on each side. Often the bottom inside was also decorated with a painted image.

- ✔ *Lekythos*: These small delicate jars were used to keep oil or, occasionally, perfume although this was usually sold in much smaller quantities.

Many other popular pottery shapes existed during the age of ancient Greece, including numerous different types of vases such as *hydria* and even wine coolers known as *psykters*.

The beautifully decorated pieces that survive in museums are generally examples of the ancient Greeks' most precious items that probably weren't for everyday use. Think of these as the equivalent of the best dinner set that you get out for special occasions.

Vase painting basics

Just like sculpture (see the earlier section 'Surveying Greek Sculpture: Men with No Noses'), the development of Greek vase painting went through a number of very clear phases, as the following sections explain.

Early vase painting (1050–700 BC)

Like sculpture, very early Greek vases mix geometric patterns with very Eastern-looking, Egyptian-style depictions of humans and animals. Sometimes the illustrations involved fantastical creatures from mythology such as the monsters that fought with Heracles (described in Chapter 20).

Black-figure painting (600 BC onwards)

The earliest form of truly Greek painting is known as *black-figure painting*. Clay red vases from this period are decorated with figures in silhouette usually depicted in black with red or white highlighting. The artist delicately incised the details onto the painted figures and into the clay.

Modern scholars attribute the development of this style of painting to the city of Corinth (see the Cheat Sheet map) in about 720 BC. By the middle of the seventh century BC artists throughout the region used the technique.

The most popular subjects during this period are inspired by mythological stories. The images are usually depicted *frieze style,* meaning that one elaborate illustration stretches all around the pot and shows figures interacting with each other. Vivid and complex scenes capturing a range of emotions were often included in the illustrations.

Figure 17-7 shows black-figure details on an *amphora* that was painted by a man called Exekias in around 540 BC. The vessel shows the Greek warrior Achilles fighting the Amazon queen Penthesilea during the Trojan War (see Chapter 20). According to the myth, as Achilles struck the killing blow, his eyes met Penthesilea's and he fell in love with her. The painter has managed to convey this complex and poignant moment by using a simple silhouette technique.

Another thing to notice about the vessel in 17-7 is Penthesilea's very white face. During this period women were often painted with white faces, whereas men were portrayed totally in black. The reason was that upper class ancient Greek women were expected to spend most of their day indoors (see Chapter 14). Men were tanned by the heat and the sun, but women remained pale.

Figure 17-7:
Example of black-figure vase painting by Exekias.

Apelles: The lost master

The most famous of the white-ground painters was a man called Apelles of Colophon, who was active in the fourth century BC. Later writers enthuse over Apelles's genius and talent for *mimesis* (see the section 'Contemplating Classical sculpture: Even better than the real thing'), claiming that his works were so lifelike that people tried to eat the fruit he painted and horses neighed at his equine images. Sadly, modern historians must take the ancient scribes' word for it; nothing of Apelles's work survives.

Red-figure painting (circa 525 BC onwards)

Around 525 BC a new style of painting – known as *red-figure painting* – was developed in Athens. This technique was a complete reversal of black-figure painting, with the background now black and all the figures appearing in the red of the clay. This approach allowed the detailing to be much more intricate as details were now painted onto the clay instead of being incised as with black-figure work. Over time, the depictions of human anatomy and clothing become more precise – like the effects achieved by sculptors of this era.

Artists could also create much more complex scenes. Notably, red-figure painters began including more than one image on a piece, sometimes showing two or more scenes that may have some kind of linking theme.

A red-figure *skyphos* was painted around 470 BC showing the young Heracles on his way to school followed by an old woman. The image is incredibly detailed, and you can easily make out the difference in age of the two characters. Heracles stands in the style of Classical sculpture (see the earlier section 'Contemplating Classical sculpture: Even better than the real thing'), and you can even see the tattoos on the old woman, suggesting that she may be from Thrace where this was a common practice.

White-ground painting (circa 475 BC onwards)

One last style of vase painting was inspired by a technique used by painters working on large-scale interior projects. Although little of this type of *white-ground painting* survives, historians believe artists covered interior walls or wooden panels with white paint or plaster to produce a neutral background.

During the fifth century BC, some painters began to adopt this style for working on vases. The most common use for white-ground painting on vases was to decorate the *lekythos* that the Greeks buried with their dead. These *lekythos* were filled with oil and accompanied the deceased to the underworld. (See Chapter 21 for more on ancient Greek burial practices.) Most white-ground vases haven't survived very well because the vessels weren't meant for frequent handling.

Finding Beauty Elsewhere: Other Arts and Crafts

Of course, the Greeks didn't just produce pots and sculptures. They were expert at a number of other art forms:

- ✔ **Clay figures** were immensely popular. These mini sculptures followed the aesthetics of their large-scale counterparts. See the earlier section 'Surveying Greek Sculpture: Men with No Noses'.

- ✔ **Decorative bronzes** were cast in the same way as larger metal sculptures. These pieces looked a bit like small versions of the friezes and metopes (smaller sculpted scenes) on temples (described in Chapter 18).

Smaller items like these would have been used as ornaments in houses and were also sometimes given as small offerings to the gods, possibly to represent the person that was asking for help.

The following sections cover a few other artistic endeavours of the ancient Greeks.

Getting dressed: Clothing

Dress-making and fashion weren't really art forms in ancient Greece, but the garments Greeks wore while going about their daily business had a beauty and simplicity that continues to inspire designers even today.

Materials

Most ancient Greeks – male and female, rich and poor – wore pretty much the same items of clothing. What did vary was the quality of the material used.

Most garments were made of wool, although in some cases linen was used. (Linen was more common for tunics or underclothes; wool must have been a bit itchy for a hot day on the plain of Attica!) White was the standard colour but the Greeks also dyed their wool (Chapter 13 has more details). Wealthier Greek women could afford to wear silk, which was imported from Asia Minor on the silk route from the East.

Types of garment

Nearly all clothes took the form of a cloak or mantle – a single piece of material that could be worn in different ways. This garment was always sleeveless, but often during cold weather it was worn over the top of a tunic that served as an undershirt.

The standard garment for women was the *peplos*, which was a kind of combined cloak and tunic. It was a large, square piece of cloth, the top third of which the woman folded over and pinned on her shoulders. Most surviving artistic depictions of goddesses show them formally attired in peploi.

Women also often wore veils when they were outside to modestly hide their faces from men. The ancient Greek word for veil literally means 'little roof'; even though women were outside, they were still kept inside the *oikos*, or home.

The Greeks didn't wear trousers and thought them effeminate when worn by men. They were popular in the Persian Empire, and when Alexander the Great began wearing them after conquering Persia (see Chapter 11), this fashion choice proved unpopular with his Macedonian generals.

By the Hellenistic period both men and women wore simpler formal garments known as an *himation*. The *himation* was a very long piece of material (up to 3 metres by 2 metres) that you draped around the body and usually supported over the left arm. The gods in the Parthenon sculptures (see Chapter 18) wear them and the Romans later based the *toga* on this versatile garment.

Looking sharp: Jewellery

In addition to sculpture and vase painting, the other great manufacturing craft in ancient Greece, and elsewhere in the ancient world in general, was the production of jewellery.

The Greeks used precious metals (gold and silver) and semi-precious stones such as bezels in large quantities to produce rings, earrings, necklaces, and bracelets in designs that are still very recognisable today. The fashion for setting a precious stone in a metal band (like a modern ring) became fashionable only around the end of the fifth century BC.

Golden combs and hair slides were also very popular. Sometimes they featured small scenes of tiny figures not much more than a few centimetres high. Incredibly skilled and detailed work, these combs were very expensive.

A great number of examples of this work still survives in museums around the world. They're hugely delicate and personal items that give a real sense of having been touched and cared for by people from 2,500 years ago.

Chapter 18

Building Beautiful Greek Architecture

*T*his chapter is about more than the types of structures and building materials favoured by the ancient Greeks; it's about architecture. *Architecture* is the art of building, the design and construction of buildings that ensure that they're technically correct and aesthetically pleasing. In other words, architecture is about making sure that buildings look good and stay up.

Of all the things that the ancient Greeks left behind, their buildings are the most obvious. You can find great big chunks of these structures – some still in surprisingly good condition – lying around all over the Mediterranean. And museums around the globe have enshrined several buildings or portions of buildings.

Even more apparent than the physical remains is the influence of Greek architecture on subsequent buildings. Indeed, many buildings in some of the world's most famous cities instantly remind you of Greek temples – such as the White House in Washington for example.

In this chapter, I look at how the Greeks built temples and other public structures, why they built them, and what to look for when you're standing in front of one.

Speedy builders

The Greeks really did love their temples. Modern scholars have added up the number of temples constructed between 599 and 301 BC, the height of the temple-building boom:

- ✔ Greeks living on the mainland built around 53 temples.

- ✔ Across the whole Greek world, Greeks constructed over 120 temples.

Perhaps these figures don't sound that impressive, but when you think of the cost involved, the pretty crude tools, and the enormous effort required, this output is the equivalent of building a new Wembley Stadium or Millennium Dome every two years or so.

Building for the Masses: Ancient Greek Temples

The Greeks loved building – and building temples in particular. The council of government (refer to Chapter 4) usually paid for these elaborately decorated structures, which were used to make political statements. The Greeks tended to build smaller private buildings like houses or shops out of whatever was available and not to any particular design. See Chapter 14 for more on these day-to-day structures.

Appreciating the role of the temple

The temple was a vital part of the Greek *polis* or city. A temple's main purpose was to honour the god that it was dedicated to, such as Zeus, Poseidon, or Apollo. Each temple normally contained a large cult statue of the god within the central room, or *cella*. The statue was much bigger than life-size and could be as tall as 10 or 15 metres (see 'Going back to the temple's beginnings' later in this chapter for a plan of a typical ancient Greek temple).

The temple was literally thought of as the house of the god. When you entered the temple, you were in the presence of that deity. That's partly why the Greeks used such massive statues – to create feelings of awe and fear. Temples were open to all and people would flee there for sanctuary in times of crisis.

Festivals, sacrifices, and ceremonies all took place at the temple. Temples were often part of a whole *sanctuary complex* in which they stood alongside *treasuries*, or small buildings used to house gifts made to the gods. A good example of a sanctuary complex is the Acropolis in Athens, which was home to four different temples (dedicated to Athena and Poseidon) and also served as the stronghold of the city in times of trouble.

Despite the temple's civic functions, each building was really about the worship of the god to which it was dedicated. In a way, the vast expense of building a temple was a kind of tribute to the god to start with. Greek religion was based around the idea of giving gifts to the gods and hoping that good things happened to you as a result. You can read more about these spiritual beliefs in Chapter 22.

Going back to the temple's beginnings

Greek architecture developed very much along the same lines as Greek history. The Minoans (covered in Chapter 2) were great builders but they didn't tend to build structures exclusively for religious purposes. During the Dark Ages the Greeks seemed to build very few massive structures. It wasn't until the seventh century BC that the Greeks began the large scale construction of temples.

Between 650 and 500 BC the classic form of the Greek temple started to emerge as towns and cities throughout the Mediterranean began to construct their temples in fairly uniform style. The temples that were built during this period were all classified as *hekatompedon*, which meant 'hundred footer'. As temples were a great source of local pride, building anything that was smaller was unthinkable. The temples also all followed the same plan of a box within a box, as Figure 18-1 shows.

The temple in Figure 18-1 is a rectangle surrounded by massive round columns. Within the rectangle is another smaller rectangle that made up an interior room. This area was called a *cella* and was where the business of the temple took place. Often the *cella* had an external porch leading into it, like the one in Figure 18-1. It was the innermost sanctum of the temple where offerings were made.

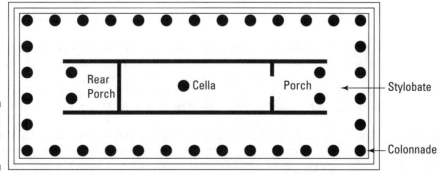

Figure 18-1:
A basic
temple plan.

The Seven Wonders of the Ancient World

Some Greek buildings were so impressive that they even made it onto the list of the Seven Wonders of the World! Various ancient writers made lists of seven wonders, including the Greek historian Herodotus (see Chapter 22). In fact, the word the Greeks used to describe these wondrous buildings was *thaumatai*, which literally means 'must see'! Here's Herodotus's list in full:

- Colossus of Rhodes
- Great Pyramid of Giza
- Hanging Gardens of Babylon
- Mausoleum of Maussollos at Halicarnassus
- Pharos (Lighthouse) of Alexandria
- Statue of Zeus at the Temple of Zeus in Olympia
- Temple of Artemis at Ephesus

As you can see, after the Great Pyramid and the Hanging Gardens, the Greeks feature quite heavily in the list with five entries. Then again, it was a Greek who compiled the list!

Most interesting for historians is the Temple of Artemis at the Greek city of Ephesus on the coast of Asia Minor. Today, only the base and a few columns of this structure survive, but this temple was considered to be the best example of its kind.

This basic format remained pretty much unchanged for the whole of Greek history. Part of the reason for this consistency was the building techniques involved (see the later section 'Making it happen: Building tools and techniques').

Other forms of temple design did develop and the Greeks introduced new materials, but this rectangle-within-a-rectangle plan was the standard. Originally, these temples were probably constructed out of wood, but by the early sixth century BC the Greeks were using stone, most commonly marble.

Evolving style: Three architectural orders

Although the design of Greek temples was incredibly regular, room still existed for expansion and elaboration of the basic form. In fact, any big temple project was a chance for a city to show off its wealth and artistry. The way that temples were decorated and adorned led to the development of three notable styles, or architectural orders: Doric, Ionic, and Corinthian.

Doric and Ionic were based around the two major regions of Greece (see Chapter 3). *Doric* mainly referred to the mainland of Greece, and *Ionic* was 'Ionian' and referred to the western coast of Asia Minor. The *Corinthian* style was attributed to a sculptor and architect called Callimachus who was active in the fifth century BC and was alleged to have come from the city of Corinth.

These styles developed during the fifth and fourth centuries BC. They weren't strict ways of building but rather styles that architects of the day felt able to experiment with.

As you can see by the three temple columns shown in Figure 18-2, the differences between the Doric, Ionic, and Corinthian styles are fairly clear. The biggest design differences are in the *capital* (the top portion of the column) and the *entablature* (the structure that sits on top of the column):

- ✔ **Doric** columns feature a very simple stone capital in two pieces that looks like a bowl with a flat block on top.

- ✔ **Ionic** columns include a carved, curling block that looks a bit like the horns of a ram. Underneath this block is a decorative pattern that some people call 'egg and dart'.

- ✔ **Corinthian** columns have a far more ornate design that mimic the look of sprouting Acanthus leaves. The thinner column is more like Ionic than Doric.

So, after you decided to build a temple and picked the order that you wanted to style it in, how did you go about building it? Read on.

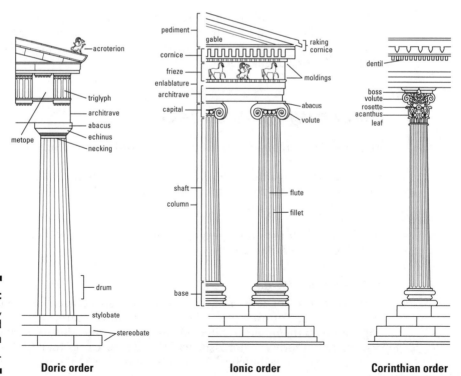

Figure 18-2:
Doric,
Ionic, and
Corinthian
columns.

Doric order   **Ionic order**   **Corinthian order**

Constructing Temples

The most important thing about any new temple project was choosing the site. Usually, the Greeks built a new temple in a sacred place like a sanctuary complex (a site with a lot of temples and religious buildings), but it was often also the most conspicuous place in the city.

The greatest temple in Athens was the Parthenon dedicated to Athena and built on the site of the Acropolis, on a massive hill that dominated the landscape. Similarly, the Greeks built many temples in Greece and Asia Minor overlooking the sea or in other commanding and beautiful locations.

Bearing the cost

Building a temple wasn't cheap. The cost was met by the public purse and sometimes donations from rich citizens. For a temple to be built in ancient Athens, the *ekklesia* (refer to Chapter 4) had to approve and budget for the project before the builders broke a single stone. The *ekklesia* then set up a supervisory committee for the project and appointed a chief architect.

For an idea of the costs involved, consider the Parthenon in Athens. This building cost 469 silver talents to build. To give you some context, the cost of building and equipping a *trireme* warship such as those in the Athenian fleet was 1 silver talent. Ouch!

Selecting an architect

The role of the architect was crucial. The position was a hugely responsible one, combining the roles of designer, foreman, and accountant. Not only did the architect design the building, but he also supervised its construction on site, hired the workforce, purchased materials, and ensured that the whole thing came in on budget.

But despite their enormous responsibilities, the Greeks still viewed architects as artisans rather than artists.

Finessing the design

Architects designed temples according to mathematical calculations rather than modelling. For example, if the temple required more columns or wider gaps between them, the architect simply had to adjust his calculations accordingly. Another major issue was the *entasis*, or contour, of the columns (in basic terms, how much wider the columns were at the bottom than the top). Architects had to go through careful calculations to ensure that the columns could support the weight of tons of stone. And if the architect got his sums wrong, the temple would fall down!

Of course, construction wasn't quite that haphazard. The fairly standard form of temple design (see the earlier section 'Going back to the temple's beginnings') meant that architects worked within fairly standard guidelines.

Hiring the workforce

Architects managed hundreds of different workers in a temple-building project. They hired skilled artisans and craftsman, along with manual labourers and prisoners of war used as forced labour.

When a major project was under way workers came from far and wide because they knew that work would be available for years to come. The Parthenon was proposed in 447 BC, and 15 years later it was finally completed!

Animals were used to transport materials and equipment. For example, during the building of the Parthenon around 400 oxen a day were used to transport materials.

Making it happen: Building tools and techniques

Ancient Greek tools and building techniques were pretty basic – which makes it all the more impressive that they managed to erect such huge, elaborately embellished edifices.

One issue that all ancient Greek builders dealt with was the lack of concrete (it wasn't discovered until early in the Roman period, during the first century BC). That's why Greek architects were so keen on columns; these structures helped support the massive weight of the buildings' roofs.

Just getting the materials together was difficult enough. Every temple required thousands of cubic metres of stone to be quarried and, given the weight and transportation difficulties, the quarry needed to be close by. The Greeks preferred to use marble, but this could be ruinously expensive. More often they used plain stone and then covered it with painted plaster so that it resembled marble.

Each individual block had to be prepared (that is, shaped for its purpose by carving and hammering) on site and then slotted together. Instead of being fabricated of one long tube of stone, columns were made of different blocks called *drums* that were fixed together with plugs coated with lead to fill any gaps. This work had to be spot on, otherwise the curvature would be wrong and the column wouldn't be able to support weight.

Moving the stones was difficult and dangerous. For the most part, a human-powered crane involving fairly simple pulley systems and lots of manpower lifted the stones into the appropriate area, and then men levered them into position.

Getting your message across through decoration

After the temple structure was up, part of the building's statement was made: The size and spectacular position of the building no doubt impressed many people. However, the Greeks conveyed more clever messages via the decoration of the temple.

Intriguing entablatures and more

Like everything else to do with architecture and temple building, the decoration of temples followed a fairly uniform set of rules. The main areas of decoration were above the columns in the series of sections known as the entablature. Figure 18-2 earlier in this chapter shows two examples of entablature.

The major decorative areas were as follows:

- **Frieze:** On Ionic temples the frieze often displayed a long, relief sculpture that showcased a consistent theme such as a procession or a continuous battle scene.

- **Metope:** On Doric temples this space was occupied alternately by *triglyphs* (triple-grooved panels) and empty panels that could be filled by relief sculptures called *metopes*. Often each end of the temple featured a different theme.

- **Pediment:** The pediment was often used as a space for large scale sculptures, usually massive, larger-than-life versions of the gods.

Like the sculptures I discuss in Chapter 17, the temples were colourfully painted – even if they were constructed of marble. The backgrounds of the metopes and pediment sculptures were painted, as well as the *triglyphs* and some details on the columns. The paints' bold colours (probably brighter colours like red, gold, yellow and lighter blue) would have contrasted beautifully with the stark white of the remaining marble or stone.

The Parthenon: 230 feet of propaganda!

The decorations of the Parthenon are a great example of ancient Greek architecture, construction, and decoration. The Greeks constructed the building over 15 years during Athens's greatest period of supremacy, immediately before the start of the Peloponnesian War (see Chapter 7). They built the Parthenon to replace a temple burned down by the Persians in the fifth century BC (refer to Chapter 6). This new building celebrates the superiority of the Athenian empire and its leading role in defeating the Persians at Marathon and elsewhere. It's a brilliantly conceived programme of decoration.

Everything about this amazing building fits with the purpose of the temple as a place of worship and also as an expression of Athens's wealth and superiority.

- The temple was dedicated to Athena, the patron goddess of Athens, and a massive statue of her dominated the inner building within the *cella*.

- Because the Parthenon is a Doric temple it doesn't feature an external frieze, but the inner building had a frieze running around it that depicted the Panathenaiac festival that took place in honour of Athena every four years.

- The building's pediment sculptures honoured Athena as well. At one end of the temple, a scene showed all the Olympian gods at rest, and the other end showed a scene from the story where Athena battled with Poseidon for the right to be patron deity of Athens.

- The *metopes* show various scenes of Greeks fighting foreign mythological enemies like Amazons and Lapiths. These images are a not-so-subtle demonstration of Greek superiority over foreigners.

You can still see the Parthenon in a fairly good state. The ruins of the temple are there in Athens although much of the decoration has been taken off and is preserved in the Acropolis Museum in Athens and the British Museum in London.

Building More than Temples

As Greek cities developed, so did the types of public buildings that were designed and constructed. Although temples continued to dominate, the Greeks did build other communal structures.

When you look at some Greek ruins today, you may have difficulty telling the difference between temples and other buildings. The similarities are because Greek architects used many of the same techniques from temple-building to construct other types of building, including *agoras*, *stoas*, stadiums, and theatres.

Agoras

The *agora* was the centrepiece of a Greek city. The word doesn't have an exact translation – the closest modern equivalent is 'town square'. (In the Roman world, the *agora* became the *forum*.)

The *agora* was where the citizen body gathered to talk, buy, and sell, and sometimes to protest or vote. Essentially, it was a large open space, but over time buildings were added because the activities that went on needed space for administration and so on. So despite originally being a big empty space, the term *agora* came to stand for a group of buildings – if you see what I mean!

Stoas

As the *agora* developed into a building, the architectural elements that surrounded it, or *stoas*, came to resemble a colonnade, like a roofed street with columns.

Over time, these *stoas* became quite ornate and complicated buildings in their own right. Some examples of *stoas* feature more than one level. Effectively, they became a kind of precinct, with small booths used for shops and businesses as well as a street that linked the *agora* to other areas of the city.

Some *agoras* and *stoas* are still partially in existence all around the Mediterranean. The ancient religious town of Delphi contains some particularly good examples (Chapter 24 has more).

Stadiums and theatres

The other major public buildings were those the Greeks used for entertainment (see Chapter 16 for all the fun). Ancient Greek athletic competitions and theatrical performances took place in the open air, so the buildings constructed didn't have roofs. Neither type of building required much in the way of architectural design; rather the key was picking the right spot to begin with. These structures were usually just cut into a hillside with acoustics being the greatest concern in the case of theatres.

Part IV
Mythology, Religion, and Belief

The 5th Wave — By Rich Tennant

AT HOME WITH ZEUS

"You know, I wish you'd be more careful about where you leave these things laying around!"

In this part . . .

In this part I explore the fundamentals of Greek mythology and how these translated into practical religion and worship. Some of the mythology, beliefs, and cults are very strange indeed. I also look at the Greek philosophers; the men who dared to disagree with the established tradition and come up with their own unique answers to the meaning of life, the universe, and everything.

Chapter 19

Going Back to the Beginning: Myths and Gods

*O*f all the things that have survived the passage of time between ancient Greece and today, the Greek myths are probably the most enduring. First adopted and altered by the Romans whilst the Greek world was still in existence (around 300 BC), the myths and their thrilling cast of gods, mortals, and creatures have proven to be a huge inspiration to Renaissance artists, English poets, and 20th-century movie makers – to name just a few.

The ancient Greek myths are stories of love, jealousy, rage, heroism, cowardice, and nearly all other human states. In short, they're brilliant – and this chapter looks at why.

Demystifying Myths

Myths were central to Greek life. They dominated the ancient Greeks' religious practices, adorned temples and buildings, and appeared in nearly all literature and poetry. The reason for the prominence of myth in ancient Greek culture is simple: Myths helped the ancient Greeks to understand who they were.

Herodotus, Thucydides, and Xenophon were the first Greek historians. Before them, the Greeks didn't really have history as such. They still had to explain the world around them – as well as the things they couldn't see or understand.

Initially, the Greeks used myths to answer the big questions – like how the world came into being and where men and women came from. Without any scientific notions to fall back on, the Greeks came up with some surprising explanations! (See the later section 'Starting Out: Greek Creation Myths' for all the fascinating details.)

Passing on myths

Before around 750 BC the Greeks didn't have writing (see Chapter 1), so they passed on all mythical stories by word of mouth, generation by generation. Eventually, these stories became part of an accepted system of belief. The gods and heroes described in them became as real to everyday folk as their local potter or innkeeper.

Myths that went beyond man's origins eventually sprang up. Gods and heroes dominated and were involved in incredible stories of adventure. The storytelling about these characters became more involved and developed into songs and poems.

Poets and epics

By the eighth century BC the Greeks began to record their oral poetry in written form. The works of poets like Homer (see Chapter 20) and Hesiod were written down, and the stories that they told became a kind of mythical fact – 'mythtory', if you like!

In many cases, the stories that the great poets produced were *epic cycles* – long stories about heroes' whole lifetimes as well as what happened to their families for generations afterwards. These stories became a kind of mythtory too, explaining the period of time before real history was written and also served as inspiration to later playwrights, poets, and artists.

Keeping track of everything

Of course, one of the problems with myths that developed through an oral tradition was that everybody had his or her own slightly different version. Often, these differences were geographical, with many towns claiming to be the birthplace of a hero or the place where a famous event took place. A good example of this confusion is the god Pan (see Chapter 13). At least 14 different mythological characters are referred to as being his father!

Collating all these many stories and their many versions was a big job, but some writers did try and do it. Not many of their works survive, but the following are two notable contributions:

- ✔ The *Theogony* by Hesiod (refer to Chapter 13) is literally a book about 'god-birth'. This long poem describes the earliest elements of Greek mythology and how the Olympian gods came into being. Several translations are available online and in published form.

- ✔ *The Library of Greek Mythology* by Apollodorus, a scholar who lived in Alexandria during the second century BC, is an expansive survey of myths. Translations of Apollodorus's work are still published and widely available today.

Starting Out: Greek Creation Myths

So how did it all begin, then? Unsurprisingly, ancient cultures offer various versions of the myth of creation – and the ancient Greeks have several of their own takes on the story.

Hesiod's version

The Greeks called the creation stories *cosmogony*, or how everything came into being. The most common cosmogony was the one that Hesiod describes in the *Theogony*:

> *Chaos was first of all, but next appeared broad bosomed Earth, sure standing place for all . . . From Chaos came Black Night and Erebos and Night in turn gave birth to Day and Space whom she conceived in love to Erebos.*

The idea is that first there was nothing but a void (Chaos) from which sprang Earth (also known as Gaia), Love (Eros), and other elemental beings. Eventually, Gaia gave birth to Uranos who became the sky; he in turn fertilised Gaia and she gave birth to more children – the *Titans*.

All fairly trippy stuff. Notice how the Greeks personified certain things which modern folks consider to be abstract notions. For example, love and the sky have humanlike qualities and even genders. The ancient Greeks relied heavily on *anthropomorphism*. They believed the creation of the world could be explained by the interaction of various forces, and these forces were best understood by making them like humans. See the later section 'Defining the gods' for more on anthropomorphism.

Other versions

Of course, Hesiod's is just one version! Loads of others pop up throughout Greek literature. Here are a few good ones:

- The earliest creation myth is called the *Pelasgian* and may have been a foreign tradition that predated the Greeks. According to this version, Eurynome produced a massive egg. Her son Ophion sat on it and hatched it. From the egg came the whole universe, including the humans and the gods.

- In Homer, the coupling of two of the Titans – Tethys and her brother Ocean – produced all the gods.

- In later versions, the first deity was Night (known as Nyx). She either produced an egg (like Eurynome) or gave birth to all gods and humans.

These three versions (plus Hesiod's explanation) are a great example of how fluid Greek mythology was and how similar stories were told in many completely different and alternative ways.

Remembering the Titans

In Hesiod's version of the creation myth, Gaia (Earth) and Uranos (the sky) gave birth to a whole range of different characters known as the *Titans*. Like a mythological version of a musical, the Titans were made up of six males and six females.

Crafty Kronos

Chief amongst the Titans was the wily Kronos, who was married to his sister Rhea. He had his eyes on power and plotted with his mother Gaia. While Uranos slept, Kronos crept up on him and sliced off his genitals with a scythe! They fell from the sky into the sea and bobbed along, until they came to the island of Cyprus where they caused a rather surprising result. According to Hesiod:

> *The genitals, cut off with adamant and thrown from land into the stormy sea, were carried for a long time on the waves. White foam surrounded the immortal flesh, and in it grew a girl . . . and there the goddess came forth, lovely, much revered, and grass grew up beneath her delicate feet. Her name is Aphrodite among men.*

The final lines inspired the Renaissance artist Botticelli's famous painting *The Birth of Venus* – but you can see why he didn't choose to depict the first part!

What goes around comes around

Kronos became the ruler of the Titans, but he feared that one of his own children would usurp him. To protect his power, every time his wife Rhea gave birth, he grabbed the child and ate it!

Eventually, Rhea swapped her latest child (a boy called Zeus) for a stone wrapped in a blanket, which Kronos gulped down. She then gave Kronos a poisoned drink that caused him to vomit up his other children. Zeus then got his siblings together and challenged Kronos to fight. Zeus and his siblings won the war: the Titans were defeated and sent down to the abyss (an empty chasm beneath the earth also known as Tartarus). The heavens had new rulers – the Olympian gods! (See the later section 'Meeting the Olympians: X-Rated Deities' for all the details on this motley crew of immortals.)

Bridging the gap between gods and man

The ancient Greeks thought that the events of the Titans happened a long time before their own day. While they passionately believed that gods existed, they considered that they only experienced the gods' actions in the form of storms and so on.

To bridge this gap between Titans and everyday experience, the Greeks believed that another age had existed in between – an age when the gods and men had existed side by side.

Of course, the Greeks being Greeks, matters weren't that straightforward! They divided this period between the Titans and everyday ancient Greek existence into various ages. Here's a quick guide:

- ✔ **The Golden Age:** This was a peaceful time when men and women existed in harmony alongside the gods, who were ruled by Kronos. This was an age of plenty when all lived easily off nature.

- ✔ **The Silver Age:** When the Golden Age human race died out another race replaced them. But this race was foolish and wicked, and Zeus decided to destroy it (see the following section 'Figuring out where it all went wrong').

- ✔ **The Bronze Age:** During this age humans discovered war and became so obsessed with it that they ended up destroying themselves.

- ✔ **The Age of Heroes:** This period was when the great Greek heroes – including Heracles, Theseus, and Achilles – flourished. These individuals fought each other and went on incredible adventures. For more on this age, see Chapter 20.

- ✔ **The Iron Age:** This was the period that the ancient Greeks considered themselves to be living in. It was an age where men were forced to work hard for a living.

The ancient Greeks firmly believed that their own period (the Iron Age) was a time of great hardship and that life had been much better during the Golden Age. In his poem *Works and Days* Hesiod gives a lovely picture of what that golden era was like:

> *And like gods they lived with happy hearts, untouched by toil or sorrow. Vile old age never appeared, but always lively-limbed, far from ills, they feasted happily. Death came to them as sleep, and all good things were theirs; ungrudgingly, the fertile land gave up her fruits unasked. Happy to be at peace they lived with every want supplied.*

Sounds pretty good, doesn't it? Then again, it isn't unusual for any society to have a romantic view of the past and complain about its own time.

Figuring out where it all went wrong

So if the relationship between men and gods was perfectly happy during the Golden Age, why did the Greeks fear and respect the gods in their time? The difference is explained by the Silver Age, where Zeus became enraged at the wicked behaviour of the race that he'd created and decided to wipe it out.

Deucalion's ark

Zeus's choice of Armageddon weapon was a flood. Much like in the Old Testament story of Noah, only one man and his family had a chance to survive Zeus's flood. In the Greek version, a Titan called Prometheus took pity on humans and warned a man called Deucalion.

Deucalion and his family built an ark and survived the rain for nine days before coming to rest on the top of Mount Parnassus near Delphi. Zeus relented and allowed Deucalion and his family to create a new race of men and women. One of the sons was called Hellen, who gave his name to the race that the Greeks were descended from – the Hellenes. Although this was a widely held mythological belief, no historical evidence for it exists. (For my theories on where the Greeks actually came from refer to Chapters 2 and 3!)

Prometheus: Always in trouble

Prometheus also helped the new race of Hellenes by defying the wishes of Zeus and giving men the gift of fire. Interestingly, Prometheus's name means 'forethought', although he didn't show too much here because Zeus's anger was considerable.

Zeus punished Prometheus by having him chained to a cliff and sending eagles to attack him. Every day the eagles tore out Prometheus's liver. The wound magically healed every evening and the punishment was repeated the next day. Eventually, Heracles freed Prometheus when he passed by on the way to one of his labours. (Chapter 20 has more on Heracles.)

The story of Prometheus is a great example of the savage punishments that the ancient Greeks believed their gods were capable of. The tragic playwright Aeschylus (see Chapter 16) wrote a trilogy about Prometheus from which the first play, *Prometheus Bound,* still survives. In the following fiery excerpt, Prometheus defies Zeus's worst punishments:

> *Let hurricanes upheave by the roots the base of the earth, let the sea-waves' roaring savagery confound the courses of the heavenly stars. Let him lift me high and hurl me into black Tartarus [the deep abyss beneath the earth] on ruthless floods of irresistible doom: I am one whom he cannot kill!*

The story of Prometheus is very much a fantastical myth but it does reinforce the way the Greeks felt about the relationship between man and the gods. People who defied the gods would be justly punished. Greek tragic plays are full of examples of characters who have pushed too far, been too bold, or too arrogant, and suffered terrible punishments as a result.

Putting the Gods in Their Place

The ancient Greeks loved gods, absolutely loved them. The Greeks had loads of gods, and through their rich mythology they turned the most surprising things – such as rivers and mountains – into gods. This section examines the various powers and responsibilities of the gods, from the perspective of an everyday ancient Greek citizen. Get ready for some surprises!

Understanding the role of gods

The gods played a vital part in how regular ancient Greeks lived their every-day lives, including what they thought, what they built, what they painted, and what they composed poems, plays, and songs about.

At the same time, people lived in great fear of the power of their gods and made sacrifices and offerings to them in the hope of receiving good fortune in return.

In the film *Clash of the Titans* (1980), the gods are depicted in quite a classical way: sitting around a temple in flowing robes, watching the world from afar and playing a game like chess with human lives. Although the special effects are pretty cheesy, the notion of the gods as beautiful and fabulous but capable of wielding enormous power is a decent depiction of these deities.

Worshipping many

After Zeus's revolt against his father Kronus and defeat of the Titans in a war (see the earlier section 'Remembering the Titans'), the gods that the ancient Greeks recognised came into existence and continued to rule for all eternity.

Ancient Greek religion was *polytheistic,* which means it consisted of many gods or deities. This is in contrast to Christianity, for example, which has one god and is therefore a *monotheistic* religion.

Greek religion had a specific *pantheon,* or collection of gods, that comprised the most important deities. I look at these top tier gods in the later section 'Meeting the Olympians: X-Rated Deities'.

Defining the gods

The Greek gods were *anthropomorphic.* This means the Greeks imagined their gods in their own terms – looking and speaking like men and women, although being fabulously powerful and magical.

Anthropomorphism is quite a reasonable thing for humans to do. (The Jewish, Christian, Muslim, and Hindu religions all include anthropomorphism in various ways.) The Greek philosopher Xenophanes summed the idea up quite nicely in his comment that '*If horses could draw, they would draw horse gods*'.

Super powers

Despite taking human form, the Greek gods were awesome in their abilities. Specifically, they were

- Able to resist wounding and disease
- Able to transform into other beings or creatures at the drop of a hat
- Blessed with eternal youth
- Capable of flight

In a way, they were like modern superheroes.

Do as I say, not as I do

Of course, the Greeks also imagined that their gods acted with some of the same motivations as normal people and experienced the same emotions. This belief meant that the Olympian gods often acted in cruel, childish, and immoral ways. In the myths, they commit adultery, rape, and murder on a seemingly daily basis and very often appear to revel in the cruel and inhuman punishments that they inflict on poor, defenceless humans.

To the Greeks there was nothing strange about the gods' actions. The Greeks didn't look to Zeus or Apollo as exemplars of good behaviour or for moral guidance. And that's just as well really! The Greeks didn't have a concept of sin or wickedness that came from religion. All the restrictions placed on people's liberty to act were based on legal or social conventions rather than religious instruction.

Visiting Olympus – a home fit for the gods

According to mythological tradition, the gods lived at the very top of Mount Olympus in northern Greece. This was where they spent a lot of time in near continual feasting and revelry, eating ambrosia and drinking nectar. It was vital for them to do this because the magical properties of these foodstuffs renewed their divine blood and kept up their powers.

Despite this seeming idyllic existence, the gods often roamed around, visiting parts of the world and interacting with their human subjects. A good example of this god/human interaction happens in Homer's *The Odyssey* when the other gods hold a sneaky meeting while Poseidon is away visiting the Ethiopians. The gods decide to help Odysseus (whom Poseidon is angry with) get home. The Greeks thought Ethiopia (their name for all of Africa beyond the Nile) was the farthest place in the world. So far, in fact, not even Poseidon could see what was happening in the Mediterranean while he was in Ethiopia!

Working like a god: Attributions and divine job descriptions

When they weren't feasting or misbehaving, the Olympian gods did have responsibilities. Each god had his or her own area of expertise, which I think of as their *attributions*.

Nearly every area of human experience had a god that oversaw it. For example, Demeter looked after farming, Poseidon sea travel, and Asclepius medicine and healing.

Inspiring ladies: The Muses

The immortals who were most closely associated with their area of expertise were the Muses. These nine female deities were led by Apollo (patron god of the arts) and each represented an area of artistic endeavour:

- ✔ Calliope: Epic poetry
- ✔ Clio: History
- ✔ Erato: Lyric poetry
- ✔ Euterpe: Flute-playing
- ✔ Melpomene: Tragedy
- ✔ Polymnia: Hymns
- ✔ Terpsichore: Dancing and the chorus
- ✔ Thalia: Comedy
- ✔ Urania: Astronomy

The ancient Greeks believed that the relevant Muse directly inspired artists working in these fields. For this reason, all epic poems traditionally begin with a request by the poet to be inspired by the Muse Calliope. Hesiod's *Theogony* is a good example; he starts the poem by describing the encounter that he had with the Muses that inspired him: 'With the Heliconian [resident on Mount Helicon] Muses let us start our song.'

The Greeks believed that the Muses lived on Olympus and spent their days entertaining the gods. Occasionally, they came down to earth and literally filled an artist with their inspiration. Hopefully, Clio paid me a visit while I was writing this book!

In many cases, gods had more than one attribution. Some, like Apollo and Athena, had loads. And yes, these attributions sometimes clashed with each other. For example, Athena was the goddess of handicrafts, wisdom, and war. Not the most obvious combination!

The way that a god got his attribution was this: People adopted a god as the patron deity of some area of human experience. It's impossible to know why the gods were given their attributions although they were usually relevant to an incident in mythology (such as Poseidon being given the sea as his realm by Zeus). Individuals honoured the god and made offerings, hoping for benefits in return. In the case of individual trades (such as medicine or shipbuilding), having a designated god led the Greeks to form guilds and organise public festivals and celebrations in honour of their deities.

Have you seen the film *Xanadu* (1980)? It probably doesn't immediately strike you as relevant to the ancient Greeks but it does feature the Muses masquerading as rock band 'The Nine Sisters'. It also features Zeus, Cliff Richard, and ELO – perfect for a Sunday afternoon!

Separating fate from dumb luck

The ancient Greeks believed that they had to worship the gods to ensure that their lives progressed happily and that bad things didn't happen to them. This philosophy may suggest that the Greek believed the gods controlled their destinies – but this isn't the case.

In addition to the gods, the Greeks believed in the idea of *fate* – that their lives were planned out and followed preordained paths. Thus, the time of your birth and the time of your death were fixed by a group of three female deities called, surprisingly enough, *the Fates*.

According to Hesiod, the Fates were very ancient goddesses who were the daughters of Nyx (Night); see the earlier section 'Starting Out: Greek Creation Myths'. These sisters spun out the thread (or the fabric) of a life and then one of them, Atropos, cut it when it was time for the human to die. The Fates existed apart from the other gods, and some accounts go as far as to state that the Olympian gods feared them.

The role of the gods was to *administer fate* as it came to pass. In *The Iliad* Homer describes Zeus as having a set of scales on which he weighs the fates of the heroes who are in combat, deciding who'll live or die that day. But although Zeus administers these fates, he can't actually do anything to change them, which is highlighted when his own mortal son, Sarpedon, is killed in battle. For a moment Zeus considers trying to prevent his son's death but then he realises that he can't.

The Odyssey includes an even better example of the gods' relationship with fate. Athena states:

> But from the great leveller Death: not even the gods can defend a man, not even one they love, that day when fate takes hold and lays him out at last.

Accordingly, people rarely asked the gods for anything related to their deaths or how long they would live. The Greeks generally accepted that the gods controlled what happened in your mortal life, not when it ended. I look at the Greek attitude towards death in Chapter 21.

Mocking the gods

Despite the awesome power that the Greeks thought the gods wielded, people still often treated them as figures of fun and amusement in art, literature, and theatre. For example, in *The Iliad* the childish and comic affairs of the gods act as a kind of counterpoint to the remorselessness of the fighting and death going on in the Trojan War.

Comic plays (see Chapter 16) frequently poke fun at the gods. In *Frogs* by Aristophanes, two of the central characters, Dionysus and Heracles, are immortals and they're lampooned just as much as the rest of the cast. In one scene, Dionysus asks Heracles for travel tips on the journey to Hades (the underworld):

I wondered if you could give me a few tips: any useful contacts down there, where you get the boat, which are the best eating houses, bread shops, wine shops, knocking shops . . . And which places have the fewest bugs.

Fun and games aside, I must make two important points about Aristophanes's comic musings about the gods:

- ✔ He isn't mocking any aspect of the gods' awesome powers as gods; rather he's making fun of them acting like humans.
- ✔ He's picked two relatively minor gods – he isn't mocking Zeus or Apollo.

This careful fun-poking reveals that the Greeks had something of a hierarchy for their gods. So without further ado, the next section looks at the most important ones!

Meeting the Olympians: X-Rated Deities

Probably the most important factor to remember about the Olympian gods is that they were, for the most part, related (see the section 'Starting Out: Greek Creation Myths' for the odd genealogical details). For example:

- ✔ Zeus, Poseidon, and Hades were all brothers.
- ✔ Hera was their sister and was married to Zeus. (The Zeus/Hera relationship was more than fit for an episode of *Jerry Springer*!)
- ✔ Apollo, Artemis, and Hermes were just a few of Zeus's many children.

Like all families, the gods had their ups and downs. Many of the stories about the Greek gods are born out of their petty jealousies and squabbles. It's like a kind of immortal soap opera – so meet the cast of Olympian gods.

Zeus, the king of the gods

Zeus was king of all the gods. When he defeated his father Kronos (see the earlier section 'Starting Out: Greek Creation Myths'), he became lord of everything. He mostly appears in myth as a great philanderer, sleeping with many mortals and immortals. Zeus regularly transformed himself into other creatures to do this: a swan (Leda), a bull (Europa), and even a shower of gold (Danae)!

Poseidon, the earth-shaker

Poseidon was the brother of Zeus. When Zeus became supreme, Poseidon was made the god of the earth (thus he was responsible for causing earthquakes) and the sea. Poseidon was also the god of horses and he impregnated the demon Medusa. When Medusa was killed by the hero Perseus, the famous winged horse Pegasus was born from her neck!

Hades, the king of the dead

Zeus's other brother Hades was given the underworld to rule and he became king of the dead. The Greeks (and more frequently the Romans) also referred to him as Pluto, meaning 'wealthy', because of the richness and fertility that come from underneath the earth.

Hades is mainly known for his abduction of Persephone (daughter of Zeus and Demeter), who he took to the underworld to be his wife. Zeus forced Hades to allow Persephone to return to mortality for six months of the year, bringing with her return to the land of living the warm weather of spring and summer.

Hera, the queen of heaven

Hera was the older sister of Zeus and also his wife. She was the goddess of marriage and the Greeks honoured her in this way. In myth and literature she spends most of her time being offended by Zeus's philandering and cruelly punishing his mortal lovers. She bore Zeus three children, including Ares the god of war. She also makes regular appearances in the stories of Heracles (setting him his tasks) and Jason (helping him to steal the Golden Fleece).

Hestia, the quiet one

Another sister of Zeus, Hestia was an intriguing, lesser-known immortal. She was the goddess of the hearth and home and is often depicted tending an eternal flame or fire. She renounced sexual love and lived a life of chastity – and consequently she never really features in any myths at all!

Despite her low profile in literature, Hestia was probably the most worshipped goddess because she was the protectoress of every household, typically receiving the first offering of every sacrifice made in a Greek home.

Apollo, lord of the silver bow

Apollo was the male twin born of Zeus's coupling with Leto, the daughter of one of the Titans (Artemis is Apollo's twin sister). Apollo was the patron god of archers and had many names like 'the far shooter' and 'lord of the silver bow'. Apollo is the god of prophecy and is also heavily associated with the sun and light. He was famed for establishing the Delphic Oracle (see Chapter 21) and is always depicted in Greek art as the epitome of male beauty and perfection.

Aphrodite, the goddess of sexual love

The goddess of beauty, attraction, and sexual love, Aphrodite was married to Hephaestus, but they had no children, and she was frequently unfaithful. Her most famous myth is that of her birth (see the earlier section 'Crafty Kronos'). She frequently appears in other stories, meddling in human relationships, sometimes with her son Eros. She plays a critical role in setting up the conflict that launched the Trojan War; see Chapter 20.

Ares, the god of war

Ares was the son of Zeus and Hera, and he was a truly terrifying god. Not only the god of war, Ares actively enjoyed the fear and chaos of battle and was credited with inspiring blood lust and savagery in mortals. He had two sons – Phobos ('Terror') and Deimos ('Fear'). He was also the father of Eros, a god of lust, love, and intercourse, as a result of a long-term liaison with Aphrodite.

Athena, the intelligent one

Athena was the daughter of Zeus and was identified with both war and handicrafts. This may seem a strange combination, but these were identified as the chief male and female occupations of the day. Unlike Ares, Athena's association with war was with the sober, correct use of it to defend cities.

Athena was also closely identified with intelligence and is often shown with an owl. The patron deity of the city of Athens, she was also the great protector of the hero Odysseus in *The Odyssey*.

Artemis, the hunter

The daughter of Zeus and the twin sister of Apollo, Artemis was the goddess of hunting and of women – with a particular focus on childbirth. Her role as huntress encompassed all wildlife, and she was seen as being wild and untamed in this way. She's often depicted in art carrying a bow and arrows and wearing animal skins.

Hephaestus, the god of the forge

Hephaestus was the god of fire and metalwork. He was the son of Hera and born crippled. In some versions, he was born without a father, developing out of Hera's rage for Zeus's infidelities. Hera was so ashamed of him that she flung him from Mount Olympus, and several myths exist about the extravagant revenges that he took upon her.

Married to Aphrodite, Hephaestus spent most of his days in his forge where he famously created a wonderful shield for the hero Achilles. Eventually, the Greeks revered him for all industry and manufacturing activities.

Hermes, the messenger god

One of the many sons of Zeus, Hermes was the messenger and herald of the gods. He appears in myth wearing winged sandals that enable him to fly at great speed to deliver messages from Olympus. Unsurprisingly, he was also the god of travellers; people made offerings to him before setting out on long journeys. He was also known as a cunning trickster – probably not the one to ask directions from then!

Demeter, the life-giver

Demeter was the goddess of corn and accordingly considered to be the sustainer of life. She was the sister of Zeus and bore him a daughter called Persephone. Due to her association with the harvest, she was very heavily worshipped by the Greeks and central to their most famous cult, the Eleusinian Mysteries (described in Chapter 21).

Dionysus, the god of good times

Dionysus was another son of Zeus and the god of wine and intoxication. Drunkenness was seen as a good thing because it helped to banish the cares of the world. Drinking and revelry fitted well with his other role as god of the theatre, where people could wear masks to change their identity. Dionysus spent his time roaming the countryside with his drunken crew, including his crazed female followers known as *maenads*.

The preceding is just a tiny introduction to the top-tier Olympian gods and their most famous stories. The myths about them are incredibly complex and contradict each other all the time. What's most important is the associations the gods had because that's why Greeks worshipped them. (See Chapter 21 for more on how the ancient Greeks went about worshipping.)

Not all fun and games

Although the gods all sound like tremendous fun, they were actually violent and unpredictable. Dionysus is a particularly good example. He sounds like a god who inspired good times and revel, and he did. But he also turned people mad. Under Dionysus's influence, people did awful and terrible things.

In Euripides's play *Bacchae,* Dionysus turns Pentheus (the king of Thebes) insane after he attempts to stop Dionysus's followers from worshipping him. Pentheus is torn to pieces by the *maenads* when he blunders in on their rites.

Here Dionysus sets out how Pentheus had broken the rules.

> *No god can see his worship scorned, and hear his name profaned, and not take vengeance to the utmost limit. Thus men may learn that gods are more powerful than they.*

Although they may act like fools and make human mistakes in many of the myths, the gods were to be feared and the Greeks worshipped them through fear as much as devotion.

The third section of Disney's *Fantasia* (1940) is an animated piece that accompanies Beethoven's Sixth Symphony 'The Pastoral'. The Greek gods on Mount Olympus are all in it. The blend of music and animation is wonderful and I can never hear that music without thinking about Greek mythology.

Transitioning from Greek to Roman

The Romans adopted gods very close to the Greek ones as their own. Greek and Roman gods were very similar and had the same attributions, but had different names. It can sometimes get quite confusing so Table 19-1 serves as a quick guide.

Table 19-1	Greek and Roman Deities	
Greek Name	*Roman Name*	*Greek Attribution*
Zeus	Jupiter	Sky, weather, storms, and lightning.
Hera	Juno	Marriage and childbirth
Poseidon	Neptune	The ocean and earthquakes
Hades	Pluto	Death and the underworld

Greek Name	Roman Name	Greek Attribution
Hestia	Vesta	The hearth (or home)
Apollo	Apollo	Prophecy, divination, the arts
Aphrodite	Venus	Beauty and erotic love
Athena	Minerva	War and handicrafts
Hephaestus	Vulcan	Fire and metalworking
Ares	Mars	War
Hermes	Mercury	Messages and travel
Demeter	Ceres	Corn
Artemis	Diana	Hunting and women
Dionysus	Bacchus	Wine and intoxication

The Roman and Greek gods aren't exactly the same but they had similar attributions, so the Romans adopted the Greek gods completely as they absorbed Greece into their empire (refer to Chapter 12).

One thing that did change in the transition from Greek to Roman was the importance of some gods. Mars (Ares) was incredibly important to a warlike people like the Romans, and Vesta (Hestia) came to prominence as the founding deity of the famous Vestal Virgins, a hugely influential cult in Rome that trained young women to be priestesses.

Chapter 20

Blending Myth and History: Troy, Homer, and Heroes

The myth of the Trojan War is very famous. For generations people have enjoyed plays, stories, novels, and films about the exploits of Achilles, Odysseus, Helen, and many other fascinating Greek characters.

You may have seen the film *Troy* (2004). It was great fun and gave the impression of an epic struggle between huge armies led by handsome, physically well-developed heroes who fought over a fantastical city for possession of one beautiful woman. When the film was released a lot of people quibbled over whether the events shown were a 'true' version of what had gone on. They were missing the point. The story shown in the film – recounted in the poetic source material, Homer's *The Iliad* – never really took place; it is a *myth*.

For the ancient Greeks, however, the Trojan War was hugely important. Their versions of the war were massively influential on the way in which they lived their lives.

This chapter is all about the Trojan myth: understanding the stories, getting to grips with its impact on ancient and subsequent Greek life, and looking at the archaeological evidence now available. It's also about introducing Homer and *The Iliad* – the man and the poem that dominated intellectual life in the Greek world.

Separating Myth and History

As I mention in Chapter 3, early Greek history is very difficult to separate from mythology. The Trojan War is a perfect example of this combining of fact and fiction.

The Greeks readily accepted the idea of what they called the Trojan Cycle (see the following section 'Mining the myth of the Trojan War') although there were various versions of it. The ancient Greeks considered the stories true and did not require any evidence. Modern minds, however, find Troy more difficult to accept unquestioningly. Historians try to balance the evidence of archaeology (see 'Seeking out the facts of Troy') with information in the original literary works, including Homer's epic poems (see 'Preserving – and Pumping Up – the Story of Troy: Homer').

Mining the myth of the Trojan War

The myth of the Trojan War encompasses a huge number of characters and incidents set vaguely around the time of the Mycenaean period (see Chapter 2), probably about 1300–1200 BC. The Greeks referred to the whole collection of stories as the *Trojan Cycle*.

Highlights of the story include the following key players and events:

- ✔ **A war spurred by love:** While on a diplomatic mission to the court of the Spartan king Menelaus, Paris, one of the sons of the Trojan king Priam, falls in love with Menelaus's beautiful wife Helen and elopes with her back to Troy. (For more on Troy's assumed geographic location, see the following section 'Figuring out the facts of Troy'.) This causes a major international incident as Menelaus's brother is Agamemnon, Mycenaean king, and the most powerful and influential of all the Greek leaders.

- ✔ **The personal becomes political:** Menelaus calls on all the other Greek nobles who owe him allegiance to join in an assault on Troy in an effort to avenge the insult to him. Agamemnon assembles a mighty fleet that sets sail from Aulis on the eastern coast of Greece, landing on the shore outside Troy (modern-day western Turkey; see the Cheat Sheet map). And thus, Helen becomes 'the face that launched a thousand ships'.

- ✔ **Larger than life warriors:** Both the Greeks and Trojans assemble armies full of the leading heroes of the age. The Greeks' superstar is Achilles, whose goddess mother bathed him in the river Styx in Hades to make him (almost) invulnerable. The Trojans' greatest warrior is Hector, King Priam's eldest son.

✔ **A brutal battle:** War rages between the two sides for ten years. The gods and goddesses both help and hinder each side; each deity chooses individually which army to support (see Chapter 19). Many heroes on both sides lose their lives, including Hector who is killed by Achilles. Paris then shoots Achilles in the heel (his one vulnerable spot) with an arrow, and he dies.

✔ **One tricky pony:** Eventually, the end to the war comes with a cunning plot devised by Odysseus, the Greek king of Ithaca. The Greeks construct an enormous horse, leave it outside the gates of Troy, and then appear to depart for home. Thinking that they've won, the Trojans take the horse inside the city and begin to celebrate. Shortly afterwards some Greeks who are concealed inside the horse slip out and open the gates for their comrades. In the bloodshed that follows, Troy is utterly destroyed, never to recover.

But the Trojan Cycle doesn't end with the war. The stories about the various characters continue. Most notably:

✔ Menelaus is reunited with Helen.

✔ Agamemnon returns home and is murdered by his wife Clytemnestra. Aeschylus's trilogy of tragic plays, known as *The Oresteia,* dramatises this veritable soap opera of deception and power.

✔ Odysseus spends a further ten years wandering the Mediterranean before returning home to his wife Penelope in Ithaca. See the section 'Returning home: The Odyssey' for more on Odysseus's outrageous journey.

The preceding is just one version of the myth. For the ancient Greeks, myths changed depending on who you were and where you lived. Another version of the Trojan story has Helen spending the whole war hiding in Egypt with only a ghost version of herself at Troy!

The film *Troy* (2004) was criticised because in it Paris and Helen leave Troy together and Achilles is present at the fall of the city. Critics missed the point. Many Greeks believed and told varying versions of the Trojan cycle so why shouldn't Hollywood?

Figuring out the facts of Troy

So what do historians actually know of the city of Troy? Unfortunately, facts are difficult to come by. What historians now know is based on a mixture of archaeological evidence and educated speculation. Despite some debate, historians generally contend the following:

- ✔ **When:** The ancient Greeks believed the Trojan War took place during *The Age of Heroes*, a period before the Greeks began recording history when they believed the great escapades of heroes like Heracles, Theseus, and the fighters at Troy to have taken place. The historian Herodotus thought that the war took place about 800 years before his time, or around 1200 BC.

- ✔ **Where:** The site historians now regard as Troy had been an important fortress throughout the Minoan and Mycenaean periods. The city was built on a low hill about eight kilometres west of the Aegean coast and just a little farther south of the Hellespont (see the Cheat Sheet map). Troy was in a superb position for trading at two coastal points and with the whole of Asia Minor and the east. Consequently, the city must have been very wealthy.

As I explain in Chapter 2, historians rely on archaeology for almost all their knowledge of the Minoan and Mycenaean periods. During the 19th century a German archaeologist called Heinrich Schliemann carried out a huge amount of excavation at sites around both Troy and Mycenae.

When Schliemann excavated at the spot that historians now think was the site of Troy, he discovered the ruins of an ancient town that was built on seven different levels.

- ✔ The earliest of these levels contained a huge amount of gold and other precious finds.

- ✔ The more recent levels were farther away from the centre, as you'd expect from a city that grew and expanded.

- ✔ Twentieth-century excavations found that these most recent levels showed evidence of having been destroyed through some cataclysmic event around the time of 1300 BC.

Schliemann was convinced that his site was Troy of the Trojan Cycle and that the treasure that he found belonged to the mythical king Priam. He announced to the world that he had found the site of Troy and proof that the Trojan War had taken place.

However, Schliemann's discoveries were problematic. Further excavations have shown that an earthquake, rather than an invading army, damaged the more recent areas. Signs also indicated that people lived in the recent levels once more very soon after the damage – not the hallmarks of a city razed to the ground by Agamemnon's army.

Other evidence for the Trojan War is literary (see the next section) and in the form of Greek art where the stories from the Trojan cycle were always a popular subject for sculptors and vase painters (Chapter 17 has a good example of a black-figure vase with a Trojan theme). However, these artefacts can't really be taken as proof of the war itself, rather as evidence of a continued interest in the Trojan cycle during later Greek history.

Ultimately, the general consensus is that the city found by Schliemann is the most likely site of ancient Troy. You can visit the site today although the fairly nondescript ruins are very difficult to relate to the story of the war. However, historians are no nearer to an answer about whether the Trojan War truly took place.

Passing On – and Pumping Up – the Story of Troy: Homer

The poet Homer and his poems *The Iliad* and *The Odyssey* had a huge impact on almost every aspect of Greek life. Modern folks often have difficulty appreciating quite why this was the case because the attitude to poetry today is very different. In ancient Greece *The Iliad* and *The Odyssey* were the first works of Western literature.

What makes the poems even more amazing is that they are huge, complicated, and lengthy works. Every succeeding historical period has acknowledged the poems as masterpieces, and people still consider them to be astounding examples of literary construction and story telling

The ancient Greeks presumed that the author of the two poems was one man – an author of genius called Homer. For centuries scholars have loudly debated his identity, despite the lack of any real evidence. One popular theory is that Homer was blind and ancient portrait busts of him (made hundreds of years after his death) often show him in this way. The most likely reason for this is the character of Demodocus the bard who appears in *The Odyssey* and performs a song about the Fall of Troy. Because he is blind some people have suggested that Homer put himself in the poem. It's a good theory anyway!

Sharing stories: The oral tradition

Part of the problem in identifying who Homer was comes from the fact that nothing Homer himself wrote actually exists!

Writing didn't develop in Greece until around the eighth century BC (see Chapter 1). Early Greeks composed and delivered poetry orally, and Homer was probably part of this tradition. (This tradition has continued around the world even to modern times, in places as far apart as Serbia and the Congo.)

Oral poets lived an itinerant life travelling around from town to town and performing their work. Ancient sources mention other epic poems such as one about the myths associated with the city of Thebes, but none of these poems survive and none of them had the influence of Homer's epics.

The skill of the poet

The *oral tradition* involves techniques such as using formulas or repeated phrases. You can see these techniques in the works of Homer. Characters are given *epithets* (words that describe their innate qualities or abilities) such as 'swift-footed Achilles' or Hector 'tamer of horses' and these are repeated throughout.

Some key scenes are repeated wholesale. A particularly good example is the description of heroes making a sacrifice and eating the meal that followed. This whole passage is repeated many times throughout both *The Iliad* and *The Odyssey*. You can find a quotation from this scene in Chapter 15.

Part of the reason for these techniques is that ancient Greek poets designed their work to be performed rather than read. The formulas and repetition enabled poets to keep the ideas and stories in their heads in order to present the works to audiences.

Fascinating rhythm

Equally important to the poems is the rhythm in which they were originally composed and that translators work hard to maintain in their modern versions. The original Greek rhythm is *dactylic hexameter*, a form virtually impossible to reproduce in English. Bearing this in mind helps you to remember that these works are poems, despite the many prose translations available today.

The Iliad, for example, is a very long poem of around 17,000 lines. Scholars estimate that the entire work would require roughly 24 hours to read aloud. When it was performed to the ancient Greeks, the poem was most likely presented in sections rather than as a whole.

The length and complexity of the poems have led most people to conclude that they were probably composed some time in the late eighth century BC and then written down around 650 BC. The written versions were more than likely the work of a group of poets but based on a tradition that started with one man, Homer.

Doing battle: The Iliad

I mention *The Iliad* a lot throughout this book, and that's because it's probably the most important work of literature that the Greeks ever produced. The ancient Greeks considered *The Iliad* to be more than just a huge poem about a mythical war. Rather, it was the closest that the Greeks had to a historical record and moral guide. It was a kind of bible; something they turned to for advice on all sorts of issues.

What about the Trojan horse?

One thing that isn't in *The Iliad* – or any of Homer's works for that matter – is the story of the Trojan horse. Although this clever ruse was well established as part of the Trojan myth, it doesn't feature in the poem which comes to an end before the fall of Troy. The incident is frequently mentioned in *The Odyssey* but isn't discussed in any real detail.

By far the best ancient version of the story of the Trojan horse is told in *The Aeneid*, a much later poem by the Roman poet Virgil (first century BC). *The Aeneid* details the story of the Trojan prince Aeneas and his travels after the war.

Historians have no idea if a Trojan horse ever actually existed but the version in *The Aeneid* is very affecting in its description of the tragedies that occurred as Troy fell.

Getting down to details

The Trojan War lasted for about ten years (see the section 'Mining the myth of the Trojan War' for an overview), but the story of *The Iliad* covers only about two weeks of battle.

The central character is the great Greek warrior Achilles, who withdraws from the fighting after an argument with Agamemnon, his commander. While Achilles is out of action, the Trojans get on top in the fighting. The Trojan prince Hector kills Achilles's great male friend (and possibly lover) Patroclus. Grief-stricken, Achilles returns to the fighting and eventually kills Hector before the poem ends with the funeral of Patroclus and the athletic competitions that followed it (a tradition following the death of a warrior).

Heroism, handicrafts, and history

Of course, *The Iliad* is about much more than Achilles seeking vengeance for Patroclus's death. The ancient Greeks considered the poem to be a source of information on:

- **The concept of the hero and the way that heroes behave:** To modern eyes, the characters in *The Iliad* seem unusual and probably quite petulant, but the Greeks loved the way these heroes were totally devoted to their sense of honour. In the world of *The Iliad* a man can preserve his honour only by fighting and killing enemies, and collecting the enemy's armour after battle serves as a visible sign of the hero's honour and skill.

- **Practical procedures:** Several scenes in the poem describe sacrifices and ceremonies that were heavily influenced the way that later Greeks conducted them. (See Chapter 21 for more on ancient Greek religious practices.)

Another good example of how *The Iliad* details everyday life comes when the god Hephaestus makes an incredible shield for Achilles to use during his return to the fighting.

At first Hephaestus makes a great and massive shield, blazoning well-wrought emblems all across its surface, raising a rim around it, glittering, triple-ply with a silver shield-strap run from edge to edge and five layers of metal to build the shield itself.

To modern readers, this passage (and the dozens of lines that follow it) may seem an over-elaborate description. But *The Iliad* and *The Odyssey* are full of details like this and that is why the Greeks regarded the poems as something like compendiums of knowledge.

✔ **Historical figures:** Homer also includes lines and lines of verse devoted to charting the histories of all the characters he introduces. Book 2 of *The Iliad* is often called the Catalogue of Ships; it's basically a long list of virtually all the fighters that were involved in the war. Many ancient Greeks would have regarded this book as the most impressive of the entire poem because of the knowledge that it contains.

For a travelling oral poet the Catalogue of Ships would also be a good way of impressing the audience: the sheer number of heroes mentioned in Book 2 meant that somebody relevant to the town that he was visiting would get a plug. This was a great way of getting the audience onside early in a performance!

Returning home: The Odyssey

In addition to *The Iliad*, the other great work that historians attribute to Homer is *The Odyssey*, which tells the story of what happened to Odysseus, the king of Ithaca, when he tried to return home after the Trojan War. Most scholars believe *The Iliad* was the first of the two poems, with *The Odyssey* being something of a sequel.

Getting down to details

Odysseus's journey takes a very long time because the gods punish him for allowing his men to kill and eat the sacred cattle of the sun god. His ship destroyed and his crew lost, Odysseus ends up stranded on the island of the sea-nymph Calypso for seven years. Along the way, Odysseus has loads of adventures with giants, clashing rocks, sea monsters, and a sorceress called Circe.

Arriving back in Ithaca, Odysseus finds that the local nobles presumed that he was dead and moved into his palace in the hope of wooing his wife Penelope. Teaming up with his son Telemachus, he kills many of the nobles and drives them from the house, finally reuniting with Penelope after 20 years away from home!

Rhapsodes: A load of know-it-alls!

Knowledge of Homer was considered to be vital to a person's education in ancient Greece (see Chapter 14), but some people went even further than that.

Rhapsodes were professional reciters of poetry, most commonly *The Iliad* and *The Odyssey*. Unlike Homer they weren't actually poets themselves but performed other people's work for a fee and often competed in games and competitions. Due to the fact that Homer's poems contained so much knowledge of the world, the Greeks saw the *rhapsodes* as authorities on almost any given subject. A little bit like a kind of walking Internet!

The Odyssey is a fantastic story and reads much more like a modern novel than *The Iliad*.

Despite the drama of the tale, the poem hasn't ever really been successfully turned into a film. The most modern effort was a mini-series from 1997 that starred Armand Assante and Greta Scacchi. It's a good effort with some great Mediterranean scenery and a particularly unpleasant set of suitors led by Eric Roberts. Otherwise try *O Brother, Where Art Thou?* (2001) starring George Clooney. Although set in the deep south of America it's a loose reworking of the story and it can be fun to try and work out the references to Homer's poem. John Goodman's character is the cyclops Polyphemus!

The rules of friendship

One lesson that the ancient Greeks took from *The Odyssey* is the concept of *xenia*. *Xenia* means 'guest-friendship', and it's the regulated system of greeting guests followed by virtually all the characters in *The Odyssey*. In short, *xenia* means you let people relax, eat, and refresh themselves when they arrive at your house before asking them any questions about who they are or what they want.

Here's a great example of the rules of *xenia* in action. In Book 4 of the poem, Menelaus welcomes Odysseus's son Telemachus and a warrior called Mentes (who's actually the goddess Athena in disguise!) into his house without knowing who they are, saying:

> 'Help yourselves to food, and welcome! Once you've dined we'll ask who you are. . . .' With those words he passed them a fat rich loin with his own hands, the choicest part, that he'd been served himself.

Nearly all the characters in the poem follow these rules – and all who don't (like the suitors in Odysseus's house) suffer violent punishments as a result. Consequently, the poem almost sets a moral code for the ancient Greeks. The idea of hospitality and offering guests food and drink was a key part of the ancient Greek mindset. As a regular visitor to Greece I've found this to be a tradition that continues to this day.

Meeting Other, Earlier Heroes

Although the Trojan Cycle that *The Iliad* and *The Odyssey* describe dominated Greek literature and mythology, hundreds of other heroes and stories are associated with the Age of Heroes. In many cases, these individuals were part of an earlier time than the age of Troy. In *The Iliad* the old warrior Nestor of Pylos says that none of the men fighting at Troy can compare with the earlier generation of heroes like Theseus (see the later section 'Theseus: Founder of Athens'). So these earlier heroes must have been pretty impressive! (See Chapter 19 for more on the ancient Greek's conceptualisation of the history of man.)

When ancient Greek literature talks about a *hero,* it doesn't mean somebody who does amazing things to help others like Superman or Spiderman. The ancient Greek concept of a hero is somebody who achieves amazing feats or shows incredible strength and endurance. Most of the time, these heroes aren't very nice and they do a lot of unpleasant things – very different to the modern version of a hero.

The following sections serve as a short guide to some of the other major heroes in ancient Greek mythology and literature, and what they did.

Heracles: A hard worker!

Heracles (or Hercules as the Romans called him) is pretty much the ultimate Greek hero. He was the son of Zeus (see Chapter 19) and a mortal woman called Alcmene.

Virtually from birth, Heracles was famed for having extraordinary courage and strength – as well as a terrific appetite and a terrible temper! A huge number of myths are associated with him, most famously 'The Twelve Labours'. Eurystheus, the king of Tiryns (whom the Delphic Oracle told Heracles to serve), sets up 12 near-impossible tasks for Heracles. There's never been a really satisfying explanation as to why he was given this much to do. Some scholars believe that it was just a clever way of bringing together some of the many stories about Heracles into one big tale.

Table 20-1 outlines and explains the 12 labours.

Table 20-1	The 12 Labours of Hercules
Labour	*Explanation*
The Nemean Lion	Kill the famous lion and bring back his skin.
The Lemaean Hydra	Kill the many-headed serpent.
The Ceryneian Hind	Capture a deer that was sacred to Artemis (see Chapter 19).
The Erymanthian Boar	Capture a savage wild boar.
The Augean Stables	Muck out stables full of years' worth of dung! Nasty!
The Stymphalian Birds	Rid a town of a plague of vicious birds.
The Cretan Bull	Capture a wild bull.
The Mares of Diomedes	Capture some man-eating horses.
The Girdle of Hippolyte	Steal the belt from the queen of the Amazons.
The Cattle of Geryon	Journey into the unknown to capture some cattle.
The Apples of the Hesperides	Steal the golden apples that grew at the end of the earth.
Cerberus	Journey to Hades and capture the triple-headed dog that guarded its entrance.

After all these labours, Heracles still isn't done. Many more stories tell of his exploits. When he finally dies, he is taken up to Olympus where he lives with the gods as one of them. That alone makes him the greatest of Greek heroes.

Theseus: Founder of Athens

As I mention in Chapter 4, many ancient Greeks believed that Theseus was:

- The son of Poseidon (covered in Chapter 19)
- The founder of many of the institutions of the city of Athens
- The hero who went to Crete and defeated the Minotaur

Of course, loads of other stories are associated with Theseus; not least journeying to fight the Amazons alongside Heracles. By the fifth century BC the Greeks thought of Theseus as the founding figure of justice, and he appears in several tragic plays as a very noble figure.

Perseus: Medusa slayer

Perseus was the son of Zeus and the mortal woman Danae. (Zeus turned himself into a shower of gold to impregnate this lovely lady!)

Perseus's most famous feat was killing the snake-haired Gorgon called Medusa who turned men to stone with one look. He also saved Andromeda from being eaten by a sea-monster. These adventures and more feature in the film *Clash of the Titans* (1980).

Jason: Leader of the Argonauts

Jason is famous for one really big feat. His wicked uncle Pelias denied Jason the throne of Iolcus, and set him the task of travelling far to the city of Colchis to steal the Golden Fleece, the skin of a ram with magical powers. On his ship called the *Argo*, Jason was joined by a famous crew of heroes, the Argonauts.

The most complete version of the myth is the *Voyage of Argo* by Apollonius of Rhodes, written in the third century BC.

Bellerophon: Mystery man

Historians and scholars often consider Bellerophon to be the forgotten man of Greek myths whose stories haven't survived as well as some of the others. A son of Poseidon, Bellerophon is sent on various impossible tasks, rather like Heracles. These tasks include fighting the terrifying Chimaera monster and battling single-handed against the Amazons. The flying horse Pegasus aids him in these tasks.

Where heroes go to die

Given that these heroes all achieved such amazing things in their lifetimes it's no surprise that myths suggested that they were equally special in death. Mortals just went to the grim underworld of Hades (see Chapter 21) but the fate of heroes was rather different.

According to mythology heroes went to a place called *Elysium*, also known as the 'Elysian Fields' or 'Elysian Plain.' This was a special section of Hades where heroes could spend all eternity feasting and hunting in a beautiful paradise. So it was worth carrying out all those heroic tasks after all!

Building them up – to knock them down

Just like historical figures and the Olympian gods (see Chapter 19), the early heroes of Greek mythology are very open to interpretation. Later Greek writers reinterpreted them in quite different ways. For example, Heracles is often shown in comedies as a drunkard and a glutton. The phrase 'a Heracles supper' evolved to describe an event that goes on long after it should have finished.

The tragic playwrights took heroes and portrayed elements of their character from very different viewpoints:

- In Sophocles's play *Philoctetes*, Odysseus is something of a villain, using his cunning to hurt others.

- In Euripides's *Medea*, Jason is proud, selfish, and arrogant.

Chapter 21

Practising Everyday Religion: 'A God Put It in My Heart to Say'

Chapter 19 introduces the many varied ancient Greek gods, and illustrates the roles specific gods were believed to have in the mythical past. In this chapter I look at how the ancient Greeks worshipped their gods and other mythical heroes in their daily lives. Get ready to uncover some strange and unusual rituals – at least for modern eyes.

Greek religion was actually very formal and full of big public rituals in the same way that modern religions make requirements on people to be in places at certain times of day and week. Public religion is the major focus of this chapter – understanding the private, spiritual beliefs of the ancient Greeks is very difficult because historians don't really have any record of them. The closest that we get to it is in understanding their cults, which were a slight departure from everyday religious practice.

Everything that I talk about in this chapter is what *most* Greeks accepted and did in their daily lives. Just like today, each ancient Greek man or woman had different, individual ideas about the gods, but by and large they carried out similar religious practices and ceremonies.

Dying – In Theory and Practice

Death and dying may sound like a gloomy subject, but the ancient Greeks had some intriguing – and perhaps inspiring – notions about what happened to humans after they passed away. Modern anthropologists often say that you can tell a lot about a society by the way that it deals with death because it proves what people thought was valuable. I think that idea is probably true of ancient Greece.

Venturing into the underworld: The mythological take

The Greeks believed that when people died, their bodies decayed, their souls (or 'shades' – like a kind of ghost version of the person) travelled to Hades (the name of both the god of the dead and the underworld) to exist for eternity.

When 'shades' entered the underworld, they first had to cross the river Styx (or Lethe) on a ferry piloted by the famous ferryman Charon. When people died, their friends or family placed a coin in their mouths so that they were able to pay Charon his fee. If a person died and didn't have the proper funeral rites, he or she would spend eternity unable to cross the river.

While crossing the Styx, the hand of the 'shade' fell into the water and the magical power of the river drained all memories from the body, allowing the deceased individual to be content to exist in the underworld without continually mourning for those they left behind.

Despite the gloomy subject matter, the Greeks were able to poke fun at the dying process. Aristophanes's play *Frogs* is set in the underworld, and Charon appears as a rather comical character.

> *Any more for Lethe, Blazes, Perdition, or the Dogs? Come along now, any more for a nice restful trip to Eternity? No more worries, no more cares, makes a lovely break!*

Other theories about the underworld and the experiences of the dead existed. For example, in *The Odyssey* (see Chapter 20), Odysseus has to travel to the underworld to speak with the prophet Tiresias. The souls that Odysseus meets are deeply unhappy and remember *everything* about their previous lives. Indeed, they spend eternity drifting around in grief and must consume sacrificial blood before they can speak to Odysseus. Yuck!

The ancient Greeks appear to have placed no value judgement on people's lives, and had no equivalents of heaven or hell. Everyone went to Hades regardless of the lives they'd led and stayed there for eternity. The only exceptions were the mythological heroes who were fortunate to have ended up in *Elyisum* (refer to Chapter 20).

Dealing with the dead: Practicalities

Mythology aside, the ancient Greeks had very specific ways of dealing with death. Indeed, the Greeks were obsessed with receiving proper burials because they believed that if bodies didn't receive proper funeral rites from relatives, then the souls of the dead were prevented from travelling to the underworld (see the preceding section 'Venturing into the underworld: The mythological take').

Funerals could be expensive affairs with all kinds of musicians and performers required and many people attending the formal meal, which all the family attended before the burial. As I examine in Chapter 14, the ancient Greeks were really obsessed with the idea of familial and friendship ties, so funerals were big events.

Poorer people had to make do with what was available. They'd still strive to ensure a proper burial, even if they weren't able to afford the attendant functions. After all, a family meal could just involve some wine, cheese, and olives.

Ancient Greece was mainly an *inhumation culture*, which means that bodies are buried, rather than a *cremation culture* in which they're burnt. Most families had a family tomb that they filled with generations of corpses.

Every year the surviving family members gathered at their tomb or grave to honour those who had died, a bit like an annual memorial service. Normally these rites would involve saying prayers and making offerings to the gods.

Often, the tombs included gravestones featuring epitaphs carved in the stone. These words were sometimes in verse form, produced by a poet for hire. One such poet was Simonides (circa 500 BC). Following are two of his best efforts!

> *Drinker, glutton supreme, supreme defamer of men. I, Timokreon of Rhodes, now lie down here.*

> *Someone is glad that I, Theodorus, am dead. Another will be glad when that someone is dead. We are all in arrears to death.*

Worshipping the Gods

Throughout their whole lives, ancient Greeks were continually involved in some kind of religious ceremony or ritual. Social life, business deals, marriage, war, and cultural entertainment all involved ritual practices focused on one or several gods in the pantheon (see Chapter 19).

Rituals were important because they allowed the ancient Greeks to ask the gods for help, approval, or a guarantee. All rituals involved a kind of bargaining: The humans provided the gods with something in exchange for their help. See the later section 'Sacrificing: Giving the gods gifts' for the fascinating details.

Seeing the gods in person: Idols

Many aspects of Greek religion took place inside temples (see Chapter 18). Within each temple was a statue that depicted a specific god. The ancient Greeks believed that the god was actually present inside the temple – or if many temples to a specific deity existed, they believed that the god always visited their temple at some point during the year or at least that they could see what was going on in many temples at once.

The belief that gods were present within the temples meant that the Greeks actually worshipped the statue within the temple – a practice that modern folks would call *idolatry.* (See Chapter 17 for more on the process of creating metal and marble statues.) In contrast, worshippers in a Catholic church for example, aren't honouring a statue but the figure that the statue represents.

As worship, the Greeks made small offerings and prayed to the gods. They sometimes dressed the statue with ribbons known as *stemmata.* The statues must have ended up being quite pretty and well-covered because a large number of people visited the temple on a daily basis.

When to worship

The ancient Greek calendar was full of official religious days and festivals (refer to Chapter 15). The Greeks didn't have a specific holy day but engaged in religious rituals during the many festivals.

This meant that normal worship at the temple took place whenever a person wanted. Individuals could worship alone or as groups and families and a temple priest would always supervise whatever activities they were carrying out. Men, women, and children were all allowed to attend temples but would probably do most of their personal worship in their home.

Having gods in your home

The Greek household (*oikos*) was itself a sacred place with its own rituals and requirements (see Chapter 14). The main protector of the household was

Zeus, known in this instance as *Zeus Herkeios*, or the Guardian. Zeus was also responsible for the concept of *xenia*, the proper treatment of guests (see Chapter 21).

The household itself was sacred to Hestia, goddess of the hearth (see Chapter 19). Every house kept a fire constantly burning in honour of the goddess, and this hearth was the centrepiece of the home. This was the spot where the *oikos* ate all meals and received guests.

The ancient Greeks also chose their own deities who they looked on to protect their houses. People placed images of the selected gods on the gates or doors of houses or somewhere within the home. Gods such as Apollo and Hermes were popular choices.

Sacrificing: Giving the gods gifts

Sacrifices and offerings were the main ways of honouring the gods. A sacrifice was the killing of an animal, whereas an offering was a gift of wine, food, money, or other item. These practices weren't Greek inventions; the tradition went back a long way into the past. The idea behind them was that you gave the gods some of your food – that which kept you alive – and in return the gods would either just continue to look after you or perhaps aid you in some way such as blessing a married couple with children or ensuring a good harvest for a farm.

Sometimes offerings were quite simple – fruits, grain, or special cakes. The more famous sort of sacrifice was livestock or farm animals, such as oxen, bulls, cows, sheep, pigs, goats, or other animals.

Little, everyday sacrifices

Although formal sacrifices and offerings (see the following section 'Big sacrifices') were part of religious life, the ancient Greeks believed that the gods could see everything and would pick up on any slight acknowledgement. Consequently people would make small, almost superstitious offerings throughout the day.

Additionally, the Greeks thought rivers, forests, and other natural phenomena were touched by the gods. By dropping pebbles or very small offerings of food in the river or wherever, people believed they were acknowledging the power and pervasiveness of the gods.

The belief that the gods were everywhere went even further. The Greeks believed that occasionally the gods walked the earth in human form to check on mankind. They also explained the fact that they occasionally blurted out something stupid with the expression, Some god put it in my heart to say'. Try using that explanation next time you say something embarrassing!

Purity is everything

Ritual purification was an essential part of any ancient Greek religious ceremony. This process literally meant washing, and in most cases just washing your hands was enough. The idea of purification probably comes from the fact that most Greeks were farmers (or had originally been farmers), and by washing you were removing the dirt from yourself and putting work aside before worshipping the gods.

Sometimes the purification rituals were extreme (see the sidebar 'The Delphic oracle') and involved a person cleansing themselves of an awful act – like a murderer 'washing the blood from their hands'.

Big sacrifices

At the temple, ancient Greeks cut the throats of the sacrificial animals. (The resulting blood was often presented as an additional offering.) These activities wouldn't take place inside the temple itself but in the grounds around it. The Greeks had two ways of making sacrifices:

- ✔ **Sacrificing some part of the animal, and serving the rest.** Sometimes people roasted the animal, and offered a portion to the gods. They used the remaining meat to make a formal meal for those attending the ceremony. This kind of barbeque-like sacrifice was the most common. In Greek poetry, the gods are often described as enjoying the smell of roasting meat as it drifts up to Olympus.

- ✔ **Completely burning the entire animal.** The total burning of an animal was usually reserved for a specific purpose. Most often people were trying to appease the gods. For example, in a case of murder, ancient Greeks considered the burned animal to count as a 'one-for-one' offering to replace the victim.

So what was the point of sacrifice? The most literal way of understanding the concept is that you were giving a gift to the gods. Animals were expensive, so killing a cow or goat was a significant financial offering. Of course, this also meant a good feed for everybody else involved too!

Pondering and Predicting the Future

Despite the mystically tinged scenes in lots of Greek plays and even more modern-day movies, the Greeks did *not* use prophecies to predict the future. Instead, they turned to the gods and asked for help in the future or advice on what to do in the present.

Divination, or what the Greeks called *mantike*, involved asking the gods questions to try and ensure a happy and prosperous future. The following sections look at these aspects of Greek religion.

Consulting oracles

The ancient Greeks believed that the gods were involved in a person's *fate*, and ensured that what was meant to happen to them did happen. The gods didn't create a person's fate but it was their responsibility to make sure that what was fated to happen actually took place.

One of the most popular ways for an ancient Greek to figure out what to do to follow their fate was to visit an *oracle*, a place where the Greeks believed they could ask someone questions and receive answers from the gods. An oracle was a place, not a person, and could be anywhere where the gods 'touched the world' such as a stream, a bush, or the inner sanctum of a temple.

Talk to the man

Usually, the person at the oracle was a priest, or *hiereus*, who was employed by the shrine or temple. The Greeks didn't think that the priest had any kind of magical powers, just the knowledge and skills required to do the job.

In addition to a priest, the temple or shrine sometimes used the services of a *seer*, or *mantis*, to understand the answers of an oracle. A seer wasn't tied to any religious institution and worked for private hire.

Many Greeks were cynical about the service that seers provided because it was pretty much in the interests of the seer to give a client the answers that they were looking for! In mythology, seers are often presented as figures who can actually see into the future, and who are beloved by the gods and in possession of magical abilities. In everyday Greece, it's unlikely that most people regarded seers in this way.

Yes, no, er . . . maybe!

Consulting an oracle wasn't quite as straightforward as it may sound. Oracles didn't predict the future. Instead, they gave advice on what to do in the present. The Greeks believed that the future was already set out, or *predetermined.* Therefore, they didn't ask to change it, but rather how to interpret what they saw around them to help predict how things may be.

So, for example, a man didn't visit an oracle and ask how many children his prospective wife would have. Instead, he asked for advice on whether he should marry her. If the oracle suggested he should marry, and he did and they subsequently had children, then the oracle developed a reputation for being able to predict the future. Of course, if the same man married the woman and the couple didn't have children, then the ancient Greeks thought the man had misinterpreted the answer!

In general, oracles provided answers that were supportive – telling people what to do to ensure a happy future rather than explaining what that future would be.

Because an oracle's response was sometimes quite problematic, the special skills of a seer were often required to interpret it.

Looking to signs

The Greeks were very superstitious and saw signs and portents in all kinds of everyday activities. The flight of birds (known as *bird lore*), the movement of leaves, and the flow of running water were all used as methods of interpreting the will of the gods. Just as with the pronouncements of oracles, a priest or seer was required to interpret these signs.

Interpreting bird lore was particularly complicated. This inscription from Ephesus in Asia Minor (dated at about 550 BC) is one of the only surviving examples of what certain flight patterns meant – and it isn't exactly straightforward!

> *. . . if the bird flying from left to right disappears from view the omen is favourable; if it raises its left wing, flies away, and disappears the omen is unfavourable; if flying from left to right it disappears on a straight course the omen is unfavourable; but if after raising its right wing, it flies away and disappears the omen is favourable.*

One of the most popular sources of signs was examining the *entrails* (inner organs) of recently sacrificed animals. The condition of these organs, especially the liver, was a method of testing whether the gods supported a course of action. People often made major decisions about war and diplomatic negotiations after examining a sacrifice's entrails.

Taking Oaths: 'I Promise!'

Just as the Greeks used divination and oracles to seek advice about what to do in life, religion was also a big part of any decisions or deals that they made. Decisions often took the form of oaths that the Greeks swore, using the gods as their witnesses.

The Delphic oracle

The most famous ancient Greek oracle of all was the one at Delphi in central Greece (see the Cheat Sheet map). The oracle at Delphi was extremely old and dated back to around the ninth century BC. The oracle was dedicated to Apollo and the centrepiece of the sanctuary was a large temple devoted to him. Both cities and individuals – including virtually every famous figure from ancient Greek history – asked for the Delphic oracle's advice.

Conferring with the Delphic oracle required a complicated process of purification and sacrifice (see the earlier section 'Sacrificing: Giving the gods gifts'). The whole thing was supervised by the *pythia*, or priestess of the temple. When asked a question, the priestess went into a trance and then babbled incoherent sentences, which arose from her communication with the god Apollo. The answers were famously ambiguous, but the Greeks believed that the gods spoke clearly; any misinterpretations came down to human stupidity!

You can still visit Delphi; it's a beautiful little town and a fabulous site which I describe in Chapter 26.

Swearing of an oath (*horkos*) meant that you were promising to do something, such as paying for goods or marrying somebody. Characters in Greek tragedy often swear oaths, particularly oaths of vengeance where they promise to avenge a wronged or slain relative and this was fairly common practice in ancient Greece too. Additionally, if you didn't do what you promised, you accepted the punishment of the gods.

Given that the Greeks only really started using writing in around 750 BC (see Chapter 1), oaths were also used as a form of verbal contract in business deals. Merchants entered into trade deals and called upon the gods Hermes or Poseidon to be the arbiter.

Having Fun with the Gods: Festivals and Cults

Most Greek cities had highly defined religious calendars based around big public festivals. (See Chapter 15 for the intricacies of the ancient Greek calendar.) Some celebrations were massive and went on for days, and others were held only by a particular town region (*deme*).

Private healthcare: The sanctuary at Epidauros

Asclepius, the god of healing, had one of the most famous places of worship dedicated to him at Epidauros. Greeks visited the shrine and asked for advice on curing their illnesses. Asclepius didn't have any real connection with Epidauros, but the priests there invented one; the site became second only to Delphi (see the sidebar 'The Delphic oracle') in visitor numbers.

Despite its popularity, people didn't expect instant cures from the sanctuary at Epidauros. As at Delphi, all answers from the gods had to be interpreted by the priests, who weren't doctors. What the priests advised usually went against what Hippocratic doctors of the time would have prescribed. Nevertheless, a huge amount of money was spent in asking the priests' advice!

Additionally, smaller religious groups gathered together in the form of *religious cults* that worshipped particular individual divinities. The rules and regulations around these cults were as strict as they were bizarre. See the later section 'Getting cultic: Swimming with pigs and other oddities' for more.

Observing the religious year

I discuss the complex Athenian calendar in Chapter 15, but the typical religious calendar of a city was even more complicated. For example, Athenians gave over 130 days of the year to specific festivals, although many more small festivals and celebrations also took place. Roughly speaking, something related to a festival or celebration probably occurred every other day.

Athenians celebrated about 30 large festivals during the religious year. The month of *Pyanopsion* (September/October) featured an impressive six festivals in honour of Apollo, Theseus, Demeter (twice), and Athene (twice).

Some of these festivals were massive; for example, the big drama festivals like the Country and City Dionysia both went on for several days and took the form of a major public holiday. Visitors came from far and wide to take part in these celebrations.

As I mention in Chapter 16, festivals included all types of activities: dramatic performances, athletic games, singing and dancing competitions, and large amounts of feasting and drinking. The public purse and donations from wealthier citizen paid for these events.

Although religious celebration was the main point of festivals, they weren't sober and restrained events – quite the reverse! All sorts of ribaldry took place with much drinking and carousing. If you want a modern equivalent, try New Year's Eve crossed with the Glastonbury Festival!

Two notable festivals: The Panathenaia and the Thesmophoria

One of the biggest festivals in ancient Athens was the *Panathenaia*, which celebrated the city and its patron goddess Athena (see Chapter 19). The festival was held every year in the month of *Hekatombaion* (June/July) and was effectively a new year celebration. The Athenians made huge processions, and the main one involved the transporting of a robe (*peplos*) for the goddess Athene. The procession is depicted in the frieze of the Parthenon, parts of which are on display in the British Museum.

The *Panathenaia* was a very nationalistic festival and was rooted in the idea of celebrating Athenian supremacy over other Greeks. The Athenians made the celebration even bigger once every four years and called it the Great Panathenaia.

One of the more notorious festivals was the women-only *Thesmophoria*, which was held throughout Greece in the autumn. Men were banned from the festival, which was held in honour of Demeter. Only married women of cities were allowed to attend and they left town and held secret rites away in the countryside. These activities were usually very mysterious and are mocked by Aristophanes in his play *Thesmophoriazousai*, in which the women spend a lot of time drinking. (Okay, there's probably some truth in this!)

The Olympian gods (refer to Chapter 19) each had a sacred day every month as well. Often these holidays included ceremonies that were specific to a particular *deme*.

On lesser religious holidays, things were often simpler. Just one relatively small sacrifice to a specific god may be required.

Getting cultic: Swimming with pigs and other oddities

These days the idea of a religious cult has slightly sinister overtones. The word is currently used to describe unusual groups that shut themselves away from the world. In ancient Greece, however, the idea of a *religious cult* was very aspirational. Joining a cult was a sign of social status because membership was very closely guarded.

All the other festivals and ceremonies that I mention in this chapter were public experiences; everyone could join in, and participation occurred in the gathering areas of town and cities such as the *agora* (see Chapter 18). Cults were different. Although cults may involve a large number of people in a ceremony, the experience of the individual was intended to be quite personal. This was the nearest that ancient Greek religion got to the notion of a spiritual experience.

The Eleusinian Mysteries

By far the most famous cult was the Eleusinian Mysteries. Even now, historians don't know precisely what went on during the cult's festivals. At the time, the secrets of their ritual were closely guarded, with dire penalties for those who broke the rules. Scholars do know that the cult was based around the myth of Persephone and Demeter (see Chapter 13) and involved a process that recreated the journey into Hades. The final ceremony apparently revealed a glimpse of the afterlife to the initiates.

The ritual took place during late summer (probably during *Boedromion*) in the *deme* of Eleusis in Athens. The ritual was open to anybody Greek-speaking, although they had to pay hefty fees to take part. The purification and initiation rituals were very complicated. Every participant had to wash a young pig in the sea and then sacrifice it, and they also had to wear special clothes and fast from certain foods. The whole experience took several days and was regarded by the ancient Greeks as a life-changing one.

The following excerpt comes from one of the so-called 'Homeric Hymns', religious songs in the style of Homer (see Chapter 20). The song deals with Demeter, Persephone, and the mysteries.

> *To all Demeter revealed the conduct of her rites and mysteries . . . dread mysteries which one may not in any way transgress or learn of or utter . . . Happy is he of mortal men who has seen these things. . . .*

Because the spiritual experience of cults was considered to be so extraordinary, the various cults were incredibly closely organised with very strict rules. This inscription from the site of the Spring of the Nymphs at Delos gives a good idea of how respectful people had to be of cult places – in this case a spring.

> *Do not wash anything in the spring, or swim in the spring, or throw into the spring manure or anything else. Penalty: two sacred drachmas.*

Major cults like the Eleusinian Mysteries were open to all but others might be restricted to people in a certain trade or guild (for example, a group of tradesmen like potters or ironmongers). Equally, the nature of the rites might prove prohibitive to some people because of the costs involved. It seems certain that more exclusive and bizarre cults took place amongst the mega-rich but unfortunately historians don't really know anything about them.

Chapter 22

Trying to Figure Everything Out: Greek Philosophy

. . . .

In This Chapter

▶ Pondering existence with the early Greek philosophers

▶ Chatting with Socrates and Plato

▶ Getting scientific with Aristotle and others

. . . .

*A*t first glance, Greek philosophy can seem quite intimidating. Most books on the subject have front covers with pictures of marble busts of serious, slightly angry looking men with big bushy beards. What's inside these books can seem just as intimidating – but a lot of the time, the ideas, insights, and explanations are actually quite simple.

In this chapter I look at how the very idea of philosophy developed in ancient Greece and share what some of the major figures thought about all manner of topics, including existence, morality, and the nature of the universe. The ancient Greek philosophers are a strange bunch with some weird and outlandish ideas – but they're quite fun too!

Making the Case for Philosophy

In Chapters 19, 20, and 21, I look at the mythical gods and heroes and how the Greek religion dominated virtually all aspects of ancient Greek life. Their religion gave the Greeks a pretty closely defined idea of what their world was like and where it came from – but for some people unanswered questions still existed.

Greek philosophy grew out of the earliest philosophers' desire to explain the world around them, including such major issues as:

  ✔ Where everything came from.

  ✔ What the world was made of.

  ✔ What happened when you died.

The word used to describe the philosopher's drive is *reason*, a desire to understand and explain things instead of accepting religious or spiritual explanations. And as I discuss in Chapters 19, 20, and 21, ancient Greek religion was full of holes and logical gaps; the gods that filled its ranks were frequently vengeful, childish, and downright unpleasant. Some folks hungered for different – and hopefully better – answers.

Writing in the fifth century BC, the philosopher Xenophanes sums up the problem.

> *Both Homer and Hesiod have attributed all things to the gods, as many as shameful and a reproach amongst mankind, thieving and adultery and deceiving each other.*

So if the gods weren't the answer to everything, then what was? *Philosophy* came into being when some the ancient Greeks tried to work it all out.

The term philosopher means 'lover of wisdom' and comes from the Greek word *sophia* meaning wisdom. Greek philosophers were all men from varied backgrounds. Philosophers like Socrates and Plato were aristocrats and a full-time philosopher would need to be wealthy to be able to spend all day pontificating!

Other people were interested in philosophy too, though, and discussion was very fashionable amongst the educated classes.

Meeting the Early Greek Philosophers

Scholars generally refer to the earliest Greek philosophers as the *pre-Socratics* because they were around before Socrates, the most famous figure in Greek philosophy. See the later section 'Creating the 'New Philosophy' with Socrates' for more on this great Greek.

The pre-Socratics weren't really philosophers in the sense that you might think of a philosopher today. Most of them didn't write books or engage in lectures or teaching. Really, these men just asked questions and looked for answers in the world that they saw about them. They were unhappy with the explanations that mythology provided (see Chapter 19), and looked for alternatives in the natural world and its elements. Truly they were 'lovers of wisdom'.

Although the pre-Socratics didn't really come up with definite answers, they started the process of enquiry, encouraging others to explore different questions and challenge orthodox beliefs.

One of the problems with looking at the pre-Socratic philosophers is that very few sources are available. Some of the earliest philosophers didn't write anything down at all, whereas the books of others are now lost. This dearth of original texts means that modern scholars must rely on later Greek writers (such as Xenophon and Aristotle) who compiled large compendiums of philosophy that include fragments of the early philosophers' work. Happily, enough material is available to get a good idea of their theories.

This section is just a small survey of what I regard as some of the most important pre-Socratic philosophers. Loads of others – including Zeno, Anaxagoras, Melissus, Philolaus, Leucippus, Democritus, and many more – are well worth looking into if you want something interesting to think about! Using the online encyclopedia Wikipedia (at www.wikipedia.co.uk) is a great place to start but if you're looking for a book try *Early Greek Philosophy* edited by Jonathan Barnes and published by Penguin Classics.

Using their eyes: Thales and Anaximander

Two of the earliest notable pre-Socratic philosophers were Thales and Anaximander. They both came from the town of Miletus on the south-western coast of Asia Minor and were active around 580 BC.

Although historians aren't fully certain, Thales's work seems to have come first, and Anaximander appears to have been a pupil or follower of Thales.

It's probably no coincidence that these earliest philosophers came from Miletus because the town received visitors from all over the Mediterranean and the east. The mixture of ideas and theories that must have been present among the population makes the location a natural place for enquiring minds.

Both of these men's investigations were based on looking at the world around them and drawing conclusions from what they saw in nature. Modern scholars call this process *observational philosophy*.

Water, water everywhere

Both Thales and Anaximander were concerned with the idea of the *four key elements*: earth, air, fire, and water. Their idea was that everything in the world was in some way made up of these four things.

Thales's big concern was water. He seems to have looked at the world around him and decided that just as the land he stood on was surrounded by water, the whole of the earth must be too. This notion was in line with the old Greek view that the earth was an island entirely surrounded by water, rather like the yolk in a fried egg (see Chapter 19).

Thales took his speculation further though. He thought that water was the essential element of all things. Humans, plants, and animals all need water to survive; therefore, according to Thales, water was the essential stuff of life and what everything was made from. The Greeks referred to this concept as the *arche* meaning 'first principle' or 'beginning'.

Thales also came up with interesting theories about other things, among them the idea that a magnet must have a soul. He based this idea on the fact that a magnet can make things move; therefore, it must have intelligence and, accordingly, a soul.

Getting cosmic

As a pupil or follower of Thales, Anaximander went on to investigate further and and more widely than Thales. Anaximander was alleged to have been one of the first people to draw a map of the inhabited world and to come up with a theory as to how the universe and the heavens were formed. This subject was known as *cosmology*, and many argue that Anaximander invented it.

The cosmology that Anaximander came up with is a bit trippy and mad! It involves all four key elements working together to produce large flat discs (of which the earth is one) that make up the universe. All natural things like humans, animals, and the weather are created when the elements stop working together and separate.

Thales and Anaximander were interesting, if misguided. Still, they were celebrated by subsequent ancient Greeks for being the two men who first thought differently and encouraged other people to theorise about big important questions. You may say that their biggest discovery was the process of philosophy itself.

Pondering existence: Parmenides, Heraclitus, Pythagoras, and others

After Thales and Anaximander opened the philosophical floodgates, many other people began to ask difficult questions about the world around them.

Some of the later pre-Socratics took huge steps forward by trying to ask questions about the nature of existence itself. What did it mean to live and die; to exist and then to stop existing?

A bit of a show-off

One of the first philosophers to ask about existence itself in detail was Parmenides, who came from Elea, a Greek town in southern Italy. Like many of the other pre-Socratics, precise birth and death dates aren't available, but he was alive and probably visited Athens in about 450 BC.

Parmenides's big concern was to answer the question of how something comes into existence and then later ceases to be. He discussed this question in a long poem called the 'Way of Truth', which seems a little like showing off:

> *How, whence, did it grow? That it came from what is not I shall not allow you to say or think – for it is not sayable or thinkable that it is not. And what need would have impelled it, later or earlier, to grow – if it began from nothing?*

In the end Parmenides decided that everything exists and that anything that you can imagine comes into existence after you imagine it. So, for example, while you're reading this book, if you imagine me, the author, riding a giant dragon, then that dragon exists because you imagined it. Blimey! A handy trick, indeed!

Further to this notion, Parmenides believed that everything that exists always has done and always will do in some form or other. This theory was known to the Greeks as *the Immutable One*.

Constant change

Across the other side of the Mediterranean in Ephesus was another philosopher called Heraclitus (circa 525–475 BC). His theory about existence was very different to Parmenides. In fact, it was the absolute opposite.

Heraclitus's major theory was that everything is in a constant state of change, or *flux*. Everything needs to move or change in order to progress and grow. Heraclitus's view was also the opposite of Anaximander's idea that the four elements had to be in order for the universe to work (see the preceding section 'Using their eyes: Thales and Anaximander').

A great example of Heraclitus's state of change theory is that, if you put your foot in a river, by the time you take it out again the water has flowed over it and the river has changed. If you put your foot in again, the river is no longer the river that you put your foot into originally. The constantly changing experience of a river is, in essence, what Heraclitus thought about the whole nature of existence.

Reincarnation: 'I think I've been here before'

Parmenides and Heraclitus tackled the question of existence and came up with some answers. In both cases, they were really motivated by a desire to explain what happened before birth and after death.

Other pre-Socratic philosophers looked at this question from another perspective. If what Parmenides said was true about all matter always existing now and in the future, then what happened to the soul, or *psyche*, after the body died? One idea that was very fashionable was the idea of reincarnation.

Reincarnation was not a purely Greek idea, having first been discussed in places as far away as Egypt and Mesopotamia. Still, several pre-Socratic philosophers promoted this concept. This quote from Empedocles (circa 450 BC) sums up reincarnation nicely.

> *For already I have been born as a boy and a girl and a bush and a bird and a dumb fish leaping out of the sea.*

The man who popularised the notion of reincarnation was Pythagoras, probably the most famous of all the pre-Socratic philosophers and a hugely controversial figure. Active in the sixth century BC, Pythagoras originally came from Samos but spent a large part of his life in southern Italy. He was also rumoured to have magically appeared in many other cities in both southern Italy and Greece.

Pythagoras is credited with a huge number of discoveries and theories, including a particularly famous geometric principle (see the nearby sidebar 'The Pythagorean Theorem: Maths and stuff'). However, because he wrote nothing down, historians know very little about him. Scholars have pieced together the following:

- ✔ Pythagoras's big theory was based around the idea of *metempsychosis*, which means the movement of the soul between physical bodies, a particular kind of reincarnation. One story suggests that Pythagoras stopped a man beating a puppy because he recognised the dog as one of his old friends by its bark!

- ✔ Pythagoras was famed for his wide knowledge, and some people attributed him with magical powers. He was rumoured to have had a thigh made of gold and to have killed a poisonous snake by biting it first.

Whatever the actualities behind these stories, Pythagoras built up a huge following. His followers became a kind of cult and closely guarded the details of their lifestyle. They built their lives around his teaching, on principles based on music, harmony, and a very proscriptive diet – such as eating beans to keep you regular! These individuals continued to work on Pythagoras's principles long after his death (or reincarnation?).

Perhaps Pythagoras's biggest achievement was to boost the interest in philosophy in those that followed him.

Jumping into the flames

One of Pythagoras's most famous followers was Empedocles (circa 490–460 BC). Indeed, Empedocles's writings preserved many of Pythagoras's ideas.

The Pythagorean Theorem: Maths and stuff

You're probably familiar with Pythagoras because you were taught his famous *theorem* at school:

The square on the hypotenuse is equal to the sum of the squares on the other two sides.

Many of the pre-Socratics (as well as later philosophers) were intensely interested in mathematics and used it to work out many of their theories. The study of mathematics and particularly

geometry was a very important concern in ancient Greece, and the work of people such as Euclid was responsible for real discoveries.

I don't delve into ancient Greek mathematics in this chapter because I think philosophy is very different from maths. What's interesting to me are the tremendous leaps of imagination that these various philosophers took in thinking about the world and nature of existence. Another reason is that I'm rubbish at maths!

Like Parmenides (see the preceding section 'A bit of a show-off'), Empedocles wrote in verse form. His long poem called *The Purifications* was one of the first attempts to align philosophy and Greek religion. In it, he introduced an element of moral philosophy that was very important to later thinkers (see the following section 'Creating the 'New Philosophy' with Socrates').

Empedocles was convinced of the idea of metempsychosis (see the preceding 'Reincarnation: 'I think I've been here before''); particularly that the soul was immortal (and thus like a god). According to a long-held tradition, Empedocles set out to prove this idea by throwing himself into the volcano of Mount Etna in Sicily, telling his followers that he would return in another form. As far as I know, the world is still waiting for his reappearance!

Creating the 'New Philosophy' with Socrates

Socrates is one of the most famous of the ancient Greeks, partly because of his terrible execution by Athens in 399 BC (see Chapter 9), but mostly because he was responsible for creating the new kind of philosophy that was developed in Athens in the fifth century BC.

Like Pythagoras (see the preceding section 'Reincarnation: 'I think I've been here before'), Socrates never wrote anything down. Modern readers are reliant on his followers (mostly Plato and Xenophon) for what survives about Socrates's philosophy today.

Socrates's major interest was different from that of the pre-Socratics. He wasn't really interested in cosmology and questions of reincarnation. Instead, he was far more concerned with why people acted the way they did. His theory was that people should always try to do well and do the right thing. This stance is why he's credited with being the person who invented *moral philosophy*.

Talking with Socrates: Socratic dialogue

In addition to his focus on moral philosophy, Socrates's method of enquiry was also quite different. The process basically involved asking questions of people and challenging their assumptions. Socrates always did this questioning in the spirit of finding out an answer, because he didn't think he knew everything. Indeed, he's famously attributed for saying, *'All that I know is that I know nothing.'*

These conversations between Socrates and his educated friends – *Socratic dialogues* – began with Socrates asking a question of the person who he was talking to and then interrogating (and eventually overturning) that person's answer.

Usually, the question was about some kind of moral quality such as bravery or friendship, although Socrates seemingly discussed absolutely everything.

In this dialogue called *Charmides* (recorded by Plato), Socrates talks about the issue of keeping to doing one's own job and whether doing so shows self-control. Have a look at the way the conversation goes – the process of the discussion is more important than the subject.

> *'Well then,' I [Socrates] said, 'do you think a state would be well run by a law like this, which commands each person to weave his own coat and wash it, and make his own sandals and oil-flask and scraper and everything else on the same principle of each person keeping his hands off what is not his own, and working at and doing his own job?'*
>
> *'No, I don't,' he replied.*
>
> *'Nevertheless,' I said, 'a state run on the principle of self-control would be run well.'*
>
> *'Certainly,' he said.*
>
> *'Then,' I said, 'self-control would not be doing one's own job when it's of that sort and done in that way.'*

This is a typical piece of Socratic dialogue. Socrates asks an opinion and then fleshes it out with examples, each of which chip away at the original opinion until the idea is shown to be worthless or affirmed in some way. The whole conversation is presented very nicely and he isn't antagonistic, but if you saw Socrates in the street, you'd probably cross the road to avoid him!

Getting better at being good

Many of Socrates's dialogues argue about moral qualities: courage, self-control, reason, knowledge, and so on. These are all qualities that you can improve by practice. Socrates argues that by getting a better understanding of what bravery is, you can act in a braver fashion. It's an interesting point of view.

It's difficult to know what Socrates actually believed himself. All the outcomes of the dialogues are exactly that – the conclusion of a conversation. Scholars and modern readers can't accept the resolution of Socratic dialogues as being Socrates's beliefs. The only real belief that becomes consistent is a true desire for knowledge and to find answers. Like the pre-Socratics before him, Socrates was a true 'lover of wisdom'.

Eventually, asking too many questions made Socrates unpopular and led to his death (see Chapter 9). He died a martyr and was responsible for fundamentally changing ancient Greece's – and indeed the world's – ideas of philosophy.

Selling philosophy: The sophists

Socrates also influenced the development of the sophists. *Sophists* were essentially philosophers for hire, although many of them had no real interest in philosophy.

Sophists took the principles of Socratic dialogue (for instance, disproving an idea) and turned them to profit. They sold their services to people who were about to go to court and needed coaching in how to represent themselves. Some people alleged that sophists had no interest in the truth, merely in winning arguments.

Some sophists also provided training in speaking and argument to the sons of rich men who wanted to enter politics. These skills were tremendously useful in the *boule* and elsewhere to gain the votes of the *demos*.

Unfortunately, all the surviving sources on sophists are very biased. People like Plato (see the following section 'Leaving Philosophy to the Professionals: Plato') wrote about the sophists but hated them for what they did with Socrates's form of philosophy. Still, some ancient Greeks must have used the services of sophists for truly philosophical purposes.

One particularly big piece of anti-sophist and anti-philosophy propaganda is Aristophanes's play *The Clouds*. In it, Socrates is portrayed as running a 'School for Sophists' in which he teaches young men not to believe in the gods. None of this was true! Socrates was no sophist and he also never ran a school. Then again, Aristophanes never let the truth get in the way of a good joke!

Leaving Philosophy to the Professionals: Plato

After Socrates died in 399 BC, Greek philosophy went from strength to strength. The next great figure was Plato (circa 428–347 BC).

Historians know very little about Plato's life, and many of the facts about him are highly disputed. However, scholars agree that:

- ✔ Plato was originally a follower of Socrates.

- ✔ After Socrates's death, Plato left Athens and travelled around the Mediterranean, returning when he was about 40 and founding the famous school of philosophy known as the Academy.

- ✔ Plato's Academy flourished for the best part of a thousand years until it was finally closed by the Byzantine emperor Justinian in AD 529.

Aside from establishing the Academy, another reason that Plato became so famous was the huge number of philosophical works that he wrote and published, many of which still survive. Nearly all of them are written in dialogue form with Socrates as the main character. They explore a wide range of subjects, although Plato's favourite themes were justice, *epistemology* (the theory of knowledge), and theories about art.

Living in an ideal world: The Republic

Probably Plato's most famous work was *The Republic*, a very long dialogue based around the idea of creating an ideal state. The dialogue starts with a discussion about the true nature of justice. In Greek the word for justice is *dike* and it has a rather wider meaning; something along the lines of rightness or correctness is one version. To try to define what justice actually is , Socrates sets out what he sees as a potential ideal society.

The model he comes up with is one with a very regulated class system. People are born into the system and do jobs according to their classes. A group known as the *Philosopher Rulers* govern the state, because only they possess the wisdom and self-control to make objective decisions for the good of the whole community.

This model was a fairly controversial set of ideas because it rejected the democratic system that Athens had at the time in favour of rule by the few – an *oligarchy* (see Chapter 4).

But why did Plato only trust the rule of philosophers?

Exploring the Theory of the Forms

The main reason Plato advocated a group of Philosopher Rulers comes from his big theory of existence known as *the Theory of the Forms*. In this theory Plato argues that everything you see around you isn't actually the real world but only a shadowy copy of it. *The Forms* are the one true version of everything. Only a philosopher is able to comprehend and understand the Forms, so only a philosopher is fit to make decisions for a whole city or state.

Plato illustrates his Theory of the Forms in *The Republic* by using the simile of the cave. He describes a group of people held in a cave who see only the shadows made by reflections on a wall; this is their whole world. These reflections are of real life going on outside the cave. Eventually, a few break free and go outside into the light while the rest remain in the cave. Those who go outside are the philosophers searching for truth. The rest are inside, still watching the shadows and believing them to be real.

If this all sounds a bit like *The Matrix* film trilogy where the character of Neo suddenly becomes aware that his whole life has been a fabrication and another, 'real' world exists, you're right. Fortunately, not even Plato is as complicated as *The Matrix* movies!

Plato was so keen on philosophers because he regarded them as the only people who were totally objective and focused on discovering the truth. Thus, only philosophers were able to make decisions that weren't corrupted by their own vice or prejudice. This quote from *The Republic* sums up the idea:

> *The society we have described can never grow into a reality or see the light of day, and there will be no end to the troubles of states, or indeed my dear Glaucon, of humanity itself, till philosophers become kings in this world, or till those we now call kings and rulers really and truly become philosophers. . . .*

At least Plato was true to his word. His whole life was spent searching for the truth and helping teach others to do so. Later in his life he spent some time in Sicily and when he died he was buried in his academy.

Meeting the Man Who Knew Everything: Aristotle

One of the most famous graduates from Plato's Academy was Aristotle (384–322 BC), the final great figure in Greek philosophy. (Aristotle also pops up briefly in Chapter 10, working as tutor to Alexander the Great.)

Aristotle originally came from Stageira in the north of Greece. Although he spent a great deal of his life in Athens, he was never granted citizen status and lived there as a *metoikos* or resident alien (see Chapter 14). He established his own school – known as the *Lyceum* – outside the city of Athens.

Thinking scientifically

Two things made Aristotle very different from the other philosophers that came before him:

- ✔ Aristotle was much more interested in knowledge gained by the five senses than by intellectual reason.

- ✔ Aristotle was interested in absolutely everything – all areas of human endeavour including politics, botany, medicine, ethical philosophy, literary criticism, and more.

In many ways, Aristotle's method was like a combination of the pre-Socratics (see the earlier section 'Meeting the Early Greek Philosophers') and the philosophers who followed. Whatever the topic, Aristotle took the same method of scientific enquiry. He became known as an *empiricist* (meaning someone having an interest in studying all aspects of human endeavour), and his methods formed the basis of scientific study that followed for centuries.

Checking out some of Aristotle's greatest hits

The sheer volume of work that Aristotle produced in his lifetime is difficult to calculate. His major works include:

- *Physics*: On nature, life, and how the mind works.
- *Metaphysics*: On logic and reason.
- *Ethics*: On ethical dilemmas and doing the right thing.
- *Politics*: A survey of all political systems and their problems.
- *Poetics*: On plays on poetry and their themes (see Chapter 16).

Aristotle also wrote books on plant and animal life, medicine, the true nature of the soul, and rhetoric. Talk about a busy guy!

Venturing into Aristotle's Ethics

With so many different books by Aristotle, choosing just one is difficult. That said, *Ethics* is a really good introduction to Aristotle's style of enquiry. Like Socrates, Aristotle believed that virtues are skills that you can improve with practice; so if you make a constant effort to be generous to others, eventually you do it without thinking, as a matter of course.

Generally speaking, Aristotle decided that good behaviour takes place when you avoid extremes and exercise moderation. Take this example of the dangers of being either vulgar or, at the other end of the scale, boorish and sour.

Those who go too far in being funny are regarded as buffoons and vulgar persons who exert themselves to be funny at all costs and who are set upon raising a laugh than upon decency of expression and consideration for their victim's feelings. Those who both refuse to say anything funny themselves and take exception to the jokes of other people are regarded as boorish and sour.

In the end Aristotle decides that the best course is to take the middle path, exhibit good taste, and be 'nimble-witted'. He comes to similar conclusions with almost all ethical issues. Later writers refer to this idea as *the Doctrine of the Golden Mean* ('mean' meaning average, or the middle path), although Aristotle never called it that.

Moving On: Hellenistic Science and Beyond

One of the impacts of both Aristotle and the conquests of Alexander the Great (see Chapter 11) was a huge upsurge of interest in the sciences during the Hellenistic period. The rich kings who succeeded Alexander spent huge amounts of money on scientific development and sponsoring the foundation of academies and libraries.

- ✔ **Geometry and mathematics** were areas of interest to such notable men as Euclid (325–265 BC) and Archimedes (circa 287–212 BC; see Chapter 24). Some principles that the two men defined last until this day.

- ✔ **Astronomy** was another area of interest, particularly the study of the position of the earth in relation to the stars. The father of astronomy was Hipparchus (circa 190–120 BC), who constructed the first celestial globe, a model of the universe as he understood it.

The discoveries of these scientists and others were very influential. Although much of their work was lost during the medieval period, Renaissance scientists like Galileo rediscovered and expanded upon significant portions.

And Greek philosophy didn't stop with Aristotle – far from it. During the Hellenistic and early Roman periods, philosophy expanded and definite schools emerged – in particular, a rivalry developed between the *Epicureans* and *Stoics.* Throughout the Mediterranean, figures of learning tended to classify themselves into one of these two groups, despite the fact that they believed in very similar things. But that's a story to check out in *The Romans For Dummies* by Guy de la Bedoyere (Wiley).

Part V
The Part of Tens

"I'm just saying, if we're able to make all these advancements in engineering, architecture, and the sciences, you'd think someone would find a way of putting pockets in a tunic."

In this part . . .

The rest of this book will have hopefully whetted your appetite for all things Greek. Here are four brief chapters giving you an idea of what Greek stuff to look at next – places to go, books to read, inventions to find out about, and slightly dodgy characters who are probably worth a second look. Enjoy!

Chapter 23

Ten Great Greek Inventions

*T*hroughout Parts I to IV, I mention all sorts of things that the ancient Greeks were the first to come up with, discover, or bring into being. In this chapter I pick out ten of the best! Subsequent generations definitely owe the Greeks a big thank you for the following.

Archimedes's Inventions

Archimedes himself wasn't an invention – but he was an incredibly prolific inventor, in addition to being a mathematician, physicist, and astronomer.

He was born in Syracuse on the island of Sicily in 287 BC and spent most of his life there. A huge number of inventions are attributed to him. Many of them are military-based and were used by the Sicilians to fight naval battles against the invading Romans. Specifically, Archimedes invented:

✔ A fearsome claw that attackers used to fix their ships onto that of their opponents. (See Chapter 5 for more on ancient Greek naval techniques.) It really worked and helped the Syracusans fight the Romans.

✔ The *Archimedes screw*, a device that was used for raising water from a low-lying source to higher ground; Archimedes screws are still found in irrigation systems today. According to the old story, Archimedes got the idea for this invention in the bath and shouted 'Eureka!' meaning 'I have discovered it!'

Much of the rest of his life was spent on mathematical calculations, particularly developing ideas about spheres and cylinders. He died in Syracuse when the Romans finally conquered and sacked the city in 211 BC. He was buried in a tomb designed according to his own principle (that a sphere has two-thirds the volume and surface area of the circumscribing cylinder – phew!). What a man.

The Railway

Yes, it's true. The ancient Greeks did have a railway – of sorts.

The first version was just a rutway with tracks dug in the ground to move heavy carts more easily, but in 600 BC a man called Einander of Corinth developed a trackway paved with hard limestone. It was used to haul ships across the Isthmus of Corinth, allowing people to avoid the long journey by boat around southern Greece when travelling from the west coast to the Aegean. The railway doesn't exist any more and ships use the Corinthian canal instead.

Modern historians have classified this trackway as a railway, although it wasn't used for public transport. Just as well because no Greek came up with a solution to the problem of leaves on the line.

The Steam Engine

Crazy as it may seem, the Greeks came very close to creating a working steam engine! The man behind this enterprise was the aptly-named Hero of Alexandria. He was born in AD 10 when Egypt was under the control of the Roman Empire. Yes, he is a little out of the period of ancient Greece covered in this book, but I'm going to include him anyway!

The device that Hero came up with was a ball fixed onto a pivot over a cauldron. When the contents of the cauldron boiled, the ball span – creating a steam engine. Unfortunately nobody really knew what to do with Hero's invention.

Vending Machines

This invention comes from Hero of Alexandria as well. He invented a machine that responded to having a coin dropped into the slot at the top. The wooden device dispensed holy water into a cup placed underneath by those visiting a shrine. If only he had invented the Mars Bar as well – he could've made a mint!

Writing

Around 750 BC the Greeks began to use a system of notation that eventually developed into the Greek alphabet and from then on into the first European language. See Chapter 1 for more details on this life-changing invention.

Writing varied hugely from place to place within the ancient Greek world, but by the fifth century it had developed into a common language. It's probably fair to say that I wouldn't be writing this book in English if the Greeks hadn't invented Greek. Well done them!

History

Okay, so the ancient Greeks didn't invent history – it's all around, happening all by itself, after all. But they did invent writing about history.

Before the Greeks had their language, events and history were passed down verbally, but eventually history began to be written down too.

Herodotus's *Histories* (written 431 BC–425 BC) were the first attempt to write down the history of Greece and are an entertaining if unreliable read. History writing really began with Thucydides's *History of the Peloponnesian War* (written in 431 BC), a lengthy historical text about a big event (see Chapter 8), written by someone who was actually there.

Comedy

Like history, comedy has always been around, but the ancient Greeks were the first to turn it into a genre.

The comic plays of writers like Aristophanes (circa 456 BC–386 BC), took contemporary political situations and mixed them with farce and fantasy to produce satirical comedies that influenced subsequent sources of laughter in everything from *commedia del arte*, pantomime, modern satire, and even late-night sketch comedy. Aristophanes's greatest plays are still translated and performed today.

Later comic writers like Menander (circa 342–291 BC) removed the satirical elements and produced a kind of comedy of manners that influenced later playwrights from Shakespeare to Noel Coward.

Money

Coinage was a very definite ancient Greek invention. The Greek towns in Asia Minor began to use formal coinage in about 600 BC, replacing the old system of bartering with goods. Initially only a few varieties of coin were used but by the Hellenistic period (from 350 BC onwards), systems of paper money transfer had been developed.

The Romans eventually took over all these monetary systems in order to exact punitive taxes on their colonies. So the Greeks are in part responsible for your council tax bill. Thanks very much!

Musical Notation

Music was a very important part of Greek life, accompanying all religious ceremonies, celebrations, and dramatic performances. The theory behind music was of great interest to both philosophers and mathematicians, in particular Aristoxenus of Tarrentum (circa 350 BC).

In around 300 BC the Greeks developed a system of melodic notation that enabled music to be written down. Two different systems were developed: one for vocal music and one for instrumental, using signs developed from letters of the alphabet. This system didn't really record melody and rhythm in the way that the modern system of eight tones in an octave does, but for the simpler music of ancient Greece it worked perfectly well and became standard throughout the ancient world up until around the fifth century AD.

About 50 scores have survived from the ancient world from various inscriptions and manuscripts. When performed, it's a spare delicate music played on only a few instruments and is quite reminiscent of traditional Japanese music.

Democracy

Whether the democracy developed in Athens was the first in the world is a controversial issue. Many scholars have come up with other examples of representative government that took place earlier in areas as far away as Africa.

In a sense the exact chronology of democracy doesn't matter. The Athenian Greeks didn't know about other regions' governmental practices but still decided through a lengthy process of social change that the whole city should vote on issues of government via a participative democracy.

Athenian democracy wasn't a perfect system (see Chapter 7). It denied any role to women, for example, but it was the first European democracy and one that many others have claimed as an inspiration.

Chapter 24

Ten Things to Read Next

A t this point, maybe you've nearly finished reading this book – if so, congratulations and thanks for sticking with it! Or maybe you're just starting to get to know the ancient Greeks. Wherever you are in the process, one of best ways to explore the ancient Greeks is through their own words, in the plays, poetry, and prose they left behind.

So if you've enjoyed *The Ancient Greeks For Dummies* or you want to gain a better understanding of some the topics, events, or people I cover in this book, here are ten things to try next.

When reading ancient Greek literature the translation is vitally important! Many translations are available of all the works that I mention in this book but I always recommend choosing the Penguin Classics. A real attempt has been made to capture the spirit of the originals in the translations. Also, all the editions have excellent introductory notes and many have indexes.

If possible, get an audio version of Homer's works. Both *The Iliad* and *The Odyssey* were originally composed to be listened to. Only when you hear the words spoken do you get a real sense of the poetic devices and tremendous powers of plotting and construction that the poet had.

The Iliad: Homer

As I state in Chapter 20, *The Iliad* is the most important work of Greek literature. The ancient Greeks looked to Homer for guidance on the widest possible range of issues – everything from fighting and shipbuilding to hospitality and honourable behaviour.

Although a relatively simple story, the poem is a treasury of mythological characters and human and deity relationships. The central figure of Achilles, the greatest Greek warrior, is powerfully dramatic as he sits out the fighting and struggles with his own pride and anger before personal tragedy brings him back into the war.

Interesting Fact: Book Two 'The Catalogue of Ships' is often a difficult read for modern readers, but the ancient Greeks regarded it as the most impressive of the entire poem for its tremendous listing of warriors and their families.

The Odyssey: Homer

The Odyssey is the companion piece to *The Iliad*. You can read one or the other individually, but reading them together brings Homer's genius to light.

In many ways, *The Odyssey* is a better story than *The Iliad* and reads much more like a modern novel. The poem is full of great stories and characters and is very evocative of a mythological time when almost anything could happen. And the dramatic conclusion, when Odysseus returns home to Ithaca to deal with the arrogant suitors that have taken over his home and are making a play for his wife Penelope, must be read to be believed.

Interesting Fact: Many modern critics have suggested that the last two books of *The Odyssey* aren't by Homer! They're slightly different in tone compared to the preceding 22 books and deal with the fallout after Odysseus has retuned and defeated the suitors. I'm not sure myself – have a read and see what you think.

Oedipus the King: Sophocles

If you read just one Greek tragedy, try *Oedipus the King*. In many ways the play is the archetypal story of how a man who is too proud is brought down by the gods. Important questions about destiny, fate, and the role of the gods are examined in detail – and aside from this the play is brilliantly constructed.

Oedipus the King is also most likely to give you the full experience of the ancient Greek dramatic concepts of *pathos* (suffering) and *mathos* (gaining understanding) because you already know the ending and therefore can give your full concentration to the process.

Interesting Fact: Aristotle regarded this play as the most perfect of all tragedies and used it to scientifically analyse the process of writing tragedy in his *Poetics*. See if you agree with him!

The Histories: Herodotus

Herodotus's *Histories* are a fantastic read. Setting out to explain the reasons why the Persian Wars started, Herodotus ends up writing a history of Greece up until his own times. (See Chapter 6 for my take on the Persian Wars.)

Histories isn't historical writing as scholars regard it today. Herodotus's text mixes history, mythology, and hearsay – sometimes even in the same paragraph! But Herodotus was incredibly widely travelled and he's sometimes the only surviving source for some of the places and events he mentions. *Histories* is a perfect holiday read because you can pick up it up, dip into it, and find some interesting place or story.

Interesting Fact: Early in his life, Herodotus was involved in an attempted revolt in his home city of Halicarnassus. The revolt failed, Herodotus went into exile, and began his travelling. Politics' loss was history's gain!

Parallel Lives: Plutarch

Plutarch (circa AD 50–120) was a Greek who lived in the Roman Empire and wrote about the lives of great men from history. He wasn't a historian in the conventional sense but more like a modern biographer whose interest was in the characters of the individuals he wrote about.

Plutarch's life of Alexander the Great is a particularly good place to start, but he also wrote lives of many other Greek figures such as Alcibiades, Pericles, and Demosthenes.

Interesting Fact: All of Plutarch's biographies were originally published as *Parallel Lives*, in which the biographies of two men are contrasted with each other, such as the lives of Theseus (Athens's mythological founder; see Chapter 20) and Romulus (Rome's equally mythological founder).

Early Socratic Dialogues: Plato

This recommendation isn't actually a book by Plato but a collection of some of the earliest of Socrates's dialogues that he wrote down. It's an interesting and accessible collection of discussions that give a really good idea of the way that Socrates's method of discussion worked (see Chapter 22).

Topics include the difference between love and friendship and the true nature of aesthetic beauty. These dialogues are a really good introduction to Plato's style and a great place to start if you want to eventually read his book *The Republic*.

Interesting Fact: All the dialogues are named after the friends of Socrates who took part in the discussions such as Lysis, Charmides, and Euthydemus. These folk don't get much of a word in edgeways after Socrates gets going, so it's nice that they get their tribute in the title at least!

The Ethics: Aristotle

The Ethics is by far the best introduction to Aristotle's style of philosophy and scientific method. Aristotle sets out to establish what makes some people good and others bad and then tries to argue why happiness through doing good should be everybody's goal. It's a cheerful argument, well illustrated by a number of sections that try to define qualities such as modesty, prudence, and generosity.

Interesting Fact: The book includes a table of virtues and vices that also incorporates a suggestion of the middle course between them that readers should take. You have no excuse for bad behaviour after you read this classic!

Frogs: Aristophanes

Frogs was produced in 405 BC and won first prize in the Lenaea comedy festival (see Chapter 16). The comedy is typical good, riotous fun from Aristophanes. The plot involves the god Dionysus travelling to the underworld to bring back the dramatist Euripides. On the way Charon the Ferryman, a greedy Heracles, and the other great Greek dramatist Aeschylus all make comic cameos. Nearly 2,500 years old and still very funny, *Frogs* is a great introduction to Aristophanes and Greek comedy. Even better, try to see a production. The most recent was a revival of Stephen Sondheim's version that played on Broadway in 2004.

Interesting Fact: The play gets its title from the chorus of frogs that live in the swamps around the entrance to Hades. Their rhythmic songs are one of the best examples of how musical the comedies were when they were originally performed.

The Idylls: Theocritus

Theocritus (circa 300 BC) was born in Syracuse but spent most of his life in Alexandria. Not a great deal of his work survives, but *The Idylls* are beautiful, sensitive examples of a very different type of poetry to the epic poetry of Homer. Set in the Greek countryside and the world of shepherds and goatherds, *The Idylls* are said to be the first examples of the *bucolic* genre. Very lovelorn and quite melancholic, the poems show a personal and sensitive side of Greek literature. (The beautiful poems of Sappho are worth looking at for the same reason.)

Interesting Fact: The selection of poems also contains a comic dialogue between Alexandrian women making their way to a festival. Very different from the rest of Theocritus's surviving work, this conversation is quite amusing and a nice snapshot of life in ancient Alexandria.

The Romans For Dummies: Guy de la Bedoyere

The companion book to *The Ancient Greeks For Dummies*, this book introduces you to ancient Rome and its incredible story. Although the Romans may seem like the bad guys who brought glorious ancient Greece to an end, they were actually responsible for adopting and then preserving a huge amount of Greek culture. The story of Rome is amazing – take a look!

Interesting Fact: During the second century AD, it became very fashionable among the Roman aristocracy to develop a big cultural interest in all things Greek. This was partly motivated by the emperor Hadrian. The name given to such an individual in Latin was a *philhellenicus*.

Chapter 25

Ten Dodgy Ancient Greek Characters

*T*he history of ancient Greece is full of interesting characters – individuals who got into some sticky situations or rose to great heights but whose motivations were sometimes dubious.

This chapter is a short list of people about whom you may be interested in finding out more sordid details!

Alcibiades (451–403 BC)

The ultimate dodgy character, Alcibiades was an Athenian general and politician who changed sides so often that keeping up with his allegiances is difficult.

Alcibiades was a young playboy about town who everyone thought was destined for great things. He was the main mover behind the idea of the disastrous Sicilian Expedition during the Peloponnesian War (refer to Chapter 8). He never made it to Sicily because a message reached him that he was being charged in his absence with blasphemy, including drunkenly mocking the secrets of the Eleusinian Mysteries (decribed in Chapter 22). These charges were probably true; throughout his life, he lived to excess.

Hearing of these charges, Alcibiades literally jumped ship, escaping in a fishing boat, and went to Sparta and worked as an advisor to his former enemy. But the Spartans soon distrusted him too, and Alcibiades ended up at the court of a Persian *satrap*. Eventually he was welcomed back to Athens and fought successfully for the Athenians for a number of years. After a defeat in 406 BC, he retired to live in Thrace. His was not a peaceful old age – the new regime in Athens assassinated him two years later.

Alcibiades was a great man who arguably dominated his era, but you wouldn't lend him a fiver!

Odysseus

Yes, that's right – I'm including Odysseus, the great Greek hero of Homer's *The Iliad* and *The Odyssey*, on my list of dodgy characters!

Homer calls Odysseus the 'master of cunning stratagems' and throughout the myths about him, Odysseus continually lies, cheats, and cons. It was Odysseus who came up with the plan of the Trojan horse, as well as many other cunning schemes. On several occasions in *The Odyssey*, he adopts disguises given to him by the goddess Athena to work some kind of con.

The ancient Greeks recognised these traits in Odysseus's character, and later portrayals of him emphasise his untrustworthiness. In Sophocles's play *Philoctetes*, for example, Odysseus is shown to be cunning and amoral in his treatment of a wounded archer when he tries to steal the archer's bow.

Odysseus was also famed as a teller of tales. Undoubtedly they weren't all true!

Pausanias (died circa 450 BC)

Pausanias was a Spartan general who earned a possibly undeserved reputation for treachery. He was the commander of all the Greek forces at the battle of Plataea in 479 BC and claimed sole credit for the victory – an act that didn't exactly make him popular. The following year he commanded a Greek fleet that captured the Persian city of Byzantium but was afterwards accused of treachery. Back in Sparta he was acquitted and unwisely headed back to Byzantium where he was again accused of treachery! Put on trial several further times, Pausanias was eventually convicted of trying to organise a *helot* (slave worker) uprising in Sparta. He fled to avoid execution, eventually starving to death in the Spartan acropolis.

Strangely, several years later the Spartans voted that Pausanias be made a hero and a cult was established in his honour. Two statues to him were eventually constructed. So was he a traitor – or just the victim of powerful enemies? It's unlikely that we'll ever know.

Demetrius (336–283 BC)

Demetrius was the son of Alexander the Great's successor Antigonus I, king in Phrygia in Asia Minor. Demetrius grew up a playboy in the Alcibiades style with a taste for military adventure.

Demetrius spent many years campaigning like a pirate around the Aegean and earned the entirely undeserved nickname *Poliorcetes*, or 'Besieger of Cities'. He was responsible for the design and construction of the '*Helepolis*' siege engine (refer to Chapter 12) during his illegal and unsuccessful attack on Rhodes.

Eventually Demetrius was defeated in 285 and surrendered his army to Seleucus (the king of the Seleucid kingdom in Mesopotamia). He spent the last two years of his life under house arrest at Seleucus's court where he indulged his other two great passions – and effectively ate and drank himself to death.

Theseus

Like Odysseus, Theseus is another great example of a classic ancient Greek hero with two sides.

- ✔ On the plus side Theseus travelled to Crete and killed the Minotaur and was one of the greatest kings of Athens.
- ✔ On the debit side he dumped Ariadne (daughter of King Minos) on the island of Naxos when she was pregnant with his child and according to another myth kidnapped the young Helen (of Troy fame) and tried to force her to be his wife.

Theseus is a perfect example of the way that the Greeks regarded a 'hero' as somebody who did amazing things, rather than helped other people selflessly. (For more on heroes refer to Chapter 20.)

Olympias (circa 370–316 BC)

As the wife of Philip II of Macedon and the mother of Alexander the Great, Olympias was always going to have an important place in history, but she's famed as being one of the great villains of ancient Greece.

Many historians believe that Olympias was behind the murder of Philip while she was in exile. Whether that's true or not, Olympias certainly ordered the deaths of Philip's second wife and her infant daughter on her return. After Alexander's death, she tried desperately to cling on to power and was responsible for several more deaths until she was executed by relatives of her previous victims in 316 BC.

To be fair to Olympias, she lived in a court where the choice was to kill or be killed. And she was just very good at killing!

Alexander the Great (356–323 BC)

Alexander the Great – a bit dodgy? A controversial choice, but a good one, I believe:

Alexander was responsible for some of the greatest military achievements in the ancient world and created population movements that ushered in the Hellenistic Age (see Chapter 11). He founded great cities and travelled farther and wider than anybody else before.

But, during his campaigns, thousands of people were either killed in battle or executed and thousands more had their homes and lives destroyed. Alexander had several of his friends killed who he suspected of treachery – at least one by his own hands. His savagery to those who resisted him was legendary. Also, his name was used as a kind of bogeyman to scare children in eastern countries for centuries after his death. 'Go to bed when I tell you, or Alexander will get you!'

So, visionary or mass-murdering maniac? You have to judge all of these people by the standards of their age. History is all about opinions. The choice is yours!

Diogenes the Cynic (circa 412–321 BC)

Diogenes was a philosopher whose controversial methods made him famous throughout the ancient world. At various times in his life he lived in a barrel, was captured by pirates, and was expelled from the town of Sinope for 'defacing the currency' – spoiling coins in an attempt at rejecting the material world. Diogenes ended up in Corinth and lived the life of a beggar, rejecting all social conventions including marriage and cleanliness. He was known as the 'cynic' because he was credited with being the founder of the 'cynic' branch of philosophy, which disdained conventional life. The word 'cynic' comes from the Greek word *kynikos* which means 'dog like'. Diogenes believed people could learn a lot from living like dogs – he did!

Although Diogenes was a proper philosopher who wrote many books, treatises, and several tragic plays, undoubtedly the best story about him concerns his meeting with the young Alexander the Great. When the young king asked Diogenes if there was anything that Alexander could do for him, Diogenes replied, 'Yes, you can move slightly to the left, you're standing in my sunlight.' A brave man indeed!

Jason

Another ancient Greek hero with a dark side, Jason is the celebrated warrior who journeyed to the Black Sea and stole the Golden Fleece from King Aietes, along with his daughter, the sorceress Medea (refer to Chapter 20 for the full story).

However, the stories about Jason's return aren't as flattering as his early exploits. Eventually he ended up living with Medea in the city of Corinth where they had two children. In Euripides's play *Medea*, Jason dumps Medea (who, because she was a non-Greek, had no legal status as his bride) to marry Glauce, the daughter of the king of Corinth, so that he would gain social status. In an act of revenge, Medea kills both Glauce and her own two children before fleeing.

For his part, Jason eked out the rest of his life alone in Corinth, eventually dying when timber from the rotting hulk of his ship, the *Argo*, fell on him. An unheroic end!

Kleon of Athens (died 422 BC)

Kleon gets a bit of an unfair press because the only descriptions that survive of him are from Aristophanes and Thucydides – neither of whom liked him at all and (in the case of Aristophanes) continually publicly lampooned him.

Kleon was one of the first demagogue politicians (see Chapter 7), whose rabble-rousing political style clashed with old-school Athenian aristocrats like Pericles. In 426 BC he tried to prosecute Aristophanes over his play *The Babylonians*, which he claimed defamed the city of Athens, but the case was thrown out.

At the same time Kleon was a brave general who won several victories and died fighting near Amphipolis. However, most people regard him as being one of the first to exploit Athens's new democracy for his own personal glory.

Chapter 26

Ten Great Places to Visit

. . . .

. . . .

*R*eading books is all well and good, but if you really want to experience some ancient Greek culture up close and personal, this chapter suggests ten places that are full of it. Visit these locations and you're sure to feel a real connection to the world of 2,500 years ago.

Of course, hundreds of other interesting sites with connections to the ancient Greeks exist, but you have to start somewhere. These just happen to be some of my favourites.

The British Museum, London

The British Museum has a superb collection of ancient Greek objects and artefacts in some really big galleries. The museum houses a great collection of vases and sculpture from all ancient Greece's artistic periods (see Chapter 17), plus many Roman copies of famous Greek originals. The fantastic Nereid Monument, transplanted from Asia Minor, gives a good idea of the scale of some of the building work that went on during ancient Greece's prime (refer to Chapter 18). You can also see some wonderful everyday objects that allow an insight into what normal Greek lives were like.

Best of all are the so-called 'Elgin Marbles', the Parthenon sculptures that were taken from Athens by a British adventurer, Lord Elgin, in around 1800. These are great examples of the metopes, frieze, and the pediment sculpture, which I discuss in Chapter 18. The Elgin Marbles are all presented with an excellent display that features reconstructions of what the original temple looked like and how it was built. In recent years there have been attempts to force the British Government to return the sculptures to Athens – so go and see them while they're still in the British Museum!

The Acropolis, Athens

Of course, Athens is loaded with things to see, but the Acropolis really is a standout. The Parthenon, the largest temple on the site, is amazingly impressive, but the other temples – such as Athena Nike and the Erectheum – are also stunning.

Just next to the Acropolis is the Theatre of Dionysus (described in Chapter 16). The current theatre is actually a Roman rebuild of the Greek original, but it still gives you a sense of the size of the performances that used to take place.

And at a really basic level, simply walking along the streets and through the gathering spaces where Pericles, Socrates, and all the others once trod is fantastic! Local guides are available to take you round but a good guidebook will suffice. Plan to spend most of the day there and get there early – the Acropolis can get appallingly hot around lunchtime, a good time to get something to eat!

Knossos, Crete

The site of Knossos on the island of Crete feels very different to the other sites I list in this chapter. As I say in Chapter 2, the Minoans, while technically Greek, were very different to the ancient Greeks who followed them.

Knossos was discovered and controversially restored and rebuilt by Sir Arthur Evans in 1900, but the site that remains is undeniably impressive. One of the highlights is the superb Royal Palace with its beautiful dolphin decorations. Equally interesting are the workrooms in the east wing. You get a real sense of a different, earlier time and age. But be warned, walking around the site in Cretan summer temperatures that can hit over 100 degrees can be hard work!

Crete itself is a fascinating island and worth visiting on its own. It's an overnight journey on the ferry from the Greek mainland and quite a distance to Knossos once you arrive. A visit needs to be part of a planned trip but it's well worth the effort.

Delphi

The site of the sanctuary complex at Delphi is amazing. A small town hidden away in the Peloponnese, Delphi is one of the most beautiful places that you can visit, boasting spectacular views from the sanctuary, which is built into the hillside. (Head to Chapter 21 for more on the historical and religious details about this site.)

A lot of buildings still remain at Delphi, including many treasuries and a large portion of the base of the Temple of Apollo. At the very top of the site are the remains of the athletic stadium where the Pythian games (held at Delphi in honour of Apollo) took place. You can also visit an excellent museum that includes a wonderful bronze sculpture of the Delphi charioteer.

Delphi is a little isolated but you can easily book a coach trip from Athens. It's worth staying over (plenty of hotels are in town) because the sunrise looks spectacular across the valley.

Olympia

Olympia is a famous Greek town that's well worth a visit. The town has become a bit more touristy than Delphi, but its archaeological site is just as impressive.

The ruins of the Temple of Zeus are still near Olympia, along with the workshop of Pheidias, where this legendary artist constructed the massive statue of the god that was considered to be one of the Seven Wonders of the World (and shown in Chapter 17).

The site gives you a very good idea of what the original Olympic games were like, as well as just how much of an event they were (see Chapter 16). If you're feeling suitably energetic, you can even run a lap of the stadium – although be careful, I fell over when I did it! Like Delphi you'll need to book a trip to Olympia (or travel there by public transport) and there are many hotels in town.

A Greek Play

The only way to really get a sense of what the Greek theatre was like is to see a performance of a Greek play. Any play – tragedy or comedy – will do. In addition to professional and regional shows, consider attending a university or community theatre production of these great works. You may even be able to find a production that's staged outdoors. (Pack a picnic and bring a bottle of wine just like the ancients!)

Greek plays aren't as action-packed as some modern theatre. In fact, you may be surprised to see how still the performers are (if the play is performed in a traditional manner). On-stage, you also have the opportunity to see the way that the chorus is used to support and comment on the action of the central characters.

Many modern productions update the play to the present or change the setting to somewhere different. But just as with Shakespeare, the modern touches usually still allow the brilliance of the original work to shine through.

Samos or Another Greek Island

If you want to get a sense of Odysseus's travels in Homer's epic poem *The Odyssey*, visit a Greek island and drink in the atmosphere. The history is great – and the peace and quiet is pretty wonderful too!

It's difficult to pick a single Greek island to visit because there are hundreds, but I'm recommending Samos because it is the one I most recently visited! The closest Greek island to modern Turkey, Samos was a hive of trade and activity during the heyday of ancient Greece, and the island still has a reasonable amount of archaeology to look at.

More than touring remains, however. Samos and many of the other islands give you a real sense of the independence of these small islands and their distance from elsewhere. You can easily see how men like Herodotus broke new ground by travelling to these areas and sharing their stories with Greeks on the mainland. You can also appreciate how each community grew and developed its own versions of myths and relationships with the gods.

Google Images

This recommendation may seem obvious, but if you want to see more examples of Greek art and architecture, go to the Internet!

A quick search (I like `images.google.com`) reveals a huge number of photos and drawings. You can very quickly assemble a good library of pictures.

Check out Chapter 17 for an introduction to Greek art and then seek out some more examples of different types of sculpture. Searching under 'Hellenistic Sculpture' or 'Red Figure Vase Painting' brings up loads of examples, each with its own story. The world of ancient Greek art is at your fingertips!

The National Gallery, London

The National Gallery may seem like an odd choice of place to visit for ancient Greek culture, but if you want to see how the Greeks influenced the people who followed them, then an art gallery is a good place to start.

Many Renaissance paintings feature scenes from Greek mythology based on written sources that were rediscovered during that historical period.

The National Gallery is a good place to start because it features Titian's fantastic _Bacchus and Ariadne_ (1520–23 AD), an amazing, colourful picture that shows the abandoned Ariadne being surprised by Bacchus and his swaggering crew of followers. Look for paintings by Titian, Botticelli, Della Francesca, Veronese, and Rubens – all of whom loved using classical mythology as a source.

All the Renaissance paintings are idealised, but looking at somebody else's interpretation of the myths is still quite inspiring. Go along and let your imagination run riot! _Art For Dummies_ by Thomas Hoving and _Art History For Dummies_ by Jesse Bryant Wilder offer further insights into the connections between ancient Greek and later artists.

The Agora, Athens

Still relatively well preserved, Athens's original town centre was the busiest part of the greatest of Ancient Greek cities. If you go, take a classical text with you and sit and read it for a while. The ancient Greeks were having conversations about the same text 2,500 years ago, probably in the same spot! You'll also be sitting in the place where Plato debated with Socrates; Pericles discussed the Peloponnesian War with his generals; and Alcibiades intrigued and flirted. Their sandalled feet trod the same ground that you'll be standing on. You can't get much more Greek than that.

The Agora is in the very centre of modern Athens and is surrounded by modern market stalls. It gives you a sense of the hustle and bustle that must have been part of city life in the days of ancient Greece. Take a walk around and pick up something to eat from one of the street vendors – just as an average Athenian would have done on his way to the assembly 2,500 years ago!

Index

Notes

Notes

Notes

Notes

Notes

Notes

FOR DUMMIES®

Do Anything. Just Add Dummies

UK editions

BUSINESS

978-0-470-51806-9

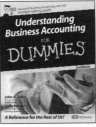

978-0-470-99245-6

978-0-7645-7026-1

FINANCE

978-0-470-99280-7

978-0-470-99811-3

978-0-470-05815-2

PROPERTY

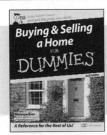

978-0-470-99448-1

978-0-470-51502-0

978-0-7645-7054-4

Body Language For Dummies
978-0-470-51291-3

Building Self-Confidence For
Dummies
978-0-470-01669-5

Children's Health For Dummies
978-0-470-02735-6

Cognitive Behavioural Coaching
For Dummies
978-0-470-71379-2

Counselling Skills For Dummies
978-0-470-51190-9

Digital Marketing For Dummies
978-0-470-05793-3

Divorce For Dummies
978-0-7645-7030-8

eBay.co.uk For Dummies, 2nd
Edition
978-0-470-51807-6

Emotional Freedom Technique For
Dummies
978-0-470-75876-2

English Grammar For Dummies
978-0-470-05752-0

Fertility & Infertility For Dummies
978-0-470-05750-6

Genealogy Online For Dummies
978-0-7645-7061-2

Golf For Dummies
978-0-470-01811-8

Green Living For Dummies
978-0-470-06038-4

FOR DUMMIES®

UK editions

SELF-HELP

Cognitive Behavioural Therapy For Dummies

978-0-470-01838-5

Neuro-linguistic Programming For Dummies

978-0-7645-7028-5

Personal Development All-in-One For Dummies

978-0-470-51501-3

Hypnotherapy For Dummies
978-0-470-01930-6

Inventing For Dummies
978-0-470-51996-7

Job Hunting and Career Change All-in-One For Dummies
978-0-470-51611-9

Motivation For Dummies
978-0-470-76035-2

Origami Kit For Dummies
978-0-470-75857-1

Patents, Registered Designs, Trade Marks and Copyright For Dummies
978-0-470-51997-4

Psychometric Tests For Dummies
978-0-470-75366-8

Raising Happy Children For Dummies
978-0-470-05978-4

Starting and Running a Business All-in-One For Dummies
978-0-470-51648-5

Sudoku For Dummies
978-0-470-01892-7

The British Citizenship Test For Dummies, 2nd Edition
978-0-470-72339-5

Time Management For Dummies
978-0-470-77765-7

Wills, Probate, & Inheritance Tax For Dummies, 2nd Edition
978-0-470-75629-4

Winning on Betfair For Dummies, 2nd Edition
978-0-470-72336-4

HEALTH

Stop Smoking For Dummies

978-0-470-99456-6

IBS For Dummies

978-0-470-51737-6

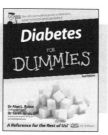

Diabetes For Dummies

978-0-470-05810-7

HISTORY

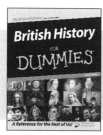

British History For Dummies

978-0-470-03536-8

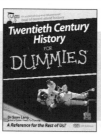

Twentieth Century History For Dummies

978-0-470-51015-5

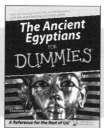

The Ancient Egyptians For Dummies

978-0-470-06544-0

FOR DUMMIES

The easy way to get more done and have more fun

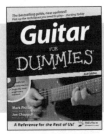

FOR
DUMMIES®

COMPUTER BASICS

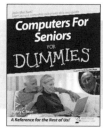

978-0-470-24055-7

978-0-470-13728-4

978-0-471-75421-3

DIGITAL LIFESTYLE

978-0-7645-9802-9

978-0-470-17474-6

978-0-470-17469-2

WEB & DESIGN

978-0-470-08030-6

978-0-470-11193-2

978-0-470-11490-2

Access 2007 For Dummies
978-0-470-04612-8

Adobe Creative Suite 3 Design Premium
All-in-One Desk Reference For Dummies
978-0-470-11724-8

AutoCAD 2008 For Dummies
978-0-470-11650-0

C++ For Dummies, 5th Edition
978-0-7645-6852-7

Excel 2007 All-in-One Desk Reference For
Dummies
978-0-470-03738-6

Flash CS3 For Dummies
978-0-470-12100-9

Laptops For Dummies, 2nd Edition
978-0-470-05432-1

Mac OS X Leopard For Dummies
978-0-470-05433-8

Macs For Dummies, 9th Edition
978-0-470-04849-8

Networking All-in-One Desk Reference For
Dummies, 3rd Edition
978-0-470-17915-4

Office 2007 All-in-One Desk Reference For
Dummies
978-0-471-78279-7

Search Engine Optimization For Dummies,
2nd Edition
978-0-471-97998-2

Second Life For Dummies
978-0-470-18025-9

The Internet For Dummies, 11th Edition
978-0-470-12174-0

Visual Studio 2008 All-in-One Desk
Reference For Dummies
978-0-470-19108-8

Web Analytics For Dummies
978-0-470-09824-0

Windows XP For Dummies, 2nd Edition
978-0-7645-7326-2